THE SNOWY BATTLEFIELD OF OHIO

A MEMOIR

by

Stanley O'Shea

Copyright

Copyright © 2024 C Stanley O'Shea

All Rights Reserved. No part of this publication may be reproduced, distributed, or transmitted in any form or by any means, including photocopying, recording, or other electronic or mechanical methods, without prior written permission of the publisher, except in the case of brief quotations embodied in reviews and certain other non-commercial use permitted by law.

For rights and permissions, please contact the author through email: auditory.synapse@gmail.com

ISBN: 978-3-2308-4152-0
Published by Success Publications SAR

Credits

Editor: Stephen M.B.
Interior Design: Zshan Ahmed
Cover Design: Aqeeta & Richa & Stanley O'Shea
Photography:
front cover "portrait": Stanley O'Shea
front cover "landscape": Pam Burley (aceshot / Adobe Stock)
back cover: Chelsie Bakken (fruitcocktail / Adobe Stock)
Beta-reader: Jennifer Robe
Marketing Consultant: Liam Publisher

Statement

This book was written with the assistance of Dragon NaturallySpeaking (version Professional Individual 15) due to my chronic repetitive strain injury (RSI). Scrivener, powerful as it is, isn't compatible with Dragon and thus was not used for this project.

To achieve maximum authenticity in this personal project, I did not avoid using sensitive terms. No trigger warning is guaranteed. Reader discretion is advised.

The opinions expressed in this book are solely my own. The readers should take my opinions with a grain of salt and apply their own judgment.

Disclaimer

My side of the story has been reconstructed to the best of my memory in order to share my life lessons with the readers. The characters' names have been changed. Other personal identifiable information has been obscured to show respect for the characters in the story. Some characters or events have been combined or omitted in order to streamline the storyline of this creative nonfiction. Some businesses' names have been altered.

The cover photo is inspired by Carl Jung's psychological theories and Matthew McConaughey's book *Greenlights*. The visual representation is a unique expression primarily based on personal experiences. Any resemblance to other works is coincidental rather than intentional, despite the author's emotional connections to some fictional characters as mentioned in the book. Any over-interpretation would be discouraged.

Table of Contents

Statement	3
Disclaimer	4
PART ONE	7
Chapter 1 Intro	8
Chapter 2 The Sunken Heart	10
Chapter 3 Where Do I Sleep Next?	20
Chapter 4 The Three Housemates and the Neighbors	24
Chapter 5 The ER Visit	35
Chapter 6 The "Shining" House	64
Chapter 7 The Worst TA Ever in Ohio State	101
PART TWO	125
Chapter 8 Played and Then Crushed	126
Chapter 9 Meeting in The Courthouse	187
Chapter 10 Student Conduct and Student Advocacy	213
Chapter 11 Searching for An Attorney	239
PART THREE	259

Chapter 12 The Last Summer and the Group Therapy   260

Chapter 13 The Last Fall and a Love Song for Myself   289

Chapter 14 "Sunshine" California   348

Chapter 15 Residues   361

Disclaimer (Reprise)   389

Acknowledgment   390

About The Author   392

APPENDICES   393

Appendix A: List of Characters   393

Appendix B: List of Songs   400

Appendix C: Questions for Readers/Listeners   401

PART ONE

"If you put yourself out there, people will open a door for you."
Then he closed his own door.

Chapter 1
Intro

"Hey Slim, you've been acting weird on Facebook lately. What happened?"

"Hey Slim, you need a blog. You can't write stuff like that on Facebook!"

"Hey Slim, who is White Coat Devil?" — A question asked by some of my friends, especially White Americans, after seeing me talk in a troubled manner on Facebook in those years.

Let me state upfront that "White Coat" refers to the uniform worn by the medical profession, and it has nothing to do with skin color: just a coincidence. I also don't hold any attitude toward the medical profession in general. The term "White Coat Devil" emerged in my mind after the incident to contrast the biased term "White Coat Angel," which refers to medical doctors and is taught to kids through media and public education in China. That being said, to minimize confusions and assumptions for global readers, I will always provide additional information for any character who isn't White or American.

The declassification of this piece of history signifies my willingness to expose my stigma to sunlight. Commiseration is not what I want from people. Moral judgment or mockery? I have received blame from some estranged relatives already. In fact, I had withheld the story from them until the aftershocks were over, knowing how critically they would respond.

INTRO

My buddy Antonio once said I would laugh at these incidents when I got old. I don't think I ever will, considering I saw multiple American therapists and wrote three songs to seal the emotional impact caused by this incident in Ohio. I choose not to forget history.

Chapter 2
The Sunken Heart

2.1 This Isn't the America I Expected

Aug 2012 – Nov 2014, Columbus, OH, grad student

My first flight was from Shanghai to Los Angeles in early August. We arrived in Shanghai by train one day in advance. On the day of my flight, a typhoon was hitting Shanghai. Meanwhile, Mr. Xiang Liu, a famous track-and-field athlete from Shanghai, Olympic champion, withdrew from the hurdling race because of his Achilles tendon injury. Though I couldn't care less about the Olympic Games that day, I witnessed my X chromosome provider, Mandy, judging him out loud in front of the TV set in the hotel lobby.

"He shouldn't have quit! How was that even allowed? He should have tried to compete, even just to fall on the ground later! Now he's a loser without even fighting! He has brought shame to this country!"

I remained silent, like most people in that hotel lobby. Anyway, I was so relieved that I could avoid seeing this controlling woman for a long time.

We arrived at the airport before lunchtime. My flight, which was scheduled for the afternoon, was delayed by several hours because of the typhoon. After 6 PM, people began to worry that the flights on that day might be canceled altogether. An old friend tagged me on his social media post, showing his schadenfreude attitude, "Can't fly to America, haha?" To his disappointment, the plane eventually took off after the rainstorm subsided.

The following day, during the third flight of my itinerary, from Chicago to Columbus, Ohio, my heart kept sinking because, in my bird's-eye view, tall buildings were disappearing and replaced by flatness. After the plane landed, we couldn't get off immediately due to the lightning. Hence another hour of waiting and starvation for me. I had starved for hours after hours because the airport didn't accept $100 bills, and I had no international bank card to use.

Upon my arrival, a local friend, Carl, hosted me for a week in his home, where he lived with his buddies and ran a home church group. Carl was 2 years older than me and enjoyed making friends with international students after graduating from college.

When I finally moved to the apartment complex called Olentangy Club, located between Grandview and the West Campus of The Ohio State University, I realized I couldn't go anywhere far from home. This was because the city bus (COTA) Line 84 came so infrequently and wouldn't run on weekends, to my astonishment.

The first week, I had hallucinations in bed (the more accurate word is sleep paralysis), and I heard God whispering to me "hallelujah" multiple times. I attributed that to elongated fatigue and the twelve-hour jet lag.

Knowing I was in the US, my friend in China wanted me to purchase something for his wife online and mail it to him, so I decided to use the UPS service inside Ohio Union on North High Street. I tried to provide a very detailed address, but the cashier said I was over-contemplative. Guess what? The package was declined quickly and returned to some weird location on campus for me to pick up. How come?

According to UPS, there was no invoice in the box. The online store would never provide one by default. When I went back to Ohio Union to ask for a refund, the cashier, an African American girl whose name I can never forget, told me that the money, roughly $80, was taken by Ohio State and I should go and ask Ohio State instead of their store. Where exactly inside Ohio State? Should I email the president of the university?

This ridiculous experience resulted in my first visit to Student Legal Services on North High Street. (Be careful not to confuse it with The Office of Legal Affairs, which serves the entire university.) I was assigned a male attorney, Mr. Parker, who would appear multiple times in my story.

Mr. Parker couldn't pronounce my legal name on file, so I told him, "My American friends all call me Slim." He laughed as if he'd never seen an Asian using a western name before. After I told him about my negative experience with UPS, he pointed out that there was a conflict of interest as Ohio Union was part of OSU. "I cannot represent you on this, as an employee of this university. If you still want to sue for a refund, you can file a small claim yourself in the city court on weekdays." Of course, I had no time for that during my first semester of grad school. My friend lost $80, and I lost my precious time.

The Ohio Union, which serves as the student activity center, was located on the east boundary of the Main Campus, while my "home" department, Communication Disorders, was on the remote and flat West Campus.

People in China had no idea I was staying in a disappointing place in America, not Los Angeles or New York City. Yet, back in 2012, it was quite common for Chinese people to ask their friends or relatives to purchase American products on their behalf, including but not limited to luxuries, supplements, cosmetics, and even electrical appliances, especially before an announced flight back to China. After all, professional purchasing agents were much less prevalent a decade ago than today. Some of the requests I had received were, admittedly, good deals, but I rarely found extra intrinsic value in the products they desired, especially the liquid and metal ones. What was worse, to most people I helped, it was my obligation to do this for them, simply because I was the only person in their circle who had made it to America. Some of you might wonder if it had anything to do with the notorious Chinese word "guanxi," whose optimal English equivalent is "networking" as opposed to its direct translation "relationship." In retrospect, a more accurate term that captures their mentality would be "entitlement."

2.2 Why Can't I Have My SSN?

I was told I couldn't apply for a Social Security Number in my first year. Why not? Because according to the rigid policy issued by Ohio State, the full-time fellowship I was "awarded" was not a paid position. Only an employee could apply for an SSN. In the meantime, a student visa did not allow me to work off-campus without permission, either. I suddenly felt disadvantaged relative to other international students with an RA or TA position, including those capable undergrads.

The fellowship was, theoretically, not taxable. But due to my lack of an SSN, they still found an excuse to withhold the tax, which meant a big cut to the monthly stipend I received. You can imagine the hindrance in multiple aspects of daily life without an SSN. To name but a few: tax refund, application for a credit card, driver's license, security deposit with AT&T… In particular, I was asked to pay the deposit twice, as their employee on North High Street misled me into starting an individual plan before joining a family plan, and I had to cooperate because most international students in OSU used AT&T... Such was my initial financial struggle at OSU.

On the surface, the fellowship is an "honor," but I wish I did not have it. As I learned from some classmates in the Cognitive Psychology program, the first-year fellowship was common in the Psych Department for new grad students accepted into the Ph.D. research program. I'm glad that an ordinary foreigner like me will have no chance of getting a three-year presidential fellowship because if I did, I would never be able to apply for an SSN. In reality, as I remember, that type of fellowship usually has its political connotation.

2.3 Why Did I Purchase Old Furniture?

The IFI (International Friendships, Inc.) volunteers took us to a store to purchase brand-new mattresses and another site for second-hand furniture. In addition to a queen-size bed with a mattress box, I bought a heavy wooden desk and a dilapidated laundry basket. They were cheap yet outdated. In hindsight, informed people should go to IKEA or Target directly. As for furniture and utilities, the more light-weighted, the better. I discarded these burdens after moving several times. To some extent, I felt stuck in the swamp because I had to rely on other people for transportation and shopping those days. It was frustrating.

I learned a life lesson here: think twice before purchasing or accepting used products. If something is high-quality, portable, and up-to-date, why didn't the original user keep using it or sell it for a better price? Goodwill is good but not always suitable for your specific needs.

The day the IFI volunteer lady helped deliver the furniture to my apartment in Olentangy Club, she said to me quietly, "I'm so glad you are involved in the Bible study here. Why? My husband is an engineering professor at OSU, and his department is full of engineering students from China. They work for labs run by Chinese professors, and they never speak English. Never." I smiled because I knew my roommate would fit her description. He could speak good English but didn't need to because his circle comprised only Chinese students.

2.4 Why Did My Eyesight Get Worse?

I've had a long-term relationship with optometry, like many people on earth, especially Asian students who grow up drowning in homework assignments and exams, and sheet music.

In high school, my left eye started to feel weak, so my X chromosome provider, Mandy, took me to the hospital instead of an eyewear store. I appeared to have mild myopia and astigmatism, but the doctor recommended some eye drops to relieve the "pseudo-myopia" so that I wouldn't have to wear eyeglasses. This idea of pseudo-myopia, despite being a legitimate concept, didn't work in my case. I had an irreversible change in the lenses. Denial was useless.

After high school, I insisted on getting a pair of eyeglasses because the discrepancy between my two eyes was remarkable. But Mandy always discouraged me from wearing my glasses, based on her fallacy, "You will never be able to take that off if you start to wear it." Of course, I didn't want to take it off at all, as I always hated the wind blowing sand into my sensitive eyes, and I wanted to look like my favorite Malaysian singer-songwriter, Victor Wong.

Many years later, Mandy supplemented her irrational justification with something even more mentally disturbing, "I didn't want the frame to spoil your pretty face." Apparently, she was imposing the feminine word "pretty" and her own aesthetic standards on me, as a lot of narcissistic parents would do. By the way, she has myopia herself, so mine is sort of genetic.

I went to a second-tier university in Shanghai for college, a STEM program. In my third semester of college, I suffered from conjunctivitis in my left eye for a few months, despite using antibiotics twice daily. The ophthalmologist in the school clinic couldn't figure out why, after I met her for several appointments. She even referred me to other eye doctors, who prescribed other types of powerful eye drops, such as levofloxacin, all to no avail. The mystery was solved when I talked to an optician in an eyewear store on campus. I was told to replace my eyeglasses with a new pair with nose pads because my eyelashes were long enough to touch the lenses and thus attract bacteria or other antigens. It did not sound very scientific to me, but this expensive "intervention" did solve the problem once and for all. Of course, the necessity of nose pads resulted from my lack of a high nose bridge, as Caucasians typically have. I have no control over my genotype on this matter. People are objectively diverse. Meanwhile, I was told that my sensitive eye linings could not tolerate contact lenses, so I've been compliant with that throughout my life.

My myopia was less bothersome than my astigmatism, but the latter made me stuck with the lenses. Then, in my second semester in grad school, after helping a lab mate edit the audio tracks for an hour or two in front of the old-fashioned CRT monitors in the lab directed by Mr. McCarthy, I felt my eyesight got worse the next day. To be fair, that was probably the last straw on the camelback because that semester, I read many difficult academic papers in multiple interrelated fields, which were printed out in tiny font — peer-reviewed journal articles are mostly like that. Then I got my first 3-hour long comprehensive eye examination with the famous School of Optometry at OSU. Why did it take that long? Because it was a teaching clinic. Although they confirmed my suspicion of worsened myopia, the student trainee and his supervisor initially gave me inaccurate prescriptions. How did I know it was inaccurate? They found out that my left eye drifted outward in certain tasks, so they referred me to a different clinician for corrective exercises. The specialist re-tested my eyesight and found out the new prescription was a bit strong, but new lenses were already ordered, for God's sake. At the same time, they introduced to me this new term called "exotropia" and later changed it to a mild diagnosis called "exophoria" after months of training. So my eye therapy went on and off for two years, with all sorts of tools except the computer software they were trying to sell me. Grad school already made me stare at the monitor all day long, so I refused to do that for therapy. A significant amount of co-pay, as you can imagine. Still, the problem wasn't completely solved, as it could relapse.

After I moved to Davis, CA, I had a 40-minute full exam with a senior optometrist in the downtown area. Yes, 40 minutes only, without pupil dilution. When I mentioned the exotropia to him, he said it might be congenital, as I'd never had any comprehensive eye exam before going to OSU. Still, I had my own theory for its cause.

Right before I went to America, a barber in my hometown, Smoke City, who is an old friend of Mandy, gave me a set of haircut tools as a gift. She told me I should give myself haircuts as many other Chinese international students would do, considering human labor is very expensive in America. I tried for the first semester, in front of the bathroom mirror, with the assistance of my Chinese roommate. However, I had to take off my glasses. My myopia had a discrepancy between left and right, and my astigmatism in the right eye was beyond negligible. In front of the mirror, I had to coordinate my eyes with extra effort. After several months, I noticed the difficulty in controlling my left eyeball. Therefore, immediately after receiving the diagnosis from OSU Optometry, I stopped giving myself haircuts.

It might sound funny or even ridiculous to you, yet very tragic to me. As a matter of fact, Mandy laughed too, when she heard about my left eyeball drifting laterally. What's wrong with humanity in this modern world? In my opinion, it is a silly idea to advise international students (or even scholars) to save money in this way, especially if they have imperfect eyesight. Think about the cost of endless therapy when it backfires. Is it worth it? Or is it just some kind of rationalization for their reluctance to interact with English-speaking professionals?

Luckily, I learned from a trustworthy Asian Canadian lab mate about Great Clips and used their service for several years. It was difficult to communicate with the barbers at first, but, as one senior barber/stylist from California pointed out, I had to learn these terms and overcome the initial barrier. The attempts and instincts to save money have created a series of disasters for international students from developing countries. What's the fundamental psychological blocker there? The currency ratio.

Years later, I learned from some rich-second-generation undergrads, mostly from major cities in China, that they were **never** told to give themselves haircuts. I got that preposterous advice simply because I had to return to underdeveloped Smoke City from Shanghai after graduating from college and before leaving for America. I took all the trouble to get into a university in a major city, but then, I fell to Ground Zero again. Similarly, while those rich kids could fly back to China on a regular basis because they had a home in a major city, I was hesitant to fly back because I never loved that "home" or that "hometown."

In my mind, this town has always been associated with smoke: the old generation among the locals used to smoke cigarettes everywhere, with no regard for other citizens; farmers used to burn straw after the harvest season, infusing the entire public space with heavy smoke; and even today, according to the IQAir app on my smartphone, this city has the highest PM2.5 pollution compared to adjacent cities in this region.

Chapter 3
Where Do I Sleep Next?

As an international student, I regret following some advice on the electronic brochure shared among Chinese international students. Given my department's undesirable location, I should have purchased a car and taken the driving test soon after arriving in Columbus, Ohio, instead of waiting until the second year. There was no way to live with dignity in a region of poor public transportation unless you had a car. In reality, I purchased a decade-old Nissan sedan from an earnest-looking dealer after intensive online research; then I obtained my driver's license in the spring of 2013, after practicing with my friends and colleagues. Antonio, my Latino classmate from the Department of Psychology, was involved throughout this process. Even after I failed my road test on the first trial, he identified the psychological root of my behavior problem in driving: I wasn't aware that I could press the brake pedal very deep.

When you're all on your own in a different country, if your visa is contingent on school or employment, or if your funding needs to be renewed every year, looking for housing tends to be challenging. The same headache applies to renewing a driver's license. For a graduate student in a research program, the legal status depends on the funding each year. After the first year, my funding became at stake, so I developed a preference for flexible rental leases. However, in reality, we were all expected to sign a one-year lease anyway.

Due to my unstable status, in total, I had lived in five different places in Columbus, Ohio, from the fall of 2012 to the winter of 2014. My roommates/housemates included Chinese students and immigrants, Caucasian Americans from multiple States, an Indian American, and a Native American, with their ages ranging between 20 and 40. Nothing to be proud of, considering I also shared rooms with people from different countries in international hostels and Airbnb homes from 2014 to 2017. In retrospect, in 2013, it was a crucial and risky step to take. Had I limited myself to seeking Chinese roommates on the Chinese website, I would never have gained access to the international community later on. What I wanted was a truly American life, not just a graduate degree.

In a way, I am thankful to people who were willing to share a place with me, given that rejection was far more normal than acceptance for an Asian foreigner in the Midwest. Technically speaking, I should even feel thankful to those who texted or emailed me back to reject me respectfully; however, I hesitate to do that, as I realize it was that inferior mindset that sometimes put me in an inferior position. One senior colleague from Texas once warned me that sometimes it's better not to know your co-tenant very well, and he was right about it. Some people care to befriend their co-tenants, but others consider themselves "independent" except when they need you.

Anyway, months of searching on Craigslist seemed to have paid off. Before the end of the second semester, in other words, before the summer term, an Irish American landlady invited me to check out her house. She no longer lived there herself, and she mentioned she had hosted someone from Taiwan before. During the visit, I met the only two tenants there: Brian, a male graduate student studying mathematics, who was moving out soon, and Jessica, a tiny lady locking herself in a tiny room upstairs and greeting me with "sorry, I'm just anti-social." I thought she was joking.

As I needed to settle somewhere near campus, I signed the lease for the next school year. Weeks later, my buddy Carl helped me move from Olentangy Club to this house. Carl and I remained good friends even after I stopped attending his home church. I once thought in order to become a true American, I had to become a Christian. But after studying the Bible for one semester, I decided I couldn't embrace the worldview of Christianity — I neither accept any omnipotent power over me nor want anybody to die for my sins.

That afternoon, the feeling of loneliness suddenly kicked in when I stepped into the huge backyard of this house — my first time seeing an American backyard. I was busy with school during the summer, but back home, I was so lonely. The neighborhood was quiet as hell but could be loud at night when the train was passing by the Lennox Center, where the AMC movie theater was located. Fortunately, Antonio, who came from Florida, introduced me to some events near downtown Columbus. It took time to get to know people who would know the entertainment resources, and certainly not those Ph.D. dads and moms in that department of Communication Disorders.

One might ask, when I had a car already, why didn't I move closer to the downtown area? Because I believed "the lab is my home" as if in China? Because I didn't know that interesting stuff was only available near downtown in that city. Because I never consciously knew what I liked or disliked. When you grow up in the city center, you fail to realize how boring and deprived the rest of the city could be.

In fact, due to my lack of advanced driving skills, my comfort zone was limited to the West Campus and the OSU Medical Center. I was overwhelmed by the daily information I had to process when living on the "edge."

Also, I could not foresee the upcoming winter snowstorm, allegedly the worst in a decade, according to the news report. I was never taught how to drive in the rain or snow — think about this: if a science teacher only explains theorems but never talks about difficult examples over a semester, you won't do well in the final exam. Since self-pity isn't socially acceptable, let me compare myself with those who had to struggle with the flood or those whose houses were destroyed in a hurricane or a forest fire. Yes, I do feel better.

At this point, it is important to note that I spent some time in Davis, California, after I eventually left Ohio.

Chapter 4
The Three Housemates and the Neighbors

4.1 Jessica, Alex, and Charlotte

It was a 2-story house with a basement. The master room upstairs had its private bathroom, while Jessica, the tiny lady who lived upstairs, shared one downstairs bathroom with us — me as well as the first-year veterinarian student, who joined in this house later.

Jessica studied digital art at a local community college, and she had her friends come over sometimes. We were nice to each other at first, but over time I sensed a destructive nature within this person. When she talked to people, she always looked and sounded like a victim. She liked to lay a bunch of scented candles on the table in the living room. Once, the sink in the tiny bathroom was clogged, and she told me she had poured hot candle wax into the sink. "Sorry," she said with her characteristic bitter smile before changing her tone, "At least it's not completely clogged." Then she walked swiftly upstairs and locked herself inside, making no effort to fix the mess she had left behind. Later that week, when the landlady came with her engineer husband, the person who fixed most problems in the house, I mentioned the problem of the sink and pointed out Jessica's association with this. Guess what? The landlady took that as my personal opinion and couldn't believe her "good" and long-term tenant to be the culprit. Similarly, despite the landlady's warning not to plant anything in the backyard, Jessica threw watermelon seeds in the soil, and several months later, the vines went rampant and conquered the entire backyard. However, the landlady remained biased in Jessica's favor, against all facts, simply because a woman would naturally sympathize with another frail-looking woman, as in a lot of TV shows.

The wood-based house was old. The stairway made a lot of squeaky sounds when people walked up and down. Jessica, who worked the late shift, always blamed me for making a noise when I closed the front door in the morning, but I never intentionally slammed the door. In the Midwest, many wooden doors won't fully close unless you exert force. I, the only minority in the house, was the only person she dared to be mad at.

Jessica also disliked the neighbors living next door, calling them "loud all the time." Indeed, this friendly couple held tailgating or holiday parties quite often in their house and had a lot of friends coming over. One afternoon, I was standing in the backyard and doing some eye therapy exercises with a tool called Brock String tied to a tree. "Hi, neighbor!" They greeted me and invited me to their house. The guy, Alex, was from Cincinnati, Ohio, and the girl, Charlotte, was from Washington, D.C.

I naturally got along with this open-minded and laid-back couple and enjoyed the precious hours spent with them as well as their cat Infinity. It was from them and their broad circle of friends that I learned very authentic American culture, without any pretense or façade. They were a naturally inclusive and creative social circle. After I moved away, I never had super cool neighbor-friends like that, and I never had so much fun playing beer pong or Cards against Humanity. They offered me help when I was in deep trouble, but I failed to maintain this relationship longer somehow.

Fundamentally, my unstable status would never allow me to belong to any circle during my stay in Ohio or California. I sincerely had no desire for that compressed nomadic lifestyle, which was like a curse on many international students or scholars, especially if they didn't stick with their "country mates" all the time. (The word "compatriots" is not used because I assume most potential immigrants can't be that "patriotic" to their country of origin.)

4.2 Jeremy and His Girls

Jeremy, from some country area of Pennsylvania, came to Ohio State as a first-year medical student. One afternoon, he arrived without notice and asked me to help him carry his furniture, including a safe, into the master room upstairs before we sat down in my room to talk about childhood fun stuff like Power Rangers. The topic gradually shifted toward the stupid public education systems in two big countries. His parents arrived later that week to attend his White Coat Ceremony, and they looked very proud of their son. He was driving this blue SUV, which his parents bought for him as a gift when he started college.

Later, I learned he had a brother who majored in Plant Pathology. Since they both went to Penn State for college, Jeremy lived with his brother and his brother's friends.

After that day of the White Coat Ceremony, his Facebook profile picture became a photo of him dressed up in the white coat, standing between his happy parents.

Jeremy was a bodybuilder with a low body fat index written on his face. According to him, he started running and weightlifting at an early age. However, his total body shape was disproportionate. He was certainly more dedicated to his arms and shoulders than any other body parts. I once saw a picture in which he was showing off his biceps in the company of several college buddies, ready to spend a fun night in a gay bar.

Despite Jeremy's movie-star face, he looked formidable rather than amicable: Brad Pitt's jawline, Robert Pattison's eyebrows, and Hugh Jackman's nose. The aquiline nose shape is shared by Doug, my Y chromosome provider. Jeremy may meet some girls' aesthetic expectations and be perceived as a "hot"/"cute," "stud"/"alpha male," but not in an urban and gentle way. I had this weird impression the first day I met him, and it had nothing to do with his bodybuilding practice. Also, his deliberate intonation sounded different from the Ohioan style— probably a Pennsylvania thing.

He had brought his guitars and amplifiers from his hometown and played a few songs in his room alone. I once asked him why he didn't sing, and he answered in his characteristic grumpy low pitch, "I don't sing… I don't play music to show off." It was only half a year later that I learned the true reason from someone else: he thought he didn't have a good voice. He wouldn't admit this to me directly, perhaps because he would never expose his weakness to an Asian male housemate who happened to be a songwriter.

Very quickly after he moved in, I noticed he didn't sleep in the house often, especially on weekends, despite paying the highest rent. Once he started socializing with a few other medical students and sleeping in their places, I barely saw him. Around that week, our fourth housemate, Shannon, was about to move here from her hometown Washington D.C. After the landlady confirmed that this was a female student, I was afraid this house would lose its gender balance. Why did I worry about that? Because I dreaded a feminine environment – like the family environment where I had grown up, like the student body in Communication Disorders at Ohio State (and many other institutions), like that special cohort in elementary school with a hysterical emphasis on arts. In particular, Mandy sent me into that artistic class to fulfill her vanity without realizing the long-term damage to my personal development.

One day, I talked with Jeremy, and he got very emotional when telling me he regretted choosing this house because he couldn't bring friends over. He'd prefer to live where other medical students were living. I did not understand what he meant by "friends" at that time, so I said he should totally bring people here. Then I asked him tentatively, "You wanna make friends with me?" He answered immediately, "I think we are already friends. Because we talk." At that moment, I was surprised by his shallow definition of friendship, in contrast with his behavior. Still, I chose to believe in the goodness of people at that naïve age, in that lonely situation.

Note to self: undeserved relationship labels should always be seen as a red flag.

He added that he spent a summer in Singapore as an exchange student, so he didn't feel uncomfortable with Asians. Unfortunately, as an English-speaking developed country, Singapore is no good representative of Asia in general.

In the first couple of months, Jeremy and I shared a big bottle of skim dairy milk, as I did with my previous Chinese roommate, mostly because we wanted to save space in the old fridge shared by four people. Somehow Jessica made a fuss about it and probably got jealous. Jeremy had his fourth meal sometimes right before going to bed, which was against commonsensical health tips. "But he's a med student, and a bodybuilder," I thought to myself. One day, he laughed at me when he saw me eating the granola soaked in hot milk instead of cold milk. But when I visited New York City later that year, I found out the breakfast cereal in a local diner was served with hot water. What I witnessed allowed me to realize this was not merely a matter of cultural or genetic differences but also lifestyle differences between coastal and inland regions. Moreover, as the Mr. Know-all, he told me more than once that vitamins and supplements were useless and that the good results yielded by many interventions were merely placebo effects.

In the second week of that fall semester, Jeremy brought a female classmate to the house for an hour because her shower place was broken. Another evening, he brought home a dark-skinned female classmate, and the girl stayed overnight. When I met them in his bedroom, I saw the girl seated on the carpet; in contrast, he was sitting on the bed. That night, I had my first intensive experience of culture shock. I knew that one-night stands or casual sex was fairly common in the modern world, especially in the West, and I knew I shouldn't feel strange after watching some American TV shows. Still, I didn't realize it could happen so quickly to a serious-looking first-month medical student with all the other housemates in the house that night. The next morning, they rushed down the stairs and left the house without knowing that he had triggered Jessica sleeping next door.

So I thought to myself, "Welcome to America." "These medical students are quite thirsty." "Well, good to know he's not a racist." I had to withdraw the last comment because he later explained to me that the girl was not black but Indian American. It wasn't that groundbreaking for a white guy to date an Asian woman, to my knowledge, if you acknowledge an Indian as an Asian.

That evening, when we were cooking dinner in the kitchen, I teased him, "You are awesome." I was implying that the "friends" he had wanted to bring home were equivalent to "sexual partners."

"It just happened." He said, with his characteristic shrug, "Did we make too much noise for you?"

"No, don't worry. I didn't hear it from downstairs. Your room isn't directly above mine." It was easy for me to process this after a short conversation, but Jessica was definitely affected, for she started acting hostile after that night.

After that one-night stand, Jeremy shifted his focus to a different classmate, a mysterious girl who lived alone in her apartment. He had been driving to her place to give her free guitar lessons every weekend since the start of their med school. Then suddenly, no more guitar lessons. Instead, he would tell me he was going to "study" at the girl's place on Friday nights. Over time, he stayed at her place more and more frequently and simultaneously enjoyed the resources of two homes. She must have also enjoyed his companionship, with or without guitar lessons.

Since he had two places to sleep, he had every excuse to avoid dealing with the trash can in our house. That entire semester, I was the person taking care of the trash can every Wednesday night, while Shannon, the vet student, was taking care of the dishwasher, which was run twice a week. Jessica, on the other hand, was religiously responsible for recycling. Good citizen.

So how was Jessica affected by Jeremy's one-night stand? She was avoiding him. To some extent, he was avoiding her too. One weekend, her half-Japanese male classmate stayed overnight on our couch in the living room, and after he left,

I asked her if he was her significant other. She said, "No, but at least he's not a rapist."

I was speechless because I knew what she was alluding to, so she said, "I was just kidding," before rushing back to her room upstairs. I initially held this scene from Jeremy, but instead, I mentioned this to our neighbors. Our neighbor Charlotte told me Jessica's irresponsible comment should earn her the B-word. Exactly. I didn't understand what kind of traumatic experience would lead to her overreaction to someone else's night business in their bedroom. As she realized that I was on Jeremy's side on this matter, she started to make things difficult for me in revenge. Honestly, she was the oddball compared to the three of us, and I naturally would take a male stance based on what I observed. Also, for the sake of networking, I would rather ally with these highly educated people than with whoever poured candle wax into the sink. However, Jeremy tended to take others' support for granted because he did believe he was a special elite.

These professional schools in a huge university like OSU played their own games, and some students never tried to conceal their arrogance on social media. They had their own sports meetings, leisure trips, and other social events all the time. Jeremy told me that some events were "free" or "sponsored" because he had no clear idea how much he needed to pay back after med school. After a track-and-field sports meeting, he hung on his wall a magnified photo of himself preparing to run on the track. It was a relay race. I congratulated him on winning the race, yet he told me his team didn't win.

When in Davis, California (2015-2017), I mentioned this piece of information to my psychotherapist, Layla (T3), and she commented, "Now you understand he is this type of narcissistic person." Indeed, his narcissistic trait was manifested in his behavior, in hindsight. However, I was blind to the sign at that age, probably because I was looking up to someone more athletic than myself, just like I always looked up to people who could play guitar professionally. When I was little, I was forced to study all kinds of arts, including the keyboard and the Russian accordion, yet discouraged from learning the guitar, the one instrument I had dreamed of. Why? Because Mandy felt that the guitar was for the countrymen while the piano and the violin were for the aristocrats — the so-called king and queen among all instruments in Chinese parents' dictionary. To me, that was complete nonsense—just one of the hundreds of reasons why I stopped loving Mandy way back in elementary school.

Jeremy's self-disciplined, knowledgeable, and thoughtful persona was nearly perfect to me and no doubt charming to his girls. One former female colleague in Communication Disorders, who was a bit younger than me, confirmed that med students ARE the elites in her eyes.

"Have you never met such a narcissistic person before?" Layla asked during one therapy session in 2015. My answer was negative, to her surprise. On the one hand, humility is valued and reinforced in East Asia, while complacency is criticized and punished. On the other hand, my classmates in college were outstanding Chinese students gathering in Shanghai, from various parts of China. Therefore, there were always people outperforming us in one way or another. I haven't even mentioned those admitted to the top 10 institutions in China. See? There was nothing to be narcissistic about. Muscles? Money? The number of sexual partners? Believe it or not, narcissism would be easily labeled as a personality problem in a collectivist culture. In contrast, according to Mark Manson's first book, *The Subtle*

Art of Not Giving a F*ck, mainstream American education, which was infiltrated with excessive non-objective encouragement and affirmation, resulted in a generation of narcissists. But, of course, there are always significant individual differences to observe.

There was a loophole in my memory. Notice that I only talked about college, not any time before that. As I now recall, there were a couple of narcissistic persons I knew of through middle school and high school, but I usually stayed away from them out of disgust and had no contact with them afterward. Narcissists may have concrete strengths or advantages, hence their fan base. They can be very good at appealing to authority to climb up the social ladder, and that's why they often end up more successful than people like me. This elaboration does not contradict my previous statement about stereotypical East Asian values. Remember, a narcissist, just like a racist, does not put the label on their face. In particular, a narcissist with some degree of fake humility and introversion tends to be irresistible to some ladies.

Although many people tend to confess to me without me asking, and I do actively listen to their complaints most of the time, I don't consider myself a so-called empath or allow myself to be constantly empathetic. I used to value it very much from a perspective of counseling, but not so much these days, out of the philosophy of rational selfishness, after years of tumultuous experiences. If you have ever read a self-help article that tells you how an empath will naturally, if not inevitably, suffer from a narcissist, you know what a dangerous position I had put myself in when interacting with Jeremy.

4.3 Shannon

Shannon, a first-year vet student at Ohio State, was well-mannered and truly studious. Her mom came with her and helped her install the IKEA furniture in her room. She also had a great dad who remotely helped us fix the AC once. Her workload in the veterinarian program was no less than Jeremy's. Still, she never used her quizzes or exams as an excuse to escape her chores in the house. Because she was a research assistant for a parasitology lab, I suppose she was at least partially funded, unlike Jeremy, who was solely living on a federal loan. Of course, I, at this age, do realize that there is nothing intrinsically glorious— it's all just a trade of values.

Shannon remained low-key and rarely got herself in trouble. She stayed very clean throughout her stay, and I figured she had her parents giving her useful advice. Probably because she grew up in a major city with a reliable subway system, she failed her driving test multiple times before moving to Ohio, where she could declare no independence without a car. The intrinsic motivation helped her, I suppose. However, would she be able to drive confidently in D.C. with her driving license obtained from Ohio? It doesn't really matter in the short run. She could live without a car in D.C.

Chapter 5
The ER Visit

5.1 Driving

As I remember, in the fall of 2012, as the temperature dropped quickly, there was one day when all the sidewalks felt too slippery to walk on. It might be the frost, but I felt like walking on the ice. Thankfully, I did not have to walk on the ice again in 2013, as I had an old car to use. However, when I learned to drive from a coach back in China, I wasn't taught things like how to drive at night, how to drive on the freeway, how to push forward against the blizzard, how to pull the car out of the snowdrift, how to perform parallel parking or reverse parking, how to use a parking structure in a big city, how to use all those extra buttons in the car, what to do with a frozen door, or what to do when the frost kept occupying the windshield despite the heater already on. So, with no exception, I had to struggle with those urgent needs myself.

I was told to figure out things over time, and they wouldn't teach me these practical skills beforehand. Why not? Most people in my life do not err on the side of caution as I do; instead, they blame me for overthinking. When the trouble happens, they are nowhere to be found. That's why basic driving training is deficient. One senior lab mate from Canada recommended I go to an American driving school. I wish I had at least partially followed his advice, if not for the time limit. However, I was uncertain if they could teach me everything I needed. Many lucky Americans had good parents who could teach them how to drive at a young age; I did not have that luxury. Driving used to be a privilege for the rich in China and thus didn't apply to the family I grew up in. Imagine if Mandy or Doug saw this, they would no doubt use "other people's offspring" as the counterexample, as usual, and call me childish or immature. However, their attempt to deny my objective disadvantage will no longer be taken seriously.

5.2 "We Are Just Roommates."

One Saturday afternoon, I met some interesting people called Redditors in the neighbors' backyard. When I saw Jeremy coming back, I asked him to come over and meet these people. During the backyard conversation, he exhibited arrogance and impatience and kept emphasizing how difficult it was to get into med school. After Jeremy jumped over the fence to our own backyard, a guy called Chris pointed out, "He doesn't like us. We can't meet his standard." This pal later became a supportive friend of mine throughout my stay in Ohio. He lived with a black cat called Elvis.

I followed Jeremy back into our house, and it was my first time seeing his frustrated face. He was one year older than me, with two years of teaching experience on MCAT with Kaplan, which implied something prevented him from getting into med school directly after college, in hindsight. According to him, he took MCAT a second time after the original score expired.

I asked him why he was so moody. He explained that normally someone would organize parties for the med students every weekend. But there was a three-day break that particular weekend, so many students went back home.

THE ER VISIT

He said he had no idea what to do all of a sudden, so he decided to go to the gym, but the gym was closed. Bummer!

I said to him, "You want to go to a bar with me? There's The Tree Bar nearby."

He responded, "I'd rather be alone." Then he started to cook his regular dinner—chicken breast, broccoli, and pasta, with his grumpy face on. It was still very early.

"You'd rather have nobody to hang with than hang with me, although you said we were friends already." My blood started to freeze at that moment.

Then he lost his temper and started his cathartic lecture, **"Nobody asks a question like that! You always ask me difficult questions I don't know how to answer. I am a med student, and I have no time to think about that! I only make friends with people who have shared goals, interests, and experiences with me."**

"But we are housemates already. I don't understand your logic." I said.

"I think when the landlady rented rooms to us, she only expected this to be a rooming house, and we didn't have to become friends. I meet so many people every day, and I just wanna be left alone when I'm back home." He said in an angry tone.

I knew he must have ruminated over his presumptuous answer to my old question. He used me as a vent, blamed everything on me, and even involved the landlady in his argument just because he had no party prepared for him that week!

In the meantime, I never expected him to "think" about the answer. But he needed to think because he had too much to hide behind his charismatic façade. By the way, I learned the word "façade" from a Scottish American personal trainer in California when we met for the first time in 2016 — he used this word to describe "the American culture" that I failed to embody.

"Yeah, I don't have anybody around my age to talk with this semester. Only when I take classes on Main Campus, or when I teach the lab sessions." I followed in a sad tone.

"Okay, so your situation is the opposite. Anyway, this house isn't a good fit for me. And the train always wakes me up at night."

Back in the kitchen, I asked him another purely tentative question: "Could you tell me why you are unwilling to listen to my songs?" That question was a dummy question, a probe, as I had no way of knowing whether he had listened or not — he had no obligation to listen to my songs anyway. As far as I knew, he was mostly into loud rock bands; besides, the lyrics I wrote back then contained some Japanese, which he would mentally block.

My hunch was right. While cooking his chicken breast, Jeremy answered in a sobbing voice, as if being bullied, "We are just roommates." Suddenly, I felt I was dealing with a teenager in need of special attention.

As I recall, when he first arrived in Columbus with his acoustic and electric guitars, I told him I wrote songs, and he became silent. Besides, I said to him, "we should **cooperate**," half-jokingly. In response, he gave me a bitter look plus a sneer— something I probably have received from people more often than I am aware. Due to my non-native English skills, I didn't know the accurate word was "**collaborate**" until Julian, my Latino neighbor at Olentangy Club, pointed it out months later. A remarkable difference between Latino Americans and white Americans was thus manifested, which many international students would echo: The former corrects you directly, while the latter typically stays silent for fear of seeming impolite. I suppose the group difference outweighs the individual variance on this matter. Another factor might be that upper-class elites, including the academics, won't allow criticism to come out of their mouths, perhaps due to social conditioning.

"But why did you talk with me so enthusiastically the first time we met?" I had never known that a person outside the field of politics could deny their previous words so blatantly and still feel so self-righteous. The next year, on hearing my story, my new American housemate introduced the term "douchebag" to me.

"Maybe I was just trying to be **friendly**." He answered. Apparently, I was seen as an appetizer to him before he could be served his main course — other med students.

"But I make friends with different types of people, and they serve different functions," I said.

"Yeah, I do the same." He looked uneasy when he realized he didn't sound thoughtful enough on that issue.

"Can't you at least give me a chance?" I fell into my low-pitch and low-blood-pressure mode at that moment, and without realizing it, I put myself in an inferior position, even when I felt played and betrayed by him.

"We'll see." He said with another bitter sneer. In retrospect, he must have felt strange to be "worshiped" like that. Then he brought his food into his bedroom upstairs, leaving the mess in the sink as usual. With a sigh, I walked out of the house and drove to my office. Unlike those big engineering departments, the buildings on the West Campus were usually empty on weekends.

Some psychological research reported that while females

like to talk to their friends when upset, males tend to bury themselves under more tasks to avoid facing negative emotions directly. That's quite true. I had a specific task to finish that night, which was to keep working on my re-application to Ph.D. programs in Psychology. After my first year's experience at Ohio State, I decided not to finish this particular Ph.D. program but only get a Master's from this department. I was trying to email a clinical scientist I wanted to work with. Yet, my mood fell into a downward spiral in that process, as I recollected my painful and lonely journey of pursuing psychology education in China. I was drowned in self-pity and, all of a sudden, burst into tears in the dark office.

Ironically, Jeremy, a pre-med in college, did a minor in psychology. He was able to RA in a Health Psychology Lab at Penn State, which helped him apply to med school. In contrast, my "famous" university didn't even have a psychology program, let alone a minor program to offer, despite my childhood dream in that field. Upon seeing or hearing this, some privileged people would take my words literally and construe this highlighted contrast as a sign of jealousy. But it simply wasn't— life has always been more unfair for people growing up in developing countries. I always knew it and accepted it.

When I came to myself, I chatted with Chris on Facebook and told him Jeremy admitted he didn't want me as a friend, against his own words. Chris encouraged me to let go of this person and move on, and I wish things could be so straightforward. If only Jeremy could just disappear from my life or stay cold to me forever.

In Shanghai, by the end of 2017, Mandy learned the detailed version of this story and criticized me relentlessly, **"You were so childish to worship a neurotic person like** that. **How could friendship be announced explicitly? You believe someone is your friend just because they told you so?**" But why had I never learned such lessons before grad school? The fundamental reason was that I had never needed to ask a specific person for friendship, except when I was having a practice conversation with an English teacher from Canada at the age of ten — I was rejected directly. I had never fallen into such a lonely situation before—no company or cohort. I had never been alienated like this before: back in college, I attended several courses together with those med students, and they were no sacred existence to us because med school started at the college level in most countries. Unfortunately, when people get lost on an island, they may even drink their filtered urine to survive. That was precisely my situation. Besides, most people in East Asian cultures would reject you directly rather than take you in and then kick you out, as Jeremy did to me. The latter would be considered as being fake and wasting other people's time. Unfortunately, it isn't uncommon in the mainstream American culture I have interacted with — to play nice at first and to find a politically correct excuse to turn you down later.

5.3 "I'm Sick."

That evening, Jeremy came back late as usual, and the noise he made walking upstairs was loud as usual. Since I entered grad school, I barely had the energy to stay up late over the weekends, but Jeremy was different: sometimes he studied in the library until midnight, and other times he partied very hard. I couldn't understand why these medical students had so many parties, mostly drinking parties. They partied after every block (the short semester in OSU School of Medicine). I originally didn't believe he would get deadly drunk because these were future clinicians who would wear serious faces, at least in the daytime. However, months later, I learned that he once passed out during a drinking contest with some other med students. Also, he would criticize religion in front of his religious classmates while drunk. This American med school culture challenged my assumptions, although I was cautious not to overgeneralize based on this particular guy. Years later, I learned from a young pharmacist in California that it is common for healthcare professionals to have different daytime and nighttime personas.

The temperature plummeted that night by about 20°F, and I hadn't developed the habit of closing the window tightly by then. By the way, I didn't know any immigrant who enjoyed adjusting to the Fahrenheit scale used in America. In the night, some cold air sneaked into my room and caught me off guard when my immune system reached a historically low point due to my sadness. By the way, psychophysiological research has shown that social rejection can weaken the immune system; that's why people, especially minorities, should be attentive to their general health after being socially rejected.

I had no symptoms in the morning, but I started to shiver in the afternoon and felt powerless when I was in the office again. Knowing something was wrong, I immediately drove back home and stayed in bed for the rest of the day. I had a fever. Then I took some meds brought from China, and soon my body temperature dropped. The next morning, I still felt weak. When I opened my door, I saw Jeremy leaving. The light in the living room was dim. He saw me and asked me, "How are you?" in a monotonous tone as if nothing had happened two days before. I answered powerlessly, "I'm sick." But he didn't seem to hear me clearly, for he left without a word. He just shut the door.

Jeremy and some undergrad girls in the Department of Communication Disorders complained that they sometimes had difficulty hearing me speak. There were several reasons:

(1) My accent plus my incapability to produce and articulate long and abstract sentences in English those days. Unfortunately, some people, such as my professor Mr. Hoffman, interpreted it as my lack of self-confidence.

(2) It was often frustrating to talk with a person like Jeremy because I saw his impatience when I failed to come up with terms like "rhinitis" (inflammation in the nose). I saw his indifference to other people's problems ("Whatsoever" or "Heh, Latino culture~"). I was afraid to waste his time and make him grumpy, as he always exhibited superb time management skills in front of me. To put it straight, I wasn't worth his time compared to his med student parties.

(3) He was listening to me while chewing food, and those students who complained were often sitting in the back rows in a small and reverberant classroom where their tireless chatting created some steady background noise.

(4) My voice has a baritone's low pitch and high sonority, which makes it difficult to perceive, among other remarkable voices, or against background noise.

(5) My breathing was very weak those days because I primarily used thoracic breathing instead of abdominal breathing. In fact, during the first semester, when I saw Melissa, a physical therapist at the Student Clinic, for knee pain, she instructed me to strengthen the belly muscles after noticing the overpronation (fallen arches) in my feet.

The following Monday, I went to school for classes and TA duties despite the fatigue. But the first two weeks of the semester were crazy. I had difficulty fulfilling the credit hour requirements for graduate teaching associates until I was advised to get research hours with Mr. Osman, whose lab I had worked in since the summer of 2013. I left the lab directed by Mr. McCarthy, mainly because he didn't let me get involved in any research project when I was there. I didn't want to waste more time with him, so I found Mr. Osman, an assistant professor at OSU Eye & Ear Hospital, whose field of study overlapped with my interest.

This "research credit" option was invisible to me initially because Mr. Osman was an external faculty member affiliated to the Medical Center. I had to request that the department staff member manually add this course to the system. It clearly demonstrates why you should consult a senior professor who is well-informed about the resources in a giant institution. I remember taking a master-level engineering course eventually, and it was laborious. Since I had no classmates from the same department, I had to figure out the problems in the homework assignments all alone, unlike those international students in the E.E. major. It should be no surprise that two-thirds of the students in that classroom were Chinese students.

That week, I had three lab sessions to teach, each lasting 2 hours. On Monday, I was doing okay. On Tuesday, my fever returned, so I went home early. On Wednesday, I started sweating and shivering again, and for the first time in my life, I noticed blood in my urine. I was terrified and had no idea what to do.

5.4 An Appointment or the Emergency Room?

My first reaction was to ask Jeremy, the 25-year-old first-year medical student in my house because his brain was full of medical terminology. He told me his health insurance was through the med school and different from our typical student insurance with Aetna. So I took out my Aetna brochure, which read like the Bible to me and called the OSU Medical Center to make an appointment with a urologist. I was told that the earliest availability was the following Monday, in the Eye and Ear Hospital off-campus. With the help of NSAIDs and cold compression, my fever was somehow under control again. Finally, I survived that week's school, but the frequent urination at night scared me.

My fever returned on Saturday afternoon, and I was lying in bed in despair. Previously, Jeremy had said I could ask him for help if I needed anything, so I called him and told him my fever had relapsed. However, he said he was at a party, so he couldn't hear me. "Never mind, have fun," I said and hung up.

When I was nearly unconscious, I made a phone call to Natalie, a trustworthy musician colleague from New Jersey. I told her I wouldn't make it to the lab meeting next Monday. I was involved in a second lab in the School of Music on Main Campus, where we studied the psychology of music: why I was attracted to Ohio State in the first place. When she learned my symptoms had persisted for a week, she insisted I go to the hospital immediately. She even volunteered to drive me to urgent care — I didn't even know the difference between urgent care and the ER at that time. Natalie was from a different state, so she used the same student insurance and had to figure out all sorts of things for herself, including the tax return, unlike many in-state students.

When we were at the urgent care in the Morehouse Hospital near my home address, the doctor took the urine and blood samples from me and decided to transfer me to the ER in the Medical Center, as they were about to close for the weekend. So Natalie drove me to the busy ER, and I waited half an hour before being admitted. The nurses took me through different tests and examinations in the next 10 hours, including a CT scan. I told Natalie about the emerging anxiety and the rough weeks I was going through, but not the tricky issues with my housemates. After several hours, a doctor arrived and informed me that I appeared to have a bladder infection, and they diagnosed me with urinary tract infection, which was less common in males. Anyway, they put me on antibiotics via IV that night. I was required to take oral antibiotics twice a day for a month after being released.

Seeing I was taken care of, Natalie said goodbye. One week later, after I recovered, I received a postcard in the mailbox with best wishes from my lab mates and my Canadian professor Mr. Anderson from the School of Music. From then on, I saw Natalie as someone who saved my life, though not technically, and I saw that lab as my true home in Ohio State, though I never collected data in their booth. After that night, I also realized that these American peers were much better at handling realistic problems, even after factoring out their advantage of growing up in this country. In China, almost everything had been preselected and packaged for us, and we were not given enough choices other than the multiple-choice questions on the exam papers. By the way, universities in China were surrounded by walls, like the Forbidden City; in contrast, Ohio State was structurally open. CUNY, The City University of New York, is even better, as the campuses are embedded in the city itself.

Everybody who has spent a night or two alone in the ER

THE ER VISIT

knows that the experience is generally unpleasant, despite my acknowledgment of the hard work of those clinicians, including the nursing technicians working the night shift. The OSU Medical Center was like a labyrinth where I could easily get lost. Sitting in a wheelchair and being pushed to different places in an empty building, I felt like in some TV show I had watched before. A little gruesome, to say the least. At night, after the CT scan and the blood tests were done, with the IV sending cold fluid into my body, and due to the lack of food intake, I started to shiver again. I managed to get a nurse to come to me and cover my body with a blanket. Meanwhile, the "accommodation" was quite gorgeous for my third-world standard— a single room with a restroom, television, and breakfast with waffles and orange juice. The bill was charged according to the outpatient service pricing, but I was still worried about the total cost. Had they ever asked whether the patients wanted 5-star-hotel service during a hospital visit? Or did they offer me high-end service because they noticed I was an OSU student? According to some news articles I read, big American hospitals pride themselves on providing home-like services and even bringing in virtual reality devices for some patients, but who will pay the bill? Sponsors? The insurance companies?

Thankfully, IV after IV, blood draw after blood draw, my fever subsided, and I was regaining some power after that horrific night's struggle. The previous evening, I texted my three housemates that I was in the ER and couldn't go back to the house that night. And their responses?

Jessica responded very quickly, "I don't know! Ask other roommates!"

Jeremy responded hours later, after his party was over, "I'm so sorry. I didn't see your text. You need my help now?"

Shannon did not respond. I expected nothing from her,

anyway. Without a car, she couldn't do anything.

On Sunday morning, after breakfast, I was finally able to pick up my phone to text people. I texted Natalie. Then I texted Jeremy with the room number and asked him to bring me some clothes from my bedroom — he was my only male housemate, so I had no other choice. Despite his hangover, he replied around 9 AM and showed up around 10 AM. I thanked him and managed to shake hands with him before he left. In retrospect, that symbolic handshake I initiated meant nothing substantive, as our relation wouldn't improve just because I was sick. Presumably, he was one of the early-stage contributing factors to my illness, but how would he realize or even acknowledge that?

Additionally, I texted my emergency contact Carl, who then decided to come and visit me with his girlfriend, Lindsay, in the afternoon.

Several hours after the last blood draw, the attending doctor allowed me to be discharged, and they also wanted to help me make a follow-up appointment at The Student Clinic. When they asked me the name of my "family doctor," I said I didn't know what that was — I didn't even have a family in the US. Then I agreed to go to The Student Clinic to select a primary care physician when picking up my prescription drugs at their pharmacy the next week. Meanwhile, I reminded the attending doctor that I was going to see a urologist at Eye & Ear on Monday morning, i.e., the following day. Unfortunately, everything turned out to be too late because making an appointment with a specialist in that healthcare system was too hard.

In case you didn't know, such a concept as "family doctor" or "primary care physician" wasn't popularized in China at all, not even today. It sounds appealing to have someone taking care of your family holistically. Yet, my first-hand experience with the healthcare system in the US has taught me that the relatively cheap HMO model isn't as scientific as it sounds. You pay for what you get, after all. A dismissive opinion of a primary care physician could seriously delay effective treatment to be provided by a specialist. How about PPO? People with an expensive PPO plan might choose the wrong type of specialist based on their subjective understanding of medicine, which could also lead to a waste of time and money. Therefore, should PPO users always rely on a family doctor for decision-making? Absolutely not; otherwise, why would they pay for the expensive PPO plan? I didn't have that insight as a foreigner at that age and thus was bogged down in an unnecessary amount of physical therapy those years.

When Carl and Lindsay arrived, they drove me home. I opened the door and saw Jeremy walking downstairs. When he threw me another smile on his movie-star face, I had this transient delusion that his change of attitude could mean something concrete and that I should forgive his past hurtful behavior. But at that time, I never dared to mention how I got sick in the first place or mention the word "friend" again, because I knew my recovering body couldn't take another relentless blow from him.

When I saw the urologist on Monday, their medical resident made simple observations on my lower body before the clinical professor showed up. They pointed out that UTI was rare for males, though my symptoms did sound like an infection. I asked them if it could be different for Asian males, and their answer was negative. "In med school, we studied clinical data from across the world," they said, which made American medicine sound even more advanced. However, they did not want to investigate further since my symptoms were mostly gone, except for the general weakness and mild headaches.

A few days later, I went to the Student Clinic and asked their African-American staff to recommend a primary care physician for me. Then I got Dr. Clark, a white male primary care physician with a low voice — sorry, no Asian clinician available in that clinic, unlike in California. After seeing my medical record, Dr. Clark thought that the urologists in the Department of Urology had not done their job, which, in retrospect, implied that he wasn't fully convinced of the diagnosis. He then referred me to Ohio Urology Group, which was independent of Ohio State Health Network, yet still covered by my student health insurance, the same PPO plan for all international students.

The MD, an African-American gentleman, told me my symptoms sounded more like prostatitis, very likely due to one's high-stress level — another clinician later explained that the signal was possibly transmitted top-down through the vagus nerve. An occasional cold or fever should NOT have led to those severe symptoms, and therefore, the missing piece of the puzzle was emotional or, say, psychosomatic. I admitted to him that the increased baseline stress I was going through could date back to the previous summer when I was walking on a tightrope toward the following year's funding. In the meantime, I didn't tell him the direct emotional trigger: I was socially rejected and pissed off by my white male housemate, a first-year med student. I knew nothing about UTI or prostatitis, but as for my susceptibility to anxiety, I'd known it so well because I grew up facing all kinds of threatening stimuli, mostly from Chinese parenting and Chinese public education.

Thankfully, once I recovered, the symptoms never came back. One thing worth mentioning was that I hadn't even noticed the suppression of my erectile function until it returned to me a week later. That night, it felt like an electric shock being administered from my brain down my spine, and suddenly, I was spiritually alive again.

After hearing about my situation, Mr. Osman, the PI of the research project I was working on, asked me to pause data collection for the experiment temporarily, despite his leaving the position soon. I reflected on my life and realized that for a long time, my schedule had been too tight because I was always trying to fill those loopholes from my childhood: the allure of the unattainable. In contrast to the hollowness of the spring semester of 2013, the fall semester of 2013 was intense, but my body was no longer young.

Back in my home department of Communication Disorders, a senior grad student from China brought me some homemade chicken soup after knowing I had been terribly sick. She offered a tremendous amount of help in those years.

I learned about stress management through those workshops organized by the Graduate School Council. However, most of them were only peripherally helpful because the fundamental threats were still there: lack of stability (I could be easily kicked out of America) and loneliness (I couldn't spend a lot of time in the musicians' lab due to the time conflict). To be fair, there is no guarantee that any international student can eventually get a job and a green card; most simply cannot stay permanently. Also, I wasn't the only minority international student to be tormented by loneliness. Our loneliness is not understood by mainstream US citizens, hardly by immigrants from similar white-dominant countries, not really by people who have never left their home countries, and not even clearly by ourselves. Unfortunately, I can't expand on this topic here, considering each individual's situation is unique.

However, I have this suspicion: Chinese students who stay within their ethnic group are less likely to be beaten by loneliness, than those who attempt to break out of the circle and mingle with the natives and other internationals. For the latter type, including myself, their social "circle" can be broad and inclusive. Still, the average intimacy level remains low — I was assumed (not perceived) to be too alien to be considered an equal by a lot of mainstream Americans. The risk is also high: once the person gets kicked out of America, everything goes futile. Meanwhile, according to online statistics, Asian males are the least favorite on the global visual market, by which I mean Tinder and even Grindr. There are some objective genetic disadvantages associated with that outcome, body size in particular, so I wouldn't attempt to argue against the facts through rationalization. Some still might, out of initial denial, and they might eventually understand.

5.5 Daniel Tosh

That Sunday morning in the ER, when I was eating breakfast, the nurse asked me if I wanted to watch some television. Gosh, I hadn't watched any television for a long time, except for football games at friends' houses. I browsed through different channels and found everything to be boring. Suddenly, this tall and cynical guy caught my attention, and every single sentence coming out of his mouth sounded so hilarious to me. The comedy acts on this show were mean and sometimes vulgar, but they made me, this patient feel my life wasn't the worst. Every single day on earth, lots of people get themselves injured and ridiculed because of their reckless behavior. The lucky ones may receive some "Web Redemptions" on this show *Tosh.0*, but how about the catastrophically injured ones? "What doesn't kill you makes you stronger?" Should they buy into this irresponsible nonsense, knowing what awaits them might be brain surgery or lifelong paraplegia?

From then on, I watched many of his episodes on the Comedy Central app on my iPad, but not in public places. Yes, my soul has always been mundane and sometimes dirty. That's the real me. I just had to pretend to be "a person with a good taste" when trying to earn my educational credentials.

Daniel Tosh was the first American comedian that stole my vulnerable heart, and, in particular, it happened inside the ER. After that, I started to explore more comic shows on Comedy Central, such as the world-famous Daily Show with Jon Stewart and @Midnight with Chris Hardwick, the genius from UCLA. I quickly developed a high tolerance for all kinds of language, above and beyond my pre-existing knowledge in anatomy and physiology.

After moving to Davis, California, I kept watching stand-up comedy online whenever I ate alone, in a subconscious attempt to remedy the negative impact of being scolded during meals by Mandy when I was a teenager—scolded for what? Typically, "why can other people's kids score higher than you in this exam?" Over time, I made acquaintance with some grassroots comedians through local open-mic shows. In 2017, I proudly spent one weekend in San Francisco just to watch my favorite comedian Anthony Jeselnik perform live in person as one of the handful of Asians in the white-dominant audience. I will never forget that Cobb's Comedy Club in SF had no barrier between the two tiny urinals in the men's room, which generated a very awkward feeling for guys lining up after the show.

Anyway, I felt fortunate to find this worldly yet intelligent art form that brings people laughter and tears of happiness. As a natural songwriter, I barely knew how to write something happy because of the consistently oppressed tone of my early life. I felt excited to see this profession that tells more brutal truth than an average human being would, considering I lacked truth-tellers in my workplace at that time, in Davis, California. People working in an academic setting often can't afford to tell the truth out loud. Political correctness is one thing, but many people grew up being behaviorally conditioned to say positive things only, and therefore, may teach their offspring to see the world through rosy lenses, which I deem a toxic influence.

Although I am no longer following any single comedian nowadays, like a zealous fan, I still believe I should belong with them if I could reincarnate in the land of America. I might be hated or receive death threats for the inappropriate jokes I tell, and that would be my destiny.

5.6 The Medical Bill and a Call from The School Staff

One week after the discharge, the hospital sent me the medical bills for the co-pay, one after another, and they totaled up to over $1200, which was shocking to me at that time. That was a substantial amount for an international student from a country with a much less valuable currency. I literally lost an entire month's stipend on one hospital visit, taking into account the 14% tax withholding. Christian and Satine in *Moulin Rouge* the musical would surely understand how speechless and helpless I felt at that moment, as you can see through the lyrics of Elephant Love Medley — It was just one "innocent" night.

I asked Jeremy how to parse all those fees and

adjustments on the bills, and he had no idea. Nor did his classmates in med school. No surprise, as I later learned that most people couldn't understand the bills. By the time I left Ohio State, I had learned a bit from the staff of the Student Clinic and realized those mysterious numbers had a lot to do with the insurance companies. After moving to Davis, CA, in 2015, the insurance plans through the employer became a choice I had to make, and it was even more challenging and heart-wrenching. As I remember, I watched many online videos carefully to make a less bad choice. Yet, because there was ZERO hospital accessible to me within the "city" of Davis, every option was doomed to be a bad one.

The Tuesday after my ER visit, I received an email from some OSU staff member asking me to meet him on Main Campus. The guy explained my rights and benefits as a teaching assistant, including safety issues, insurance, sick leave... Wait, sick leave? I could have called in sick when I was sick instead of teaching those lab sessions with a sick body? But at the beginning of the semester, how could I miss anything? How could I know whether I would be able to carry on safely or not? Will work always make your sickness worse? Who would take my place if I needed to take sick leave? Who would attend lectures on my behalf? Was everything just a formality? If I had stayed home that week, could I have avoided the ER visit, which cost me over a thousand bucks and posed a risk to my liver?

Why didn't the concept of "sick leave" come to mind when I was sick? Was I dumb? In some people's eyes. Lack of work experience? Maybe. Anyway, I'd never seen examples or precedents on this issue. Nobody ever mentioned the term before this meeting. The phrase "sick leave" was not in my English vocabulary yet, despite my knowledge of the Chinese equivalent, or at least had never been activated before. For the most part, my life in English and my life in Chinese were like two parallel lines, with much less overlap than needed. Strangely enough, nobody around me ever mentioned something like a primary care physician or suggested the idea of sick leave, either. Mandy blamed me for this in 2017, "Why are you so stupid? Sick leave is common sense." No, it's not common sense when a man is swamped with a busy schedule with responsibilities.

By then, I had already realized that my English skills would never reach the level of a highly-educated native, let alone a lyricist, simply because I did not grow up in an English-speaking environment. I wasn't a *1.5-generation immigrant*, a term that refers to people who move to a foreign country in their childhood or adolescence, and usually with their family. While I used to envision that my English skills would grow asymptotically adequate, my observation over time has informed me otherwise — I would never be able to write like Mark Manson or debate like Ben Shapiro. Even today, there are lots of loopholes in my knowledge, objectively speaking, as I am unaware of what I don't know until some mistake pops out. However, many people were inclined to construe my objectivity, honesty, and rationality as a sign of low confidence or high modesty, consistent with a stereotype about Asian students from an American perspective. In retrospect, I shouldn't have been surprised, as it is widely perceived by the international community that American pop culture rewards overconfidence and even pomposity sometimes. To me, this partially explains how some incompetent yet narcissistic politicians can have a huge fan base.

Don't you wonder why the OSU staff contacted me so late? Did they expect people to be totally healthy before that

THE ER VISIT

point? My guess is that they always prioritize big departments on the Main Campus, and small programs like Communication Disorders on the West Campus would be put toward the end of the queue until it's too late.

I didn't tell the staff member that I just came out of the emergency room, which means I repressed my emotions only to be polite. I wonder how he would react to it. Looking back, I regretted not attending that free talk regarding the Aetna insurance, which was held in the Ohio Union on Main Campus the previous semester. What I did instead was stay at Mr. McCarthy's lab meeting to join the celebration of some girl's birthday. One should always put their health benefits first over other people's rituals— I learned the lesson the hard way. However, it's still hard to implement or stick to in real life, especially in a collectivist culture. Whereas my case wasn't the most tragic among international students, I have become strongly opposed to the idea of learning everything through making mistakes, i.e., error-based learning, instead of organized coaching.

As an international student, I wasn't equipped with the skills to seek healthcare for myself strategically because I was unaware of the framework of the US healthcare system, including things like HMO and PPO plans. Moreover, because I was told one's health condition is private in America, because I was told to separate personal life from work, and because I was scared and ashamed, I didn't know how to ask for help. Had I known that I could see a primary care physician first and let him provide early intervention, there was a probability the costly ER visit could have been avoided. He could probably refer me to a more trustworthy specialist as well. I know it's essentially hindsight, but no one can be too prepared for dealing with healthcare issues. Besides, it might sound funny to you, but at that age, I didn't even know what ibuprofen was, or how to differentiate between nonsteroidal anti-inflammatory drugs (NSAIDs) and antibiotics.

Here's the price you pay for independence; when you are a kid, your parents make the decisions on your behalf, good or bad, and mostly mediocre, instead of teaching you how to make rational decisions. However, when you are an adult facing multiple demands, you have to learn through making mistakes if nobody ever warns you of the pitfalls beforehand — for example, I have learned that one should just take days off when sick. Of course, it's easier said than done, especially if you have been conditioned to prioritize duty over health since the former was what your Chinese parents mostly cared about. By the way, in this context, "duty" means studying for higher test scores to please the adults or to avoid punishment from the adults.

At the same time, there is an underlying competition between waiting to see the doctor through an appointment and asking a pharmacist directly for quick solutions. Unfortunately, there is no universal answer to that dilemma. Looking back, I wish I had at least tried the CVS walk-in clinic, but in reality, my attention was fixated on those few healthcare providers listed on the insurance brochure. Seriously, how could I even know or notice the extra resources without someone telling me? I only learned CVS walk-in clinic from a classmate who was a 1.5-generation Asian immigrant, and she was a decade older than me!

I know whatever I say might look ridiculously unsophisticated to an insider, a senior clinician, or an insurance specialist. Yet many other international students have to stumble through the healthcare system once or twice in a similar fashion unless they are fortunate enough to have a guide or mentor in daily life. Or they can make a half-

THE ER VISIT

joking comment, "I dare not get sick because of the high cost of healthcare in America." Is our health situation totally under our control, though? Or shall we pray? Sometimes, the senior like to tell the young that "all you need to do is ask." Let me point out the hollowness or fallacy in this piece of advice: without knowing that something exists, how do you know what to ask for? Plus, the overused slogan "No Whining" seems to tell us to "suck it up" no matter what.

Speaking of education, who should be responsible for filling the knowledge gap for international students? The institutions? As I recall, Ohio State required all international students to take an online course that was quite formative, i.e., superficial. They were more interested in teaching us to hand in homework assignments through Carmen, the online teaching platform, and not to vandalize school properties than in protecting ourselves and our rights. They are aware of the big loophole in our knowledge, but they can't teach us anything useful without first acknowledging the negative side of the American society. Therefore, they choose to say nothing substantive.

It's my understanding that navigation through the "healthcare" industry should be mandatory courses or workshops offered to all international students and employees. Why necessary? Things that baffle the locals could paralyze the foreigners, despite many foreigners being the most learned, resourceful, adaptive, and independent back in their countries of origin. Yet, in reality, the institution only focused on mild routines: they provided superficial orientation to mainstream landmarks, including the Thompson library, RPAC, and the football stadium.

I don't expect a mid-tier institution like Ohio State to take concrete action to improve itself in everything. However, I think they should at least take these concerns seriously if they care about sustainable competitiveness in higher education.

5.7 Working with Mr. Osman

Mr. Osman, who was a non-tenured faculty member at the OSU Medical Center in 2013, immigrated to the US from the tumultuous Middle East with his family in the 20th century. Like many other families of a Christian background, they had to escape from both warfare and persecution. After finishing college in California, he first became a Canadian citizen by getting a Ph.D. over there. As a US green card holder, he said he didn't want US citizenship. Presumably, being a US-based Canadian citizen spares him with unnecessary cognitive dissonance. For example, he needn't worry about accidentally voting for some POTUS who might someday launch a military attack on his home country.

Mr. Osman was initially reluctant to let me work with him because he was fighting a battle against his employer in the spring of 2013, as he later revealed to us. According to him, he was plagiarized by his superior, Ms. Foster, who stole his research idea and submitted a grant proposal without him. As a result, he filed a case against that senior professor. Yet, to maximize their interest, the Medical Center decided to silence him and asked him to leave his non-tenured position by December 2013, against his original work contract.

After I told him my option to only get a Master's degree from OSU, Mr. Osman finally accepted me into his spacious yet deadly quiet lab. He was indeed helping me work toward my degree by assigning me an exploratory project to work on ("exploratory," according to a senior professor in Canada). In return, I was, indeed, making his project progress faster. Remember, nobody accepts a graduate student out of mere kindness. The student has to be capable and valuable, to be accepted. Mentoring would improve the faculty member's CV, especially for junior scientists like Mr. Osman. When one person considers helping another person, "having nothing to lose" is the bottom line. While a good relationship usually arises from a win-win situation, many people in power won't let go of that sense or notion of hierarchy: they covertly want to be worshiped.

Due to the time constraint, I couldn't collect sufficient data for my master's thesis project, which stressed me out as time passed. Meanwhile, he was unwilling to change the ostensibly flawed experimental design when he was preparing to leave. Despite his effort to design good experiments independently without feedback from senior researchers, reality always showed he was incapable of doing that. It is common sense that, for experimental psychology, if your design has any conspicuous flaw, such as failing to control for some confounding variable, the whole study is vulnerable to intellectual attacks. Unfortunately, with his bet-on-chance rationale, he habitually hoped to get away with non-trivial problems by adding caveats at the end or hoping that reviewers wouldn't notice the crack.

When referring to his precarious job situation, Mr. Osman even said to me once, "My life is already like gambling." At that time, he had just submitted a proposal for a new NIH grant and was waiting for the result. I learned that "gambling" comparison from him, which made me look madly desperate later on. Looking back, I'd say about 30% of his daily influence was harmful to me, not even including the repetitive strain injury in 2015.

Due to his persistent fight for his employment rights, he was able to stay a few more months, which allowed me to collect enough data for the project. But why did it have to take so long? We only needed less than 30 participants for this small study, anyway. The truth is, during the snowy winter, which lasted for months, very few people were willing to drive to the hospital off-campus for the research study. OSU students who didn't have a car could theoretically take the medical shuttle from the main hospital on campus if they didn't have a tight schedule. Still, the finals, the winter break, and the debilitating snowstorm created a vacuum period for us. To amend that, we offered free rides the following spring to get more participants in one particular category, namely musicians. In the meantime, I had started drafting the thesis way before finishing the data collection and had prepared the data analysis pipeline by February. The statistics I studied in the Department of Psychology turned out to be very useful, if not adequate. It's worth mentioning that during this stage, Mr. Osman suggested certain data "enhancement" techniques that would be labeled as dishonest by the psychology professor who taught us statistics. No, thanks.

For those outstanding students who are considering a research program for grad school, based on my life lessons, maybe it's a good idea to drop your idiosyncratic interest and aim at an established and renowned professor with sufficient research funding. However, the most successful and charismatic MIGHT be the most draconic in nature, just like in politics, and there's almost no reliable way to tell before you enter a program. Meanwhile, the chance of getting your own research funding is close to zero unless you have some privilege — sorry, but intelligence and diligence don't count because those are common traits in grad school.

I insisted on working with this mature-looking yet junior scientist, an ethnic minority with remarkable victimhood,

THE ER VISIT

based on the partially overlapping research interests. See how I ended up? When I only met him once in a while in Ohio State, it was merely chronic stress. When I became his full-time research assistant at UC Davis in 2015, what awaited me was shock, frustration, and despair. Yet, I had to repress my negative feelings, as my legal status in the US depended on the visa sponsored by my employer in academia.

Now I implore you to think about it: centuries ago, rigorous scientific research was for the upper class like Isaac Newton; these days, it's just a glorified yet unstable career track for academically successful individuals with a lower or middle-class family background, generally speaking. If you are self-motivated about research or making this world a better place, you should consider applying your talent elsewhere, perhaps in the private sector, and you can still reach your values in life if you're lucky. Of course, there is no guarantee of success, as in every field.

I remember telling Mr. Osman about my intention to settle down in some city in the US. Mr. Osman responded in his usual arrogant tone, "I'll tell you what, you will never be able to settle down." He would have been correct if I had cared about academia as much as he did. After reading extensively on Quora, I was sure that the academic nomad lifestyle was not for me, someone who wants to belong to a good city. In case you're curious, those posts on Quora do provide more detailed reasoning on this issue. Simply put something like "why you shouldn't get a Ph.D." in the search box. People seem to share their opinions more honestly on Quora than in real life for some inexplicable reason.

Chapter 6
The "Shining" House

6.1 Stacy's Visit and Jessica's Eruption

In this world, it's hard to speculate why one person dislikes another. Outsiders can rarely figure out the story behind a weird relation. From the day Jeremy moved into the house, Jessica held some prejudice against him. She told me he looked like a "bro dude," and I wasn't sure if that meant he looked like a frat boy. Due to Antonio's influence, I frequently used "bro" when speaking to minority dudes but rarely to white guys.

One weekday evening, as I was grading the undergrads' homework in the office, i.e., the dark Ph.D. room in the basement, I got a text from Jeremy, "I have a friend coming over, and they need to park at your regular spot by the road. Can you park behind Jessica's car?"

I replied, "Okay. When you say 'they,' you mean a female?"

"Haha, you figured me out. She'll be here for a while." To me, the word "they" was self-revealing—The more you try to hide something, the more suspicious you appear. Incidentally, the landlady once told me that "they" can be used when you don't know whether a unisex name refers to a male or a female. For instance, "Shannon" is a unisex name, but the individual's gender identity doesn't have to be non-binary.

As I suspected, the visitor was "the girl" who had provided him with a free harbor now and then. When I arrived home, I parked my car behind Jessica's car in the driveway, and then I met this mysterious girl for the first time. They were sitting on a mini couch in his master room and watching the famous drama series Breaking Bad on TV. I entered his dark, smelly master room and walked behind the couch to chat with them.

This small, young blonde from California had a tan on her skin. Her low-pitched voice made her sound like a boy and therefore was unattractive to me. She seemed exuberant. In front of me, they argued over academic nuances like a pair of birds. In particular, he was trying to show off he had memorized the names of those tiny bones in one's wrist.

"Hi, my name is Stacy." She said.

"Glad to finally meet you. I'm Slim." I said, "How many guitar sessions did he teach you?" I asked.

"Three or four, I guess. But later, I realized he isn't that good. Plus, we're busy with school, so..." Stacy laughed.

"I've been trying to use my guitar to attract girls since college, and she is the only person ever falling for it," Jeremy quickly sought revenge.

As the chat went on, she told me she went to a private college in Massachusetts. Her parents were divorced, but they supported her through college. When I asked her where her apartment was, she revealed it was next to Olentangy Club, where I used to live. Unlike Jeremy, who would park right next to the Medical Center with the most expensive A parking permit, she chose to park on the West Campus with a C permit and then took the school bus to med school every day.

When I told her I didn't have a sense of belonging in my home department because the student body was too feminine, she said, "You should come to the med student parties. These events are mostly off-campus."

"He doesn't want me to enter his circle," I shrugged.

"I don't even have a circle," Jeremy said.

"Those guys who you regularly take photos with... you seem to get along with them pretty well. You even brought them here once, you remember?" I said.

"Ah, I'm not friends with those guys. They basically kidnapped me into their photo every time there was a party," he said with a sneer. I didn't argue further. I would be happy to meet his fun classmates again, but he would never give me a chance.

Based on my subsequent conversation with Stacy in his absence, I could tell she couldn't empathize with him regarding the house drama. Instead, she exhibited the inclination to defend Jessica, a seemingly non-menacing lady, and felt that Jeremy was making a fuss about it. Had she formally met Jessica at all? Never. When Stacy visited this house, Jessica locked herself in her tiny room.

Men tend to make themselves look composed, knowledgeable, thoughtful, considerate, empathetic, and ethical when their female partner or colleague is physically around or CC'ed in the email. Jeremy and Mr. Osman were typical examples. The tendency is, I suppose, largely subconscious. Meanwhile, I have also noticed my own inclination to speak highly of my buddies in front of their partners over the years. The remarks were mostly spontaneous and sincere. Here's an interesting fact I only noticed retrospectively: I couldn't say positive things about Jeremy that evening in front of his "guest," probably because, from deep within, I knew he didn't deserve it. Remember, I was just out of the ER.

As I felt exhausted after a long day, I decided to go to bed

THE "SHINING" HOUSE

and let them enjoy themselves. Shortly afterward, Stacy left our house for her own place, which was nearby. My interpretation back then was that Jeremy remembered the lesson that he could not keep a girl overnight in his room without triggering the lady across the wall. Later I realized another important reason: her two-bedroom apartment was far more comfortable for them to perch in than his room. By the way, this lucky girl got a super deal because the apartment complex failed to provide the studio she had booked— she didn't pay that much, and she wouldn't.

I was shocked the next morning at 6 AM when Jessica barged into my bedroom and yelled at me, "Move your car! Now!" She possibly had a particular reason to leave so early that weekday morning, unless she did it on purpose, which wasn't unlikely. Usually, she wouldn't leave the house until 10 AM, considering her evening shift at Sandy's, a chain restaurant.

"Oh, sh*t, sorry." I got out of bed, quickly put on my jacket and jeans, and moved my car for her. "Why couldn't you knock at my door first," I said.

She stared at me with hostility in her eyes before driving off like a tornado. I knew my day was ruined: being woken up abruptly would cause me a headache for the rest of the day. I knew she was jealous and smart enough to understand that my usual parking spot was taken. I also knew she would never have the gut to do that to Jeremy, but an innocuous Asian was an easy target for her to bully. I knew she, an employee at a fast- food chain, would spit on your onion ring if she didn't like you. I texted Jeremy during the day and told him my awful experience, and they felt bad about it. As a consequence, he never brought Stacy to this house again. That evening, I told my neighbors, Alex and Charlotte, about

Jessica's intrusion. They offered to let me sleep in their vacant room if the situation worsened.

To nobody's surprise, it did exacerbate. One Friday night, Jessica brought a team of her friends into our house to party without giving us any notice. The real problem was that they crammed into her tiny room, drank, and played loud music until 11 PM. Shannon and I would usually be asleep by then, but we tolerated these strangers in the house. I had not dared to interrupt their party all alone because Jessica had previously chopped up something like crazy in the kitchen in an attempt to establish her dominance in front of me. Knowing how vengeful she was, I temporarily retreated to the neighbor's house because I couldn't tolerate the noise anymore. Alex and Charlotte were watching a movie on the couch, so I joined them, ready to spend the night there. In the meantime, I texted Jeremy, "You'd better stay at Stacy's place tonight. Jessica is throwing a crazy party in our house that never seems to end." He told me he was on his way home from the Thompson Library, so I decided to return to my room and see what we could do.

Then I heard the sound of his car and saw him rush upstairs and lock himself in his room. After 10 minutes, I heard him knocking very hard at Jessica's door. After 5 minutes, Jessica's drunken-head friends left quietly one by one, with guilty looks on their faces. Jeremy came downstairs, sighed, and told me he scolded them about their disrespectful behavior in this quiet neighborhood. He also told me Jessica was sobbing alone in her room after they all left. His body was shaking in anger, and I told him those were just the alligator's tears, something I had already become immune to. In high school, I became unaffected by women's tears after witnessing Mandy sobbing alone in the kitchen — she was shedding tears at night because I failed to get ten bonus points for the college-entrance exam in my province.

During those weeks, Jessica was very passive-aggressive. As we shared the bathroom downstairs, we had a Cold War over whether to put the bottle of hand soap on the faucet's left or right side— people have different proclivities, I guess. Then one day, I saw the half-full bottle thrown in the dustbin. I bought my own hand soap that day because I felt sick dealing with her. Why not let her win? As you can imagine, she later took it out of the dustbin. That was nasty.

One weekend, when I went to the basement to do some laundry, I saw someone else's clothes inside the washing machine and a handwritten note on top of it, "DON'T PUT MY LAUNDRY ON THE FLOOR!!!" She was referring to the fact that I had once laid her washed laundry on a big clean trash bag spread on the floor when I needed to use the washer myself. I admit it wasn't the best way of handling it, considering the humidity in the basement, but I didn't have an extra laundry basket for other people. In fact, the one I had back then was second-hand. Neither Jessica nor Jeremy cared to prepare an empty basket when they couldn't unload the machine in time. These two people usually just threw the laundry into the washer and disappeared for the day. Jeremy would make a "solid" excuse later, "Sorry, I stayed in the library all day long. This block is very busy." Honestly, I couldn't discern when he was partying with his classmates and when he was genuinely studying. By the way, as I recall, he had a laundry bag instead of a basket, which he had used since college. It came in handy when he gradually migrated to Stacy's apartment. Understandably, he would make use of the better washer and dryer at her apartment because… why not?

Jeremy also told me something I didn't know. One night he heard Jessica shouting in her room and punching the wall, like in those horror movies, and he woke up, frightened. "I thought the house was on fire!" he said angrily. His reaction corresponded to one of his "ancient" Facebook posts, which popped onto my newsfeed months later because Stacy clicked the LIKE button several times when traveling through his Facebook timeline. So what was that post about? When he was a freshman in college, some prick set off the fire alarm in his dorm building the night before a chemistry final. That false alarm made all the students panic. Needless to say, getting some good sleep is crucial before a morning exam. Hence he cursed in that post after the exam, "I hope that guy will be burned in hell." Someone commented down below, "That's harsh." Well, that's Jeremy's character, believe it or not. For instance, he once found out the dairy milk he purchased from Kroger was stale, so he went to Kroger and poured the sour milk on the floor in front of their manager. You might think, "Can this kind of blunt behavior solve any problem better than peaceful negotiation?" Well, it could make his little girl look up to him even more, at least from a Darwinian point of view.

6.2 The Confrontation

As everybody in the house was affected by Jessica, Jeremy and I discussed what to do next. He had been searching for a studio to live alone; however, he was bound by the one-year lease, just like everyone else. He regretted choosing the house way back in September, and the escalating house drama pushed him to the breaking point. He wrote a serious email to the landlady and told her about our struggle and suffering. At first, we got no response. Later, the landlady commented that we adults should try to resolve the problem between ourselves, especially since she and her husband lived an hour away. One noteworthy thing is that, back in 2013, online group chat wasn't that popular for handling casual meetings yet, and people still preferred face-to-face communication whenever possible.

That Saturday evening, Jeremy was allegedly studying in the library. Alex and Charlotte invited me to hang with their friends in a local brewery in Grandview. I did go, but my mind was preoccupied with the house drama. I greeted Stacy on Facebook and told her that Jeremy was lucky to have her support during this house drama. She responded immediately.

"Oh, Jeremy told me everything, and I'm so sorry that your housemate barged into your room because of me," she said.

"Well, I guess I am the easy target for her. But what I don't understand is, why doesn't Jeremy wanna move in with you? You know, as boyfriend and girlfriend," I said.

"I don't know if I can call myself his girlfriend." She said, "I asked him if he wanted to be my boyfriend when he taught me the guitar. He said he didn't want a girlfriend now. I feel I'm still in his trial period. American guys are wimps."

I immediately looked up the word "wimp" in the dictionary app and started to giggle. She then told me she had a boyfriend back in college, and they broke up earlier this semester.

"It's very kind of you to host Jeremy when he's in trouble," I said.

"I was brought up Christian and taught I should help people when they need me. It also doesn't hurt to have a study pal," she said.

As I knew Jeremy was an atheist, it made me feel uneasy.

She wanted to help him, so she slept with him. That's what I just heard.

"As a Christian, you're okay with premarital sex?" I was confused because those folks in my old Bible study group taught me very different things about Christianity.

"That's fine. My family are pretty casual. We aren't Catholic or evangelical," she said.

"Thank you for being so frank with me. I have a lot to learn in this country every day. All these new concepts I learn in daily life require a lot of comprehension… sometimes even more difficult than grad school," I said.

"I guess that's because I'm from California. I understand it's hard for you. The Midwest is quite a different environment for me, too. I don't have many friends here, except Jeremy and some undergrads," she said. At that point, I felt I bonded a little bit with her.

The next time I met Jeremy, I meticulously mentioned my chat with Stacy, "Hey, I'm going to ask you one thing that might tap into your privacy again…"

"Go ahead," he said.

"Stacy told me she felt she was put in a trial period. I thought you loved her." I said what I had to say.

He sneered, "People just want a label."

"Yes, they do." I said no more, and he didn't respond. Remember, he once gave me the friendship label and later withdrew it from me.

In 2017, Mandy also criticized me for messing with the private business between Jeremy and Stacy. Like always, Mandy had a lot of 20/20 vision. If not for their "medical student glory" and my long-term purpose of networking, why would I even spend my precious time on them? We weren't kids anymore. People like me take actions to maximize their self-interests. A big government, such as the US government, never interferes with other countries' domestic or regional affairs unless they have something to gain from it or some potential loss to minimize through this intervention. They won't do it simply out of some sense of justice on a global scale. Taxpayers won't allow it.

The house drama was still going on. Then, one night, it occurred to me that in an old email sent by the landlady, Brian, the former tenant, was included as the co-recipient. Brian was the grad student in mathematics who remotely transferred his lease to Shannon. I only met him once, for less than a minute, during my first visit to this house. He was walking through the living room with a bottle of Budweiser or Corona in his hand.

Anyway, I found Brian's email address and told him we were haunted by Jessica and shackled by the leases. He replied the next day, telling me that Jessica had also frightened him and his other housemates. As he said, the master room used to be rented by a different med student, but that guy was so scared of Jessica's erratic nocturnal behavior that he moved elsewhere with his girlfriend and paid double rent for several months. Brian also mentioned that Jessica lied to the landlady about him and his friend, who only temporarily slept on our couch as a makeshift. As the self-appointed house manager, Jessica reported to the landlady that Brian brought in an illegal tenant who failed to pay the bill. Admittedly, there should be room for dispute on this matter— conflicts between roommates or housemates are rarely black and white. However, because Jessica had been a senior tenant, the landlady trusted her accusation so quickly, without knowing all the grudges Jessica held against her. In retrospect, Jessica was tiny yet subtly manipulative. Ironically, the landlady's husband, the engineer who fixed everything in the house, was the first to say aloud that we should work together to persuade Jessica to move elsewhere. Unfortunately, he wasn't our landlord. The landlady disagreed immediately.

Seeing no prospect of justice from the landlady, I decided to seek help from the OSU Student Legal Services again. Jeremy agreed to be there, while Shannon said she couldn't make it because of an upcoming exam. The appointment was at 4 PM. Before arriving at the Student Legal Services, I bought three donuts from a nearby convenience store. I only needed one, but I thought my "comrade" might also benefit from some energy supply before meeting with the attorney. When we met, I asked Jeremy if he wanted one, and he said no, he wasn't hungry. I ate two of the three and saved my favorite pumpkin flavor for the last. Then Jeremy suddenly said, "If you can't finish it, I can help you with that." I totally could, but I knew he was hungry behind his strong and invincible façade, so I handed my favorite flavor to him. He was not thankful because he thought he was doing me a favor by eating it. While I chose to repress my feelings for the global benefit, he stayed self-righteous and found a way to climb up to the moral high ground. He always won.

As soon as we finished the three donuts I bought, the attorney showed up and brought us in. This attorney, who looked a decade older than Mr. Parker, quickly got the idea that Jessica hated "dudes" in general, not just "bro dudes." First, he was trying to see if we could find any loophole with the rental property itself, something we could use against the rental agreement. For instance, "Is there a fire extinguisher in the house?" We weren't even sure about that. Then, after doing some research in his law book, he suggested that we offer the landlady some kind of buyout, such as two months' rent, if we each decided to move out. I sensed that the whole situation was to our disadvantage, legislatively speaking. It's not that easy for a house drama per se to escalate to a legal issue, with or without evidence of disturbance. When we left the Legal Office, Jeremy was wearing a demoralized and broody face. The sky was gloomy. He drove back to the Med Campus while I decided to stay on Main Campus for a free movie at Ohio Union. Ironically, the movie was called Safe Haven (2013).

That night, he returned to Stacy's apartment and emailed the landlady again under the previous email. No reply still, after several days. Because Shannon and I were CCed in the emails, I was able to see that he referred to Stacy as "my girlfriend" for the first time.

I texted Stacy, "Congrats! he finally acknowledged you as his girlfriend."

"He probably just didn't know which word to use." She texted back. I was surprised she knew she was mentioned in the email.

"Wimps need to be whipped," I replied.

"Oh, haha, no, that was out of frustration. I didn't mean it. He's a sweet guy." Her sudden change of attitude made me feel uneasy again. Apparently, this label meant a lot to her. It was a reward for her. It would continue to motivate her.

One evening, Jeremy came back to the house with a strange promise that he would write an apology letter to Jessica. I was bewildered because he had said that Jessica needed to go to therapy and that she was the person who should move out. I didn't believe he felt apologetic to her at all, considering he didn't even feel sorry when he had hurt me ruthlessly. Why? What kind of trick was he playing? The answer might be he was scared of Jessica, who kept haunting us, instead of me, an innocuous Asian trying to earn his friendship. Or maybe Stacy suggested this idea? Anyway, I waited for him to carry out his plan that evening, wondering why an American stud would fear a direct conversation with a lady — remember, it was he who kicked her friends out of the house that night.

When I saw him eating his cheerio the next morning, I asked him about the letter he'd planned to write. "I... I didn't write it..." he answered, "I didn't know what to write. I mean I'm the only person she hates. It's all because of me. I've been checking out several places these days. As soon as I move out, this house will have peace again."

"Okay. Fine. You wasted my time again." I repressed my disappointment and went on to eat my breakfast. That morning, I felt betrayed by this med student a second time because he wouldn't even bring it up without my prompt. He had hoped to get away with it somehow, unnoticed. In the meantime, he was seriously planning to escape from the battlefield alone while letting me taste the embarrassment.

What was worse, I was angry the whole day and couldn't focus on my classes. I began to feel disgusted by that house as well. That afternoon, I emailed him,

"... No problem. You can just move out now and do nothing, and let me clean up your mess all by myself. You think Lady J won't hurt other people? You think it's only about you? I wouldn't deceive myself like that. You can do whatever you want, but I will have to tell your next tenant everything. I won't let you hurt innocent people. I'll help you move as I promised, and I won't ask you for any credential of friendship anymore. It's just a label. Good luck."

I sounded more concerned about the future tenants. Still, I was primarily worried about my own safety in this already-ignited battle. I had this gut feeling that he couldn't wait to cut off clean from anybody in this house, based on his persistent effort to keep me outside his personal life. Incidentally, I had started referring to Jessica as Lady J in all my written correspondence with people. To some extent, I felt her existence contaminated that innocent name, "Jessica."

He texted me very quickly, "I'm sorry. This block is busy in general. I'll definitely write something to Jessica this time, just to make sure you guys are not in danger after I move out." According to him, their med school program moved the Neurology course from the third year to the first year, and the students were pushed very hard, yet all I cared about was whether he could stick to his words or not. Considering my body was still recovering, and I had my own grad school to survive, I put low expectations on him this time in case I got stood up again.

When we returned home in the evening, around 5:30 PM, he wrote a sticky note and stuck it on Jessica's door. The note said, "I'm sorry. Can we talk? — Jeremy" When I saw his childish handwriting, I thought of how kids from China were mandated to practice handwriting of the English alphabet and the Chinese characters in elementary school. I envisioned that upon seeing that note, Jessica would throw it into the dustbin and lock herself inside.

When we were planning on the conversation with Jessica, I brought Jeremy to the neighbors' house to seek advice because I knew Charlotte would have something constructive to say. He looked embarrassed and amused when standing in their living room because he had previously signaled that these random people didn't meet his standard for "acquaintances."

Charlotte offered some practical advice based on her experience in college. She recommended that the three of us, including Shannon, intercept Jessica when she came back and initiate a conversation with her without judging or attacking her personality. Considering that our landlady was biased and refused to intervene, I decided to record that conversation and send it to her to show proof of our genuine effort to communicate with Lady J.

Then, naturally, the next big thing for us to do was intercept Jessica the second she came back. Guess the facial expression of Jeremy at that moment? He wore a wacky smile and kept reminding me that we should get rid of that sticky note on her door as if there was nothing more urgent than that. "Let's get back to the house. She'll be back soon." He left the neighbors' house flippantly without saying "thank you," only "goodbye."

The recording I made wasn't sent to the landlady eventually— after Jeremy, a federal loan recipient, decided on a studio apartment near downtown the next week, he wanted to make sure he could move out smoothly with no entanglement. I complied for his benefit but probably sacrificed some of my values. In retrospect, I don't think the recording could sway the landlady to our side— it wasn't her job to be the arbiter, after all. I was simply doing what I was supposed to do after Shannon reminded me once that I had no evidence to back up my accusations. In the meantime, concrete evidence doesn't guarantee the victory of the innocent or the righteous party, especially if justice isn't the ultimate goal in that process, as shown in *The Trial of the Chicago 7* (Netflix, 2020) in modern American history. Okay, so what's the ultimate motive for a landlord/landlady? Unsurprisingly, maximization of the total rent paid by the tenants. Similarly, this realistic motive explains why some giant IT companies hesitated to intervene in those ad campaigns spreading ostensible misinformation on their platforms: ads and engagement bring them loads of income. (This analogy struck me after I listened to one episode of the *TechStuff* Podcast by Jonathan Strickland; this particular episode about Internet algorithms was published in December 2020.)

When we were back in the house again, I finally revealed to Jeremy the "rapist" comment from Jessica, which left him aghast. I had refrained from mentioning this to him, as it was insanely slanderous, but he showed curiosity about it after knowing I was keeping something from him. "Could that be her innocuous joke?" He responded after two seconds. Apparently, that was a lot for him to process.

"Do you ever joke with such a word?" I asked rhetorically.

Then he took a deep breath and said, "Now I know what kind of person she really is. Like my dad said, she needs to go to therapy."

Cheerfully, Shannon agreed to join us this time in the confrontation. Then we heard Jessica's car coming up the driveway. Then the front door opened. Jessica saw us and sensed the unusual atmosphere, so she rushed upstairs and locked herself inside. Jeremy knocked at her door and asked her to have a conversation with us. She didn't answer. I turned on the recorder quietly. Then Jeremy kept talking and asked her what she wanted and why she was doing all the scary things to us. Finally, she started to communicate in her high-pitched voice, in the style of a victim. "I have already started to look for a different place to live, but it won't be that quick…" I figured she had no intention of answering our questions directly, just like some online customer service representatives in China these days. Meanwhile, she appeared to be unaware that Jeremy had been looking for a different place here and there already. Once she knew that, she wouldn't bother to move away, which was undesirable for me. Things had become unexpectedly complex, as several threads were moving forward simultaneously and intertwining in an exhausting fashion.

After Jeremy finished his talk and questioning, I added mine, "let me ask you, why did you always target me and try to scare me? Is it because you think I am easy to bully?" The house fell into complete silence at that moment. The two future clinicians in my sight lowered their heads. I withheld my urge to question her rationality and her moral codes, but I really wanted to ask just one essential question: "Did you get any pleasure by trying to wreak havoc on us?"

I knew I couldn't simply label it as a matter of race, but I couldn't help but think that way.

What I have observed over the years: white people in some regions of North America and Europe still treat the "innocuous" Asians as the first or second course of a sacrifice. For instance, in the arts and entertainment industries, Asians are often recruited to play roles that die early, e.g., *Les Miserables* (musical), *Hadestown* (musical), *Humans* (TV series), and *Brave New World* (TV series).

In my personal life, some white Americans have belittled me for my smaller body size, openly, in real life or on social media. Unlike those idealistic "fighters," I'm not so optimistic about changing white people's general attitudes toward Asians, Asian males in particular, in the short term, knowing these attitudes have biological, historical, and political bases— in other words, beyond superficial prejudice.

THE "SHINING" HOUSE

How did I come up with this term called "innocuous Asian"? It initially arose as my self-mockery in front of my Western friends, as I tended to be the only "model minority" in a group of people.

The confrontation inside the house was over, and we went out of the house. Jeremy was trembling and asked me for a hug. That moment I felt needed, and naïvely thought I had developed some comradeship with him. In retrospect, this mindset of "feeling needed" by others rendered me prone to exploitation after I had suffered extreme hollowness toward the end of the second semester of grad school. As a reminder, for two semesters, I wasn't assigned any research project by Mr. McCarthy; due to his misguidance, I also missed the opportunity to start a project with Mr. Anderson, one of my favorite professors in Ohio State. As a result, my first year in grad school wasn't fruitful at all, compared to many lab mates.

Since Jeremy asked for a hug, I gave him that hug.

At that time, I couldn't understand why he was so afraid to confront Jessica. But perhaps his fear was legit, and I was the reckless person. The following summer, when I was looking for housing and was required to fill out some application form, I referred to Jessica as "a borderline lady" when asked why I moved out of the previous places. The informal diagnosis based on the undergrad-level Abnormal Psychology course I took was probably questionable. I didn't know her background or personal life well enough to check all the boxes on a DSM scale. The one fact attesting to my suspicion was that she had difficulty maintaining interpersonal relationships, even with her purported "best friend," who I had met a few times. As a dude, I don't really have a best friend.

Days before The Confrontation, Jeremy texted me, "Some people are just bad people, and there's nothing we can do except protect ourselves." After I told him her problem was likely rooted in problematic family dynamics and inadequate socialization, Jeremy immediately changed his tone into a philanthropic one, "Yeah, I often feel sorry for these people because I don't know how to help them with their problems." I wondered if he knew he sounded very hypocritical with this blatant change of stance.

I shouldn't judge him, considering many people's childhood dreams are based on mental complexes, which we tend to sugarcoat with altruistic motives. One needs to introspect seriously: do I primarily want to help those in need, or do I essentially want to make up for what I had no access to in my early life? A complex usually indicates one cannot evaluate a concept objectively and holistically. If you think a particular profession is heroic or glorious, then you are ignorant of what that position entails. Will you lose your privacy? Will you lose your free speech? Will you risk your mental and physical health? Will you have to do things against your values?

After deep introspection through writing, I came to comprehend the misfortune-based complex behind my idiosyncratic childhood dream, namely, to become a psychologist, which technically required a doctoral degree. While I did view this profession as respectable because they actively listen to those living in miseries, it was an underlying motive that drew my attention toward this profession: As I grew up, Mandy and Doug often minimized or neglected my pain and struggles.

Here's another example: in the TV drama *The Flight Attendant* (HBO, 2020), the protagonist, played by Kelly Cuoco, dreamed about becoming a flight attendant after witnessing a plane crash in her childhood. But, as the story went on toward the climax, she proposed a new interpretation of her motivation: nothing altruistic but simply schadenfreude. It sounds cynical but fits the storyline seamlessly.

Anyway, at this age, counterintuitively, I no longer encourage the idea of childhood dreams; instead, I think it's crucial to figure out the looming drive behind the mental complex in order to detect any potential problem at the early stage, i.e., before it infiltrates into big life decisions. Notably, because a person's parents and school teachers are likely the contributors to the formation of the complex, they should NOT be the ones to judge or intervene. Only a trained psychologist or an educationist, i.e., a fourth party, can be considered as totally qualified to modify a developing brain. However, that only happens in a utopian world. That's why human suffering often starts in childhood, unannounced and unnoticed.

6.3 Escaping from the "Shining" House

The snow season came quickly, and Jeremy finally moved out to an expensive studio far from campus but close to downtown, with assistance from Stacy and me. One SUV and two sedans in tandem. We learned the following when we helped him move that Saturday afternoon: first, he had several bottles of pills in his bathroom vanity, including supplements; second, in his walk-in closet, he had more clothes than Stacy did, as she pointed out.

It was past dinnertime when all three of us returned to the "Shining" House, as in the movie *The Shining* directed by Stanley Kubrick. After cleaning up his room and fetching his belongings from the kitchen, Jeremy asked Stacy if she wanted to cook dinner together at her place. She said no because she had a babysitting gig that night. Then she drove off in a hurry.

He looked disappointed, so I teased him, "You wanna have dinner with me? There's a Chipotle nearby." He immediately responded in a serious tone, "No, I'm running out of time. I need to go to Kroger to buy some kitchen utensils. There's nothing in my apartment yet." I kind of knew that his answer would always be negative. I sensed he would allow himself to create zero positive experiences with me so that he could adhere to his post-hoc conceptualization of friendship and use that to exclude me from his circle.

Before he left, he hugged me and said kindly, "Sorry I have to abandon you here." Spring of 2017, my co-worker Mr. Shapiro said exactly the same sentence to me when he quit his postdoc position under Mr. Osman. Mr. Shapiro was excited to leave this tiny lab for a more rewarding career while I was stuck with my J-1 visa.

The evening we were discussing with our neighbors on how to confront Jessica, Charlotte encouraged me to find a different place as Jeremy had been doing: it was too risky for me to continue living with a mentally unstable opponent in this house. Besides, given the dark history of the "Shining" House, it would be tricky for Jeremy to find another male to take over his master room. But the new task was super challenging for me. I had to find a more flexible lease in the snowy winter and explain to the potential housemate or landlord why I had to move. Not everybody in this world prefers to hear the unpleasant truth, and most people only want to introduce positivity into their surroundings. I tried to find a room near campus to minimize the risk of driving in the snow. Like last time, I was ignored or politely rejected, again and again, like many other housing seekers. The semester was close to the end, and the snow got heavier.

In retrospect, it was foolish of me to include Upper Arlington, a wealthy, vast, and quiet district on the northwest side of the Ohio State campus, in my desired, or, shall we say, acceptable, locations on Craigslist. One day, a lady in Upper Arlington replied to my post on Craigslist, telling me she had an extra room to sublet. Days after I visited her place, this lady Kayah admitted she was looking for someone to look after the entire condo, as she was about to enjoy her 3-month trip to Southeast Asia. When we met initially, I thought she was Italian or Indian American, but she revealed she was Native American and that her family had been assimilated for several generations. Kayah was a connoisseur of artisan jewelry. In our conversation, she was surprised to know that I wanted roommates and urged me to make a quick decision because her departure was approaching. She also said I looked trustworthy, which didn't make me feel any better about myself, and here's why. During the hunting process, I also met some white male grad students living on the east side of the Main Campus. One lad, in particular, didn't even try to hide his disappointment when I showed up. He was waiting for me to leave while I was sitting and chatting with his then housemate, who was moving to Cincinnati.

On my request for some "endorsement," Jeremy generously went with me to check out one place on Henderson Rd, on the north end of Upper Arlington, away from campus. He also demonstrated his advanced driving skills on the freeway— the left hand holding the smartphone and the right-hand steering. The guy reaching out to me on Craigslist turned out to be a Doctor of Jurisprudence (J.D.), who daunted me with his legal stipulations printed on a stack of paper, including the possibility to buy me out when his girlfriend came to live with him. He also requested that I take care of his dog for him when he was out of town — I had always been a cat person since childhood, with very limited experience or patience with dogs, unfortunately. This smart and gentle guy remained respectful to me, and I had no doubt that the "endorsement" I got from a white med student was more or less helpful. This kind of white "tag" seemed indispensable to my success in getting accepted throughout my second year in Ohio, except for summer sublets. It was adaptive yet burdensome. While it may seem obvious to those who have grown up in a racially and ethnically diverse country, it took me years to understand that most people only feel connected to others who look and sound like them. That revealing process also involved eradicating the outdated and misleading idea of a "melting pot" from my brain, which did not manifest itself in the Midwest, not in the slightest sense. Caution: If you only surround yourself with open-minded, empathetic internationalists, you will never understand what's happening in the real world.

 I told Jeremy about the challenges I was facing and explained that I didn't want to live alone as a stranger in a strange land. I didn't have a cohort because I belonged with neither the clinical trainees in Communication Disorders nor the graduate student body in Cognitive Psychology, let alone Music Theory. My home department only accepted two students into the research program in 2012. The other person, a mom of two toddlers, had worked in a famous hospital for a decade. I did have many local friends scattered in different circles, but still, something was missing. From Jeremy's perspective, he would naturally want me to make a quick decision so that he would feel he no longer owed me anything. My insecure gut feeling about this person's behavior was legitimate for the most part. However, I told myself I had to play along and live day by day.

Besides, I told Jeremy I wanted to ensure I could have at least one roommate because I sensed he would eventually treat me as a stranger. He texted me back to reassure me, "I'm not abandoning you. This block is busy in general. After my finals, we can probably do some social stuff together." I felt moderately insulted by his word "abandon," but I repressed my emotion so that I could focus on my own finals and TA duties. It's shameful to admit that when looking at Google Maps, I even thought it was convenient to drive from Upper Arlington to his new place on Riverside Drive, along the Scioto River. I also naïvely reckoned that if he could live alone, I should be able to do that too— totally forgetting to add Stacy into his equation. By this point, my pathological attachment to this person was only burgeoning, and I underestimated the plight yet to come.

The word "attachment" is used because Layla, my therapist in California, brought up this explanation, which made sense to me. I was ambivalent about this person: liking him because he was hard-working and ambitious, just like me, disliking him because he betrayed me several times without any sense of guilt. I couldn't forget the bad things he did to me, nor could I let go of this individual because I had invested so much time and energy in this relationship. A similar mechanism can explain why people in a casino would lose their sanity little by little until they go bankrupt.

The "charm" of this socially recognized elite was manifested in that he never directly rejected me but always gave me some hope, using uncertain words like "maybe" and "let's see" to manipulate me into trying harder. For instance, after helping him move into his new apartment, I said to him, "You can host a party here now."

"Maybe. Probably." He looked around his studio and sneered.

"But are you going to invite me?" I followed up.

He sneered again and didn't answer.

I was 95% certain that he would never host a party unless his girl volunteered to host one for him. As I remember, Stacy did organize a birthday party for him when she was pursuing him, and she even baked a large cake for him. He brought home the untouched cake, left it in our extra refrigerator located in the basement, and never tasted it. Ironically, I was the person who tried a piece of the cake with his permission before he dumped the bulk of it two weeks later. Honestly, I didn't enjoy the free slice of cake because it was coarse, dry, and full of nuts, unlike a regular cake. Of course, my unbiased evaluation was made because I didn't know who made the cake back then. It was only weeks later that I first met Stacy in Jeremy's bedroom. However, I refused to withdraw my opinion of the cake in front of them.

I was 99% certain that he would never allow me into his circle. In fact, I just hoped he could directly say no to me, once and for all, but he wouldn't. To make things worse, every time he said sorry, I felt obliged to forgive him and thus fell into a limbo between trust and mistrust, which deepened my frustration. That's why I once suspected that I had developed Stockholm Syndrome toward this person, but Layla thought my condition wasn't that pathological.

Jeremy was manipulative, but his behavioral style wasn't uncommon. Many people in this modern society like using silence or ambiguity as a replacement for explicit rejection. To them, everybody is supposed to agree upon the protocol

THE "SHINING" HOUSE

that no reply is a reply. I suspect that's linked to the seemingly noble education they have received and internalized: don't say anything unless you have something nice to say. Based on my observation of certain people who preach this, this notion has its utilitarian connotations: first, let the other party go down the rabbit hole, and it's none of your business; second, you are allowed to stab the other party in their back, as long as you remain silent; third, let the brutal truth come out of the mouth of someone else so that you can stay dissociated from negativity. If we all follow that dogma of nobility, then no journalists should speak the truth for our society.

The night we were discussing how to talk with Jessica, I took the opportunity to question him why he would always keep me out of his world — simply because I was not in med school? His first excuse was uttered from a pouty mouth, in a girly tone, "But nobody would ask a question like that." He was referring to my initial question: do you want to make friends with me? If you remember, he initially acknowledged the existence of friendship but overthrew it after a couple of weeks when he was having a disappointing weekend.

And my response was, "I'd never done that to anybody else." He felt flattered and thanked me. But, frankly, I felt a bit disgusted by what he said and how I responded.

After 5 seconds, he came up with his second excuse. "It's because of the bad association." In his theory, he couldn't dissociate me from Jessica or this unpleasant house, despite his sufficient mental maturity for med school. How could I be convinced?

And my response was, "But it's unfair for me."

His answer then turned to "Okay, let's see," with another

sneer. What I perceived was he, under multiple stressors, took pleasure from playing me, an Asian male that he tried to alienate in essence. My encounter with him the next spring on Main Campus reinforced this impression: He threw me another vicious sneer when seeing me, a depressed person, across West Woodruff Avenue on Main Campus, when he was running in the sprinkle. I was waiting for the campus shuttle at the bus stop, dressed in total green, among a crowd of students. Many of those students seemed to be Chinese undergrads, so we, standing together, must have looked like a bunch of frail alien nerds in his eyes. I watched him running away in his Penn State hoodie and shorts and couldn't feel anything.

In hindsight, I was still useful to him at that time, and he kept wasting my precious time by sending me mixed signals. I had doubts about my judgment in the past, but not anymore. He was who he was.

6.4 Bad Omens

When I agreed to move to Upper Arlington and stopped searching in the winter storm, I wasn't excited at all, as other places I desired didn't want me. The same logic applied to me ending up in Ohio State for grad school— since Ivy or sub-Ivy League institutions didn't want me for their prestigious Ph.D. programs. Not surprisingly, they reject the majority of the applicants each year. I knew I wasn't that competitive despite my steady efforts, high GRE score (except in the analytical writing section), and high GPA. I knew my alma mater in China wasn't top 10 and wasn't well-known to American institutions. Still, it felt like a compromise, or, say, the destiny I had to accept; nothing to complain about and nothing to celebrate for. Ordinary and palpable life, it was. At least I tried to enjoy the honeymoon

THE "SHINING" HOUSE

period with Ohio State and make the most out of life when I could.

The brutal truth is, if you have difficulty paying for an expensive master's program out-of-pocket, you may have to get into a Ph.D. program in an institution one or two tiers lower in exchange. First things first, you're competing against the entire third world when applying to any solid program in America. Meanwhile, if you factor in the implicit discrimination and the political correctness embodied in the recruiting process, which they will officially deny, you should generally expect a worse outcome than what you deserve. It's particularly true when you are the so-called "model minority," since the discrimination involves you while political correctness doesn't compensate you. Furthermore, some of them will favor the natives over those from America's rival or enemy countries, based on human nature, if not policies. Again, they won't admit it. According to Annalise Keating, the protagonist attorney in the TV series *How to Get Away with Murder,* "Justice is the exception." As I see it, one should just accept the brutal truth when setting goals for oneself instead of seeking sporadic evidence to back up their denial.

The only silver lining was that I no longer needed to see Jessica's victim face. Actually, it was naïve of me to assume that because the following summer, Alex and Charlotte invited me back to their home party to celebrate their cat Infinity's birthday. Who'd have thought Jessica also showed up with her friend at the party? At that moment, I felt disgusted because, from the day I moved into the "Shining" House, she was critical of Alex and Charlotte. I couldn't believe she sincerely accepted those neighbors. That awful feeling lasted a few days, which made me dread going back to that neighborhood.

THE SNOWY BATTLEFIELD OF OHIO

It was time for me to move to Upper Arlington. In December 2013, Kayah, the new housemate who was NOT actually going to share the place with me during her trip, left the key to her neighbor, a female hairstylist, for me to pick up after her departure. That evening, around mid-December, the city was covered in snow. Driving into that wealthy and quiet neighborhood on the northwest side of the West Campus, so far from downtown, I felt every decision in my life was compelled to be a bad one, but I couldn't figure out why exactly. The hairstylist gave me the key and intended to show me around the condo again to ensure everything was working. The condo was different from other places I had lived in. Apart from the feminine-styled interior decoration, it had a laminated wooden floor throughout. In contrast, a low-end apartment complex in the Midwest, such as Olentangy Club, would be fully carpeted. As we know, carpets conceal the dirt and the filth. Kayah had left the heating system on before she left for the airport, which was not uncommon for households in cold regions. She was nice and considerate, even under my somewhat cynical standard.

The last time I checked out the place, I was told not to take off my shoes, so I didn't this time either, thinking it would take no more than 5 minutes. Three seconds after stepping into the house, I slipped over and fell right on my buttocks. I instinctively used my left hand to support my body at that moment. Aside from the shock, my left wrist was swollen. Apparently, the snow underneath my shoes melted because of the indoor temperature, and the shoes I had purchased from FootLocker in Easton Town Center weren't anti-slip enough— that's why I threw them away afterward to get rid of the bad luck. The doormat covered with snow and ice provided little help in this situation. After

THE "SHINING" HOUSE

hearing my "ouch," the neighbor immediately brought an icepack to me, and we chatted a little bit on the couch. I failed to realize that the first 3 seconds were just some bad omen for the ensuing nightmare.

Feeling hungry, I drove back to the "Shining" House, where I had to face Jessica again. Without any prior experience of such an accidental fall, I lacked the wisdom to have my wrist examined by a doctor as soon as possible. The pain subsided the next day, and I was busy. Only when I traveled with a Chinese friend on the Greyhound to New York City during the Christmas season did I start to notice that hidden symptom: I sensed a sharp diffuse pain across my palm when trying to push my backpack onto the overhead cabin. I went to see my primary care physician after New Year's Day. I received physical therapy for months until I graduated, acupuncture for months until after graduation, two cortisone shots from the best hand specialist in the Medical Center, two medical massage sessions, an x-ray, CT, and MRI spread over half a year. Ironically, I didn't get any convincing diagnosis until I emailed my friend back in Shanghai, a hand surgeon in a top-tier hospital.

To make things worse, I had to cope with multiple sources of musculoskeletal pain at that time. One clinician with access to my electronic medical record told me that my medical history could be printed into a thick book—physical therapy being the bulk of it. "I must be a disaster for the insurance company," I thought to myself. Plus, Frankie, the new PT at the Student Clinic, told me that it would become increasingly difficult for one's body to heal from an injury after reaching a certain age due to "the increase of entropy." Here we go. My body was broken in and out.

To some extent, I wish I had never been to Ohio. I know I could get injured in other states as well, and I know I wasn't the only person regretting going to Ohio State. However, the reasons could vary a lot from person to person. When I lived in Shanghai and looked at Ohio versus California on the same map of the United States of America, it was as if I was looking at two crates on the moon's surface from the earth. I had to be physically there to get a sense of the difference. Despite people's mild warnings, I had no idea how deeply I could be affected by the snowstorm in a less urbanized region with poor public transportation. By the way, I witnessed a girl falling on the ground while walking out of a bus stop on West Campus that same winter. She was downhill from me, so I couldn't even help her before she stood up herself. I hope she had a better level of "entropy" than I did. But first, I hope she was diagnosed correctly.

Want to hear some positivity? Our female housemate Shannon did us a great favor by inviting her two female friends to live with her in the "Shining" House, so both Jeremy and I were able to find our substitute tenants without too much struggle. We had both posted ads on Craigslist, but most applicants failed to meet the landlady's criteria, such as "no pet allowed."

Before I put an end to this section, there was another twist I'd like to mention. Jeremy agreed to help me move on that Sunday afternoon "to return your favor," as he called it in a text message. I resisted that wording, but he didn't respond. My gut feeling told me that Judgment Day would come sooner or later. We were to meet outside the "Shining" house, and he told me to call him when I was ready, as he would be in his lab preparing for a dissection exam. I called him around 2 PM, and his phone was out of the network. I tried several times within half an hour and even left voicemail messages. Then I started to panic, like the protagonist in the sci-fi movie *Her*, who was chronically worried about being abandoned by the AI virtual assistant with a female face and voice. It turned out the AI had been lying all along and did abandon him in the end. That panicked feeling I had was beyond the typical disappointment when being stood up by someone. In retrospect, this was a red flag for my attachment to him.

By the way, I actually watched this movie in the Ohio Union in the subsequent semester. I watched it with great empathy for that protagonist, as I spotted the same psychological mechanism which had engendered the same somatic response in me. Although my attachment wasn't romantic in nature, my fear of being cheated reached the same magnitude. Of course, I could pretend it WAS romantic and make the entire story juicier for some readers, yet I chose not to ruin its authenticity.

Standing in front of the "Shining" House, I thought this was his way of saying farewell on my Judgment Day so that my hope would be destroyed. With no time to drown in misery, I started to move my luggage bags and other accessories by myself, onto my Nissan sedan. Jessica was trying to talk with me about the air conditioner that morning as if nothing had ever happened, but I was determined to make that Sunday the last day to see her face or hear her voice.

After I had moved two rounds between the "Shining" House and the condo in Upper Arlington, I received a text response from Jeremy around 4 PM, "Sorry, I didn't realize the phone signal is blocked in the dissection lab. I was waiting for your call and thought you didn't need me." I texted him back in anger because I thought he should have at least checked his phone, let alone called me. He defended himself by explaining that it was inconvenient with his hands already in rubber gloves. To be fair, it's hard to tell which operating room or lab in a hospital building needs to be shielded from external electromagnetic signals. I only knew its necessity for electrophysiology and imaging, but clearly, those two were not all.

The feeling of agitation while waiting wasn't new to me. Dating back to my college years in Shanghai, I once waited outside a recording studio for hours until leaving in despair because the person who agreed to usher me in couldn't receive the mobile signal from inside, not even text messages. Also, the guard couldn't recognize my friend's artist name and wouldn't let me in. Therefore, this was the second time I waited anxiously, which inevitably brought back the bad memory. The difference was that in the previous case, that guy was a friend I generally trusted. Jeremy was not someone I could naturally trust, but someone I felt obliged to trust under his "med student halo." He was self-centered and self-righteous as usual, but I still needed his help to move my wooden furniture that day. It was too late to rent a U-Haul, and none of my friends drove an SUV as he did. I had to admit his SUV had its advantages.

In the condo, when he heard my new housemate Kayah was of Native American heritage, he looked at her group photo and possibly mistook her younger friend for her. "She looks cute," he said, "I wanna meet her someday."

I thought to myself, "You just wanna try different things."

Where did that suspicion come from? One evening in the "Shining" House, I told him how much I admired Benjamin Franklin when I was a teenager. Ben Franklin was portrayed as a legendary scientist in our physics textbook in middle school. I always thought he was either very lucky or favored by Mother Nature, for he didn't die of electrical shock when his kite was hit by the lightning bolt. The fact that he became one of the United States' founding fathers made me think "God bless America" was kind of serious.

Yet Jeremy taught me a new word to be used on this historical figure.

"Do you know he was promiscuous?" He asked with a smirk on his face.

I answered, "I'm not familiar with that word." It was true.

He said, "He was very close with multiple women."

I responded, "Oh, you mean like a Playboy?"

He said, "Pretty much."

"Just like you?" I followed.

He couldn't stop laughing and didn't defend himself this time. Somehow, I didn't withdraw my comment with something as cheesy as "I was just kidding." Come on! He didn't confirm or deny it! And it was just my educated guess! If American founding fathers like Ben Franklin and Alexander Hamilton (see *Hamilton* the Broadway musical) had desires, how could I judge my housemate, a charming bodybuilder with high testosterone?

After the moving was finished, we hugged each other again before he drove off in a hurry to prepare for the quiz. He did not want to hear me complain about racial discrimination, which I thought was why I ended up in this condo alone. "It's not about race. It's about cultural differences. Sorry I gotta go." How could one ever refute that thoughtful justification without conducting a social psychology experiment?

I told him that my life would have been very different if I had a brother like him when I grew up. He said calmly in his low voice, as low as Mitch McConnell, "Well, there are lots of brothers out there." Being rejected by one German American didn't make me feel bad because I understood that he already had a biological brother and that his life was kind of saturated. I later mentioned the same thing to Carl, another German American, and he clearly stated that a good friend was not the same as a sibling. I accept that.

My generation of Chinese-born folks tends to be the only child in the family due to some historic administration's corrective policies. I, like many people, assumed life would be easier if we had siblings who could share the pressure from the parents and the teachers. However, Chris told me otherwise — siblings don't necessarily get along and may compete for parental attention or other resources. Prince Harry from the UK knows that very well. My observation of some relatives' love-hate relationships with one another also confirmed that. Taking one step back, did I actually know what it entails to be someone's brother? No, and I probably never will. Not hard to understand, the one-child policy, despite its rational purpose to control the population, created an objective loophole, or blind spot, in the mental health care industry in China: clinicians from my generation have difficulty understanding the family dynamics among the generations above and the future generations below.

I call my very close buddies "brother" in an Irish or Latino sense, but do the Irish or Latino Americans take this word seriously? I doubt it. Be realistic: If you call every dude a brother, then that title of "brother" is pretty much worthless. In analogy, the ubiquitous question "How are you?" actually means nothing to many Americans. It's impossible that everybody sincerely cares about you. You

THE "SHINING" HOUSE

realize how hollow and tricky it is when you're not doing great and hesitate to answer the question honestly to people outside your inner circle. Will they be able to handle a negative answer? Will they help you navigate the situation or walk away after showing some ritualistic sympathy? My therapeutic song *"How are you?* (2016)" alluded to this subtle issue of adulthood. In the lyrics, I said I wish I could answer 42. While discussing the lyrics with my therapist Layla, I explained that the universal answer "42" originated from the fiction *The Hitchhikers Guide to the Galaxy* by Douglas Adams. She wasn't familiar with that science fiction, but she said she could relate. In contrast, some of my peers back then didn't exhibit awareness of this kind of struggle. "Just say you are good!" Either their lives were truly pain-free, or they wouldn't show their vulnerability in front of me, and vice versa.

Weeks later, during the winter break, the landlady of the "Shining" House and her husband drove to Columbus from a small town called London, OH, to sign the lease-transfer paperwork with me. Another week later, I received a check from her: about 50 bucks was deducted from the original deposit. According to her, she had to drive one hour each way, and I was solely responsible for her gas and time costs. In retrospect, everything could have been done digitally, as my condo-mate in Upper Arlington always did. After all, the landlady, a pharmacist, was only in her thirties. She had the ability to learn modern technology.

That Sunday afternoon, on the same roundtable where we signed the original lease, when I told her we had tried to talk with Jessica, she said coldly, "It's already over." And in the meantime, my haunting memories would stay with me forever. I thanked her husband, the engineer who had been on the lads' side through this battle. As I remember, he came to fix the weird sound out of the heat tunnel from the basement several times. When I asked the landlady if Jeremy had also done the release paperwork, she said his lease was slightly different from mine; in other words, no hurry. I wonder which factors justified her differential treatment. I also doubt she would eventually ask Jeremy to pay for her commute in the same way. He wouldn't have cared as much as I did because 50 bucks was literally nothing compared to his enormous student loan for med school. Not for these binge-drinking elites.

Chapter 7
The Worst TA Ever in Ohio State

Another stressor for me during that fall semester of 2013 was the graduate teaching assistant position. I intend to show you how my life turned from bad to worse after I undertook this TA appointment, which was intended to benefit my career development.

7.1 What I Learned from the TA Training Course

I was required to enroll in an intensive TA training course during the summer of 2013, because I didn't pass the Spoken English Test administered by Ohio State. I only stayed a few sessions in that course before the instructor reassigned me to a weekly seminar. However, those few sessions informed me how international teaching assistants and faculty members tended to be reviewed when English isn't their first language. As I remember, based on one academic paper we were asked to read, Asians are the least favored, which indicates a statistical interaction between language skills and race.

The paper also pointed out that students who speak English as their first language find it more effortful to perceive and comprehend the speech uttered by their international TAs. Our accents may significantly obstruct effective communication, though it's definitely not the only factor. Aware of its impact, I took an accent reduction course with a private instructor one year after moving to California, and I wish I had taken it earlier. I was sad to learn that I had been pronouncing several English phonemes incorrectly, thanks to the public education in China — not only for American English! It's gruesome to realize that non-English majors in college would never have the privilege to learn the truth unless they receive training outside their major programs. To make things worse, out of politeness or even political correctness, the US institutions generally would not impose this type of "corrective" training on international personnel, despite its remarkable benefit for the individual's career development. Such a benefit can be confirmed by any individual who strives to speak authentic English in front of native speakers.

Mr. Hoffman, the primary instructor for the course, gave me early precaution that the students would be rude to me because the way I spoke English was "different." I couldn't understand why, but later I realized his prediction was correct. Mr. Hoffman had a senior status at Ohio State; his stern look resembled Professor Samuel Oak (or in Japanese, Dr. Yukinari Ohkido), in Pokémon, the world-famous Japanese game and anime series.

Besides, Mr. Hoffman warned me that I needed to be patient with these students who had never touched any math or physics after high school. Yet I still overestimated the students' ability to handle algebra. In retrospect, he could predict almost every type of challenge that I would face, TA-wise, despite his certainty in my mastery of the course material. And I inadvertently acted like that "obnoxious" TA from India, who was mentioned as a negative example in the original TA training course. According to the instructor, that Indian TA told the undergrads in their department, "This is something you should have learned in high school." His students rated him as overly harsh.

Another noteworthy fact was that most trainees in that TA training cohort, i.e., those who failed The Spoken English Test, were graduate students from Asia. I was uncertain whether it was arranged that way or I could draw any profound conclusion regarding Asian students' English skills. Maybe the conclusion has always been clear to the entire world: students from non-English-speaking countries can hardly speak professionally fluent English without intensive training and long-term exposure. Life in America allowed me to see my objective disadvantages as well as my position on global coordinates. As for language skills, compared to kids growing up in Singapore and Hongkong, or kids studying in private international schools, I was already behind at the starting point. It's just an undeniable fact. Not my fault, but my problem to solve, according to Mark Manson.

7.2 Why Did the Students Hate This Course?

In the department of Communication Disorders, the undergraduate students were predominantly female. Sorry to disappoint those sexists, but those few introverted male students weren't necessarily stronger at math than the ladies. They were, however, all composed and respectful. Between the professional programs of speech-language pathology (M.A.) and audiology (Au.D.), it is easy to guess which student body is more feminine than the other. To be honest, I could not understand why these scientific clinical professions could not attract more male students. Among those existing male students, how many would feel comfortable in that environment when they are the gender minority? I have no idea. While my research program's official name had the word "science" in it, the program code didn't fall under "STEM" by official standards in Ohio State, as I later found out, which was unfortunate for international students seeking employment in the US.

Most students in that undergrad program did not embrace quantitative coursework. The course I was assisting with covered basic acoustics and audio engineering without involving trigonometry or calculus. Yet, to make it sound even less daunting to the undergrads, Mr. Hoffman named it "Art & Science of Sound." One would think the "art of sound" should include music, which happened to be part of my expertise; sorry, but the textbook's music-related chapters were skipped because the acoustics and psychoacoustics of music were not mainstream topics in these particular clinical professions. Fair enough. Another old name for this course, "Bioacoustics," seemed to be a misnomer to me, as the field of bioacoustics mainly studies the sounds made by different animal species. Because the majority of these undergrads wanted to become speech pathologists eventually, they couldn't care less about quantitative physics, based on my overall impression. No matter how enthusiastic I was when teaching the lab session, their faces told me they were baffled and tormented. This course's depth was commensurate with high school physics, but the content itself was too specialized for high school.

To some extent, I admire those students who are more willing to memorize anatomy or historical facts than practice algebra or computer programming. Some relatives in China were stunned when I told them I was assigned to teach American undergrads, but I didn't feel accomplished at all—neither with this course (something I loved turned out to be daunting for other people), nor with this master's degree in hand (the name of that unfinished Ph.D. program did not reflect my true expertise but gave me some disadvantage during job applications instead). Chinese people in China, especially those who had never been to college, refused to acknowledge my objective failure until I told them every detail of my experience. They would rather speculate that I lacked self-confidence than accept the bitter truth I told them, even though they knew how serious I'd always been since childhood. Ironically, these were the people who sometimes blamed me for being too rational. Hence my multi-layered frustration.

Honestly, the course touched upon a variety of topics, and some of them were challenging and abstract for a lot of people. Any STEM person who has been tortured by the demanding coursework in college would sympathize. The department canceled the prerequisite math course in order to increase the enrollment number of this course, which was legitimate. But who was there to suffer? I have witnessed White American students who were strong at science and math, and that's why I would never criticize American education as a whole, unlike many people who do so indiscriminately. As I once told a friend who had worked for Shanghai American School, most Chinese students do not understand math or science more thoroughly; their high performance in the written exams merely reflects the long-term effect of memorization and repetition. A senior American pharmacist in Columbus told me he had realized that international students from Asia were not necessarily smarter but that only top-ranking international students could come to study in America. Unfortunately, even this is no longer true. Overseas education has become a global business; one can gain access to higher education in various programs in developed countries as long as their parents are willing to pay extra.

One thing worth mentioning: While I did excel at physics in high school and even trained for Physics Olympics in my province, I was never as good at math as some of my peers. In other words, I failed to live up to the Chinese standard of being a top student. This shortcoming made me an easy target of public humiliation by math teachers such as Tao (male). Consequentially, when a staff member in the Department of Communication Disorders called me "the mathematical guy," I corrected him, "I'm not qualified, man, compared to the Ph.D. student who uses differential equations in his research." I was flattered. It's all relative.

7.3 I Did Everything I Could, but…

Except for my initial errors, I was on duty every week, even when I was sick. If you remember, I ended up in the ER. I took the initiative on many tasks and coordinated well with the other TA, Emily, an intelligent and enthusiastic girl who graduated from their undergrad program. However, it was not an enjoyable experience working with some of these undergrads. Some students in my sessions went to Emily's sessions, as Mr. Hoffman predicted. According to these students, they learned far more from her than they could learn from me. Understandably, Emily knew American students' needs better. She knew girls better, had taken this particular undergrad course herself and knew what to expect in the exams. Interestingly, some of her students came to my review sessions to ask questions. I learned from her students that Emily didn't actually go over the exercises in the textbook during her sessions. I couldn't understand her rationale, but I did spend the entire summer term doing all those exercises myself, as instructed by Mr. Hoffman. I was certain that these exercises would help the students achieve higher exam scores. Higher education wasn't all about exams, but one shouldn't let a bad-looking GPA become the roadblock on their way to grad school.

Based on my observation, most male professors like nice girls and expect guys to be as obedient. During that semester, there were several times the email correspondence between Mr. Hoffman and me led to some misunderstanding. Mr. Hoffman seemed to be irritated because I didn't **appear** to prioritize the TA duty in the face of incidental time conflicts.

Similarly, during the second week of my employment in Davis, California in 2015, Mr. Osman, who had become my boss, once scolded me for no legitimate reason other than to establish dominance over me, "You never look happy!" "What? You said you didn't have time? It's a job!" I was the only other person in his lab, hired full-time to set up the lab for him, and exhausted every day because I had to figure out everything by myself without a colleague. Months later, when the only lab mate, his postdoc savior Mr. Shapiro, was finally here, Mr. Osman said to me, "Every time I talk to you, my blood pressure will increase." I told him my blood pressure tended to get lower when I talked to him. Dear readers, don't try to convince me that aged dudes are all that grumpy because it's not true. If it were true, I would rather live a relatively short life span.

Like many male teachers, professors, landlords, or Y chromosome providers, Mr. Hoffman would rarely admit his own mistakes unless the evidence was displayed right on the table. However, this authoritative persona was very mild compared to the authoritarian and narcissistic personality of Tao, the male math teacher who traumatized me throughout the final year of high school.

To be fair, Mr. Hoffman wrote me a recommendation letter for my re-applications to Ph.D. programs outside Ohio State; he also helped me with the thesis project at its early stage, scrutinized my manuscript sentence by sentence, and eventually allowed the pitiful project to pass his checkpoint. Therefore, I should be very grateful. Indeed I was. But here's the thing: research and teaching are separate dimensions. Despite his patience and sense of responsibility, it was hard to portray him as an agreeable person when focusing on this TA issue alone. Every time he perceived he wasn't held as the dominant party, he would use all uppercase for certain words in his email or cc Mr. Williams, our department chair. I had rarely seen uppercase words in any email before coming to the US, except for spam, ads, and one reply from my first-year supervisor Mr. McCarthy after his ego felt insulted by my neutral question. Unfortunately, my interaction with this professor is beyond the scope of this story.

How did the UPPERCASE affect me, a person constantly walking on a tightrope? Whenever I saw angry words such as "YOU" or saw Mr. Williams cc'ed in his email, my heart would beat faster. As mentioned before, the anxiety which had accumulated for months and climaxed at the start of that busy semester laid the foundation for my ER visit. Anxiety for what? I feared that I would lose my only source of funding, which would mean me getting kicked out of America right away, which would mean more traumatic or depressing experiences for me, or even a major Apocalypse. In reality, the Apocalypse was postponed by four years but eventually struck me in 2017.

Those days, I tried to convince myself that ALL CAPS simply indicated emphasis and warning, so I mistakenly assimilated and amplified this method, which turned out to be disastrous in the following semester. When I mentioned this email thing to him in his office once —pretty sure he was trying to daunt me on purpose —he justified that Mr. Williams, as the official supervisor for the TA appointment, wanted to be informed regarding my performance. In fact, Mr. Hoffman was always super meticulous with his wording. He rarely judged anybody in front of me directly, especially since we were not in a deep or long-term mentor-student relationship. I suspect he must have acquired this advanced academic etiquette for self-preservation through some effective learning process. Renowned professors like him radiate professionalism and diplomacy, which are adaptive traits among academics. Understandably, in a human world where telling the brutal truth will most likely get you in trouble or even danger, people tend to find their artistic way of expression, sarcasm or innuendo, for instance.

Like my former co-worker Mr. Shapiro, you might want to tell me that I should accept the difficulty of interacting with my superiors as part of life. Yes, in the animal kingdom, this kind of slave mindset may be de facto the adaptive one. Yet, I will tell you that's why many people with integrity dislike teachers, bosses, surgeons, authorities, law enforcement, Big Brothers, and in an extreme case, human society in general. Knowing such unidirectional suffering due to the status gap is pretty much inevitable throughout a civilian's life in a hierarchical human society, I have been determined not to bring another life into being since I was little. Beware that I haven't even added into the equation the biological features that will subject my potential offspring to discrimination and prejudice on the global market or to exploitation in a collectivistic world.

It's quite an illusion for outsiders that an ivory tower is a safe place for rightful debates. In reality, the society in academia is intricately hierarchical rather than democratic. Jeremy once told me he would never go to grad school—he was referring to research-oriented Ph.D. programs. After years of struggling, I have come to agree with his standpoint, but from the unique perspective of mental health. There is a constantly under-reported probability that one will develop some kind of mental disorder in grad school for various reasons, even before a grad student enters the real society! The actual stressors include the financial difficulty and the p-values, i.e. the pressure of publication. Still, for many people, the most remarkable one is the unequal interpersonal relationship: Edward Snowden called it "the imbalance of power" in his memoir *Permanent Record*. While there are good people in every profession, you won't know exactly which ones beforehand because no one outside or inside the system can be absolutely certain or 100% transparent with you. It's normal to have risks and setbacks in one's life, but as a personal trainer once told me, you will get injured more if you push through the pain. So ultimately, it's up to you whether to take the risk or not.

Innocent students, especially international students, be careful what you learn from your professor or superior, whether this person appears solemn or frivolous. The potentially harmful influence comes with no alarm, and you'll only have yourself to blame in the end due to your lower status. I, personally, had learned bad things from my professors. However, those little things won't hurt them because they have power already. Moreover, I strongly warn against using a supervisor/mentor as a father figure for yourself because, in the complicated adult world, your essential relationship with them is professional. However admirable they seem to you, the boundary should always be held sacred to prevent any emotional "conflict of interest." The teacher-father analogy promoted by the ancient Chinese culture, Confucianism in particular, is maladaptive and even toxic in some ways. Under extreme circumstances, you will be sacrificed, not sacrificed for, because you can't be their top value. It's universally true, not just my personal experience.

As far as the lab/recitation sessions are concerned, there is no denying that my pedagogical skills couldn't compete with that of trained teachers, despite my deeper understanding of certain engineering topics. Teaching in a classroom has never been my pursuit, but I think anybody who understands a topic thoroughly should be able to explain that topic and get proficient with practice. Unfortunately, knowledge alone was NOT what those undergrads wanted. Looking back, I was too slow to realize I should have treated these students as clients whose parents had paid for the expensive service. Higher education was essentially a business in the United States, just like healthcare or litigation. These "clients" felt entitled to 5-star service in addition to knowledge and skills. Interestingly, other international TAs I've conversed with have reached similar conclusions, as I later found out.

Something to admit: I had no idea what a satisfactory teaching assistant should be like until I experienced college-level courses in psychology and neuroscience taught by some senior Ph.D. students. They either brought candy treats for midterms or sent individual emails to congratulate some students on their outstanding test scores. Eye-opening. In contrast, when I was in college, I barely received special assistance from any teaching assistant. Such a luxurious service did not exist for us. In college, we once complained to the instructor of Human Anatomy that the final exam was too comprehensive. She defended herself with an English proverb she had heard, "God helps those who help themselves." Under her teaching style, students either had to study extra hard or just quit. Years later, Carl, an expert on the Bible, told me he had never heard of such a proverb, despite its unfathomable popularity in China. "What? God helps those who help themselves? I think God helps those who **can't** help themselves," he said.

I didn't master the skills to "describe" acoustics to students who couldn't figure out algebra. I lacked the willpower to cater to a noisy crowd that showed little respect and sometimes hostility. I didn't receive rectification for my teaching style from Mr. Hoffman because, according to him, he didn't want to add to my stress by coming to the classroom; nonetheless, I suspect the students would behave better when he was watching from behind.

At the end of the semester, I received an email notifying me that the results of the students' mid-semester and end-of-semester evaluations were ready to be seen. I admit I was shocked and infuriated by some students' comments. A student rated me as "the worst TA ever in Ohio State" despite the fact that "Ohio State is an institution of excellence." A student took my words out of context and accused me of "having no interest in teaching." In a serious tone, I once mentioned that my stipend didn't correlate with the class average. The intended message was that I didn't want to torture my students in the same way many school teachers in China tortured us for their own agenda, namely their salary, bonus, and promotion. Some comment was fair by pointing out, "he just doesn't know how to control this messy class." However, there were zero good comments, not even from the students who interacted with me a lot and got very high grades after coming to my review sessions. I suppose hard-working students rarely took the optional review seriously because it was a waste of their time.

Honestly, nobody had ever warned me that I would be rated by the undergrads; I myself didn't have the privilege to enjoy an expensive college education in America, so how would I know? Would I have acted differently? Absolutely, but only verbally. I would impose censorship on myself and do my best to please these patrons. I understand that some great professors in Ivy League institutions have received venomous comments, too. However, at that age, it was quite a blow to me. I received comfort from colleagues, friends, and travel mates. A grad student told me, "Oh, students hate that course." My housemate Shannon said to me, "Those are spoiled undergrads." A postdoc from Europe astonished me by saying, "They're stupid." I didn't know how to respond. On my trip to New York City during the winter break, when I expressed my worries that my TA appointment was at stake, an Egyptian hostel roommate, who was a grad student in Canada, said to me, "Take it easy, bro. You will be okay. Don't take it personally." But my gut feeling told me otherwise. What about a Chinese friend, Lily, who studied in OSU's Master's program for Teaching English as a Second Language (TESL)? After hearing about my trouble the next semester, she commented, "Ah, of course, you guys don't know how to teach." She wasn't completely wrong. Unfortunately, the person who knew how to teach had to return to China soon after graduation—foreign ESL teachers are not in high demand within America for obvious reasons.

Regarding my service to the students, I remember one thing I didn't do well: before the final, the students were told to email the professor and the two TAs any questions they had— all three of us at the same time. One student from Emily's session emailed me and me only (unless she sent three separate emails) with one question involving high school trigonometry. I was surprised because I'd never taught her in person. I told her not to worry about it because the necessary formula was never mentioned in the textbook or during the lab sessions. Thinking it would not be in the exam paper, I didn't open Pandora's box for her.

However, it did show up as a multiple-choice question in the final exam the next day. I found that out as I was working manually on the key to the exam paper designed by Mr. Hoffman. This student's concern turned out to be legitimate. It's not impossible that due to my negligent response, she could not figure it out and thus lost the two points, and through the chain of the butterfly effect, her future was destroyed. I wouldn't know because it wasn't I who graded her exam paper.

Let's look at the bright side of reality: that student was probably the only Asian in that entire cohort of students (around 150), so I suspect her grade in this relatively quantitative course should be better than average, if not outstanding. Stereotype, I know. Trying to downplay my sin, I know. In retrospect, I could have explained everything on a piece of paper and sent her a picture taken with my HTC smartphone. It's worth noting that some colleagues of mine were still using "stupid" phones back in 2013.

Well, this undergraduate student probably expected me to be the only person willing to answer her question, but why? Had she asked Emily this question already but received no answer? Or did she choose me based on my race or country of origin? It was a long shot for her since I didn't know her at all. As a grad student in a small department, I didn't treat people differently based on their ethnic background or country of origin when working in an American institution; however, it wasn't the case for immigrants who couldn't speak fluent English and had to live by their group labels. I decided to bring this issue to attention so people would drop the misassumption that every individual would, by default, feel close to anyone who looks similar to themselves. For instance, one can't expect Asian Republicans to vote for

Andrew Young, the Democratic candidate who has promised universal income for American citizens, simply because he is Asian. One also can't expect all Latino Republicans to vote against Trump just because he built up the border wall against the Mexicans. That kind of logic is too simplistic, as I see it.

7.4 The Removal

A week before the new semester, I noticed that my TA access to the course on Carmen, the online learning system at OSU, was no longer available. So I emailed Mr. Hoffman, who was still out of town those days after the staff member failed to explain what happened. Guess what? He didn't reply to me until the night before the new semester— sent from his iPad, with Mr. Williams cc'ed. According to him, the course enrollment had dropped substantially compared to the fall semester, so he only needed one TA. He decided to retain Emily, who would stay in this department for longer, not me, who was planning to leave, "for continuity." Apparently, that was a partial cover-up— who doesn't want an extra helping hand for free? Note that I was funded by the department, not by his research grant.

Later in the spring semester, I saw him teaching one session of the lab/recitation himself, but I never brought this up, as I construed it as his "diplomatic" way of abandoning me (or segregating me from those undergrads for mutual benefit). I view that as a lack of transparency, which was very common in any centralized human organization, but back in 2013, I could only try to look at the bright side: some extra time saved for my thesis project. One might tell me to suck it up or, say, "process" this undesirable part of adulthood; let me tell you: even when I was a teenager, I hated Mandy's "conspiracy" with those school teachers behind my back. In reality, Mr. Hoffman's unannounced rearrangement did more harm to me instead. Due to his belated email, our department chair Mr. Williams had to come up with some new TA duty for me, but it was already too late. I was asked to hold office hours every week for a different course under a different professor, but students rarely showed up to ask questions. That emptiness was combined with other empty aspects of life and eventually asphyxiated me.

If you believe that the way he handled everything was due to his magnanimous virtue, you are mistaken. His loads of repressed emotions were released cathartically during my thesis defense, which happened months later. The project had its major and minor problems, but Mr. Osman and his collaborator thought he was overreacting. Mr. Hoffman explained to Mr. Osman that he was unhappy he wasn't consulted before the experiment was run. However, from our perspective, Mr. Hoffman overlooked our original email asking for his feedback, presumably because he was too busy or unwilling to open the link. He didn't respond at all, so how should we interpret that? It varies from person to person. We thought he didn't care much. I wish he could stand on my side to persuade Mr. Osman to upgrade the defective experimental design in the first place.

Frankly speaking, I envy these American students who have free speech against their instructors. In contrast, growing up under the authoritarian education system, I never had the gut to rate those awful teachers negatively, no matter how much I disliked or despised them, for fear of reprisal by these tyrants. In fact, we were usually encouraged or mandated to give good ratings by the headteacher of the class right before the evaluation questionnaires were handed out. We students, except the bluntest ones, were aware of snitches in ambush around us. These snitches were loyal to the tyrants due to shared personalities and values. Believe me; most of those teachers wouldn't survive students' free speech.

Growing up in Smoke City, I never liked the teaching profession because of the horrendous things some school teachers did to me. The worst individuals tend to create the most everlasting traumatic memories in me, casting a shadow on the rest of my life. This once-in-a-lifetime TA experience in grad school exacerbated my aversion toward that industry, just from a different stance — I would suffer either as a student or as an instructor. According to my correspondence with some other international TAs, I wasn't alone. I wouldn't even call this failure my Waterloo because it was doomed from the very beginning, just like a hypothesis has been factually wrong even before you run experiments to test it. To be fair, those professors had not intended to give me extra setbacks in life; they were trying to figure out how to help everyone, but they first and foremost needed to protect their own reputations and the department's public image.

Facing this diplomatic demotion after the exhausting house drama against Lady J, I was on the edge of falling into a misogynistic attitude, as Eminem did, according to his lyrics. Fortunately, I didn't have to, as I was in touch with many rational and mature females in my life. What I dreaded was a feminine environment, like the one I had in elementary school. Contrary to some people's imagination, it was a nightmare to a man, not a paradise.

7.5 Was I Obnoxious?

Mr. Hoffman called me "obnoxious" once during our preparation for the lab session. Emily, who was also present, told me not to take it to heart. Based on my understanding of human behavior, I knew it couldn't be his Freudian slip. I knew something wasn't right. Some students must have complained about me, "How can he even say something that's not nice and sweet?! We American girls need affirmation and encouragement! He is not here to help but to intimidate us!" I knew Mr. Hoffman understood the whole situation better, as he had had decades of experience with people of various backgrounds. Still, he couldn't tell me directly in his position that those students would only accept praise and encouragement. Mark Manson discussed this issue in his orange-covered bestseller *The Subtle Art of Not Giving a F*ck*. In a nutshell, some American psychologists and policymakers in history misguided the entire American education. I also think the silence of these educators in the system has indulged this unhealthy trend. Unfortunately, unless they have their tenure already, they have to be extremely careful with the "cancel" culture themselves. As an international employee who was canceled by these undergrads very quickly, I could only learn the truth by reading, gleaning, and retrospecting over the following years.

There is no doubt that an objective person like me will offend some people in some way because the truth hurts those who benefit from the falsehood. Meanwhile, I had not learned the ideas of cultural sensitivity and political correctness until I moved to California, which means my honest opinions or genuine questions have inevitably hurt some people's feelings. I am no senior US citizen, so I won't join the voice to call the younger generation snowflakes.

However, it doesn't mean I don't see that cohort of students as problematic. For a 2-hour lab session, many would leave after half an hour instead of using the precious time to ask questions. Some girl asked me in a flirtatious tone before a fest in downtown Columbus, "Do you want to hang with me, Slim?" Some girl wanted to take a dominant position in a conversation and then accused me of yelling at her when I simply raised my voice to emphasize my point. Fortunately, when I was in bewilderment, another girl explained to me, "She is just sassy" — I learned a new word that day. I know many people like to use "cultural differences" as a shield for personal traits. Therefore, I would like to point out the cultural difference here: in China and Japan, girls who work in the rehabilitation field do not behave like that.

That fall semester, I was going through some internal change, and I had a feeling that I would become a controversial person someday, more specifically, a person hated by those who lack objectivity, brevity, profundity, and curiosity. Controversiality, unlike notoriety, isn't a bad thing to me because human beings naturally have clashing values and beliefs. Throughout my life, I have never considered myself as "excellent," unlike what those authoritarian teachers had hoped for— they were accustomed to using me as their puppet or so-called role model. Accordingly, I can't live up to the standards of an "excellent" institution like Ohio State. Taking one step back, isn't it funny that high-ranking students from other countries are treated like garbage in some regions of America? I know I wasn't alone. Yet as for the wrong choice, I only had myself to blame for it. Yes, I blame myself for not seeing through the mesmerizing and hyperbolic advertising in human society and not taking a lavish field trip across America before making all the grad school applications. We had imagined the entirety of America to be like heaven, but it isn't remotely true. I only liked a few big cities in the end.

Anyone who plans to jump from one field to another for grad school: I urge you to consider what kind of courses you can TA for in that specific department. Do the undergrads in that department need your knowledge and skills in the long run? Funding for RAship most likely won't be guaranteed throughout the duration of a Ph.D. program unless your professor treasures you like a formal employee. It's possible, yet just rare, when you first start grad school. The first-year fellowship is just the initial attraction, similar to a seed grant for assistant professors. It might be a bit provocative to call that "funneling," the business model we see online nowadays, but you should treat that "honor" with caution because other people are paying their way into better institutions at more desirable locations. There is no free lunch in this world if you think carefully and notice the time, attention, and opportunity cost involved.

7.6 The Good Ones

To clarify, I did assist some students who were respectful to me as a teaching assistant and to STEM fields in general. They were inquisitive and treated the physical mechanisms seriously. Meanwhile, some students were also athletes winning medals for the university. A student older than me was dealing with her divorce while taking this course. She asked me to extend her deadline for the homework assignment; of course, I had no problem with that. A married student from Puerto Rico had to struggle with algebra, just like most of her classmates. Besides, she felt alienated during the group discussion and the group projects, which she attributed to her accent. She could be partially correct, but her introversion and decision to sit at the back of the classroom also gave her some disadvantages from my perspective. I communicated with her with no difficulty, aware of my own foreign accent; however, I had no control over how these American students would accept or reject her, especially since I felt repelled by a fraction of the students myself.

I had no idea whether or not these students eventually entered those clinical programs. I was there to "assist" them, providing knowledge and tips when needed.

Can I confidently say the other students who hated me or that course aren't good people? Negative. If their goal is to become a regional speech-language pathologist, they don't need advanced quantitative skills in daily practice. For audiologists with a doctoral degree, yes, they do; the deeper, the better, within a reasonable range. However, according to the enrollment sizes of these two clinical programs, the market seems to demand far fewer audiologists than speech-language pathologists.

Educationists would agree that math education is a national issue for America. But does everybody need a lot of math in their job? We all know the answer, regardless of which country you live in. As some American professor once said to me, people have different expertise, so no one should be overlooked. I agree. However, through human interactions, I have learned that the gap between those who can reason and those who cannot is objective. Quantitative reasoning is a crucial part of reasoning.

I wish those hard-working students success, as every responsible instructor would say. However, life is highly unpredictable, and top-notch individuals with high integrity are also prone to exploitation within a hierarchical system. With that in mind, I also wish my hard-working students good luck.

7.7 The "Nerdy" Minority

Mainstream Americans, including but not limited to White Americans, tend to stereotype Asian Americans as STEM nerds, often in a pejorative tone. They only dare do this to the so-called model minority, as the "model" label prohibits one from expressing grievances— a psychological gag, so to speak. My intuitive interpretation of this phenomenon is very straightforward: (TRIGGER WARNING) it reminds me of that crazy point in human history when the mainstream population of Nazi Germany persecuted one smart ethnic group. They demonized the Jews out of jealousy and tribalism, although the latter did nothing illegal or immoral.

Broadway actor Patrick Page, who played Frollo in *Hunchback of Notre Dame* and Hades in *Hadestown*, once made a thoughtful Instagram post addressing this type of ridiculous bullying on campus and in American politics (as I paraphrase it): the mediocre tend to harass the achievers, the so-called nerds, because, from the perspective of the former, the latter are the "weird" ones who draw the attention and rewards from the evaluators. Bullying is one of the cheapest ways for the mediocre to compensate for their sense of inadequacy and inferiority. When they constantly feel like an underdog in a ranking system, they attempt to win in a non-standard dimension or in an unethical way. Be careful: if you are among the top 5 to 10 percent of your cohort, you know you automatically fall into one specific type of minority, as every normal distribution has two tails. The word "minority" indicates you may suffer from the tyranny of the majority, although outsiders tend to only see the glory around you.

In my opinion, mainstream Americans who put a stigma on Asian Americans based on math skills are making the comparison along the wrong dimension: race. That's racism and, therefore, unacceptable. Instead, they should hold the variable of skin color constant and compare themselves with people of the same color from other nations, such as European countries, Australia, New Zealand, and Russia. In that way, they will suddenly understand what it feels like to be a minority, not a "model minority," though. Perhaps we should consider that as some unconventional evidence for American exceptionalism? Only if you buy that term.

PART TWO

No tree, it is said, can grow to heaven unless its roots reach down to hell.

— *Carl Jung*

Figure: Carl Jung's Trees, original photo

Chapter 8
Played and Then Crushed

8.1 A Trip to the East Coast

During the winter break of 2013, I went on a trip to New York City with a Chinese friend, who was in his thirties and also a Ph.D. student. It was right before Christmas, and I did not get to see who I had planned to meet. NYC was usually 10°F warmer than Ohio, and Manhattan was always vibrant. The metropolis was to my taste, though my colleague Joe said it was like a giant machine. Because the original host fell through on me, I had my first experience of hosteling in the US, which meant I shared a room with guys from different countries. I couldn't remember the name of the tiny hostel, but I did remember that a roommate from Australia told me I had an American accent. The Ohio natives speaking "standard" American English certainly wouldn't agree with that.

We visited Times Square, saw the Statue of Liberty on a ship, and even took the ferry to Staten Island out of curiosity. I shot some video clips for my song *"Can you hear me?"* which was written as a gift to my former lab mate in Communication Disorders, who was getting married that year. Ironically, she didn't like music very much. Such people do exist.

I didn't tell people it was my birthday that day. Nor did I use this fact to persuade the aforementioned Egyptian roommate to go to a bar with me that night. However, that evening, I had a very memorable dinner at a local fast-food

PLAYED AND THEN CRUSHED

diner. The Egyptian dude laughed when I told him I ate some honey-flavored chicken wings. It was amazingly unique to me, considering I was living in Ohio. Years later, in Davis, California, when I had Irish breakfast tea bought from Safeway for the first time, I was amazed by its flavor. My co-worker, Mr. Shapiro, ridiculed my reaction. "You rock my world," he said, "It's just black tea." Unlike him, I didn't have the privilege of growing up in America, especially in California. He attempted to use my distinct sarcasm against me in revenge, but I wasn't affected at all.

That morning, my buddy Carl said "Happy Birthday" to me on Facebook. Then, Stacy did, as the second person. No more. I saw Jeremy on Facebook a lot those days. I had no doubt he received the notification on the front page of Facebook, but he chose to stay silent in contrast to Stacy. My heart felt as bleak as the weather on that day. I did wish him a happy birthday on his birthday, though I was kept out of his circle. The next morning, I texted him about the granola thing as a probe, and he started to lecture me like a pro— the same trait Doug has. In the end, he said, "Happy birthday, by the way. One day late, I know." He avoided doing it earlier to signal that he didn't consider me a friend. So why did he still mention it? I suspect he didn't know how to label me because I would never meet his friendship standard. I had to say thanks, but my heart felt nothing, maybe a little self-pity. That was the last day I allowed my birthday to be open to the public on Facebook. I have never since celebrated my birthday as a special day. One might say I did this purely because of Jeremy's apathy, but the truth was, I realized that the more I want something out of the ritual, the more dismay I will bring to myself. I hate mixed feelings.

Then my Chinese friend and I booked a rushed tour along the East Coast up to Boston, run by a Chinese company, and saw several scenic spots within two days. I stepped onto the campuses of Harvard and MIT, touched John Harvard's head in front of their library, and felt nothing magical. Chinese tourists adore these places because they dream their kids can someday study in these Ivy League institutions and bring glory to their families. But for me, I was only going to a public school in the Midwest and rated as "the worst TA ever." I stayed as an ordinary person and subsequently became a multidimensional sacrifice, if not a failure. The East Coast had a lot of good things that Ohioans could never dream of, and I was just a tourist, not a resident, in a big city. I knew deep in my heart that applying to the Midwest institutions for grad school was a stupid mistake, despite the existence of some distinguished professors over there. Years later, I lived in Davis, not SF, not LA, or San Diego, resulting in yet another depressive period in my life.

Back in New York City, with nobody else to hang with during the cold winter, I decided to go back to Ohio to spend Christmas and New Year's Eve with friends like Carl and his then-fiancée Lindsay. I wish I had the money and shelter to stay in NYC through the New Year because what awaited me in Ohio was no fun. Honestly, I didn't even know much about the Ball Drop back then as a devout academic researcher. The travel pal, who was from the north of China, referred to Christmas and the New Year as "foreigners' holidays" for some reason. I did not stay in touch with him after he dropped out of his Ph.D. program at OSU because, through much interaction, I got the idea that we were not from the same world. Similarly, I rarely get close to those who refer to psychology as pseudoscience or a scam. They are not completely wrong, though: there are a lot of quack experts out there doing harm to people.

8.2 The Judgment Day

Back in Columbus, Ohio, it was freaking cold. With the snowstorm getting worse, in the streets of Upper Arlington, the entire world was so white except me — because I am Asian. According to some natives, the city would not shovel the snow in these neighborhoods. Suddenly, I realized I was locked up in the snowy world, all by myself. "No wonder Kayah went to Southeast Asia," I thought to myself. I was away from my close friends, though not too far from the boring West campus by car. Grocery shopping was no longer as convenient as before, especially in the snow. The nearby Giant Eagle and Whole Foods were more expensive than the Kroger near Olentangy Club and the "Shining" House. Anyway, it was my first winter driving in the snow.

My condo-mate Kayah had left me with access to her Netflix and Amazon accounts. Unfortunately, I wasn't very familiar with American T.V. shows at that time, so I didn't know what to look for. I opened Facebook and typed a status showing my loneliness, which Jeremy presumably saw. He appeared to be online, so I messaged him, "Hey, what are you doing these days?" Then he logged off immediately. I started to panic. How? That moment, I saw the giant snowflakes falling outside the window, and I couldn't move my body, as if I was frozen, despite the heater on. I guess I would have had a stroke if I wasn't young back then. After a minute, I gathered myself and dialed his number, but he hung up on me. I tried several times until the phone told me to leave a voicemail. I did, in a polite tone. I fell into a depressed state as soon as I realized I was being cheated again. He said he did not want to say goodbye to me forever, but he was lying. And in particular, he chose to cut me off this way, right after Christmas and before the new year of 2014, so that my whole new year would be doomed while his could be saved. At this age, after watching many American T.V. shows and movies, including documentaries, I realized that deception is too common in this world. I was just a naïve alien ready to be kicked off.

When I discussed this with therapist Layla in Davis, she was surprised by my frozen state but not by my depression. According to her, extreme isolation could easily drive a person insane. But I figured there was something else: the shame I was struggling with. I was ashamed to be cheated by this man again and lured into this lonely and helpless situation. No offense, but if the individual cheating me was the opposite sex, I could simply use the b-word on her, but in the face of a man like him, I couldn't do anything for fear of being judged as being oversensitive.

I texted Stacy and asked her if she knew what was going on. She told me he was relaxing at home and reading a book she had sent to him as a Christmas gift, but she failed to persuade him to respond to me after several attempts. He seemingly had forgotten that I was still in touch with her—people like him tend to believe their interpersonal connections and specific skills are exclusive to them. She told me she would meet up with me once she flew back from Los Angeles, where she had been surfing with her uncle that week. I trusted her, but not the excuses made by Jeremy. I knew he wanted to appear righteous in front of her. I felt disgusted and belittled when I thought of his lies, such as "I am not abandoning you" or "we should hang sometime."

Starting the next morning, I woke up at 5 AM and couldn't move out of my bed. There was a constant battle in my brain as to whether he considered me a friend at all or just intended to play me, as I seemed to have evidence for both sides. I was struggling internally. Along with the bad sleep was nausea in the morning, or heartburn, for the first time in my life, and it lasted until I got prescription drugs from my physician, days before the new semester. Later I learned from my friends in China that this condition was not uncommon for people who were emotionally strangled by another person. Again, I could not directly tell the physician what happened because it was too personal. At the same time, the doctor referred me to physical therapy for my injured wrist.

I managed to spend Christmas and New Year's Eve with Carl and his family. While watching the Ball Drop on Times Square on television, Carl and Lindsay were solving a 1000-piece puzzle on their big table, and they couldn't finish it before midnight. I sighed because my life was like a large puzzle made up of innumerable smaller puzzles in the manner of fractal geometry. I sighed because I knew Jeremy would have a better year after escaping from the "Shining" House, as seen in his group photo in which he wore a new gray shirt, with his big jaw raised very high in front of the camera. In contrast, my new year turned gray, and I didn't even know how to make myself look happy on Facebook. Charlotte tried to convince me that his disappearance wouldn't affect my success in life, but she didn't understand how much I had invested in this tricky relationship with him. I naïvely believed that by helping a medical student, I was indirectly contributing to the medical cause in general, and I didn't think that a first-year medical student could be so immoral. I am aware that many young people still, perhaps subconsciously, believe what I believed at that age due to the type of education they have received. However, these days I have realized that if you are helping a hypocrite, you are indirectly causing harm to innocent people.

8.3 The First Email and the Song

On the 2nd of January, in great pain, I wrote a long email to Jeremy, imploring him to explain why he would cheat me like that again and again. I detailed my difficult situation and told him I couldn't belong in that feminine department, and I wanted to "align myself with the elites like him." I even mentioned that my E.R. visit was triggered by him, something I had never said before for fear of causing him stress. In retrospect, that painful email could be summarized as such: I wanted you to treat me well, not only because we are on the same level of diligence but because you made my already challenging life even more miserable. At that time, I didn't know that the word "elite" sounded stigmatized, if not derogatory, to many people in modern America. I didn't care how he would see me after reading this email. He probably would escape farther away because I pointed out that he pushed me into the abyss. Based on my analysis of cause and effect, had he not given me false hope of friendship, I wouldn't have made the regrettable decision to move into solitude so quickly, which in turn led to a series of tragedies for me to face. I could have continued searching for shared housing near campus or even stayed in the "Shining" House. But at that time, I chose to blame myself on Facebook for trusting someone untrustworthy. He could see my Facebook status, but he never unfriended me thoroughly.

According to Stacy, he read it, but he would not respond to me. Instead, all the information was relayed by her. When I visited her, she said, "He said he was just stressed. He doesn't want anyone to rely on him. Besides, he likes me because I am independent." She was referring to the day she changed a tire by herself on her way to the airport, with a friend coaching her over the phone. Jeremy liked her Facebook status. I was infuriated inside because it was a totally different type of relationship. They had their intimacy as a couple, but Stacy juxtaposed herself with me subconsciously. I had no idea when I relied on him because it was he who always relied on me to communicate with Jessica, and he pointed out I had more friends than him in Columbus. Months later, when I told this to my sensitive friend Julian, he said he once had a male friend who also disappeared from his life after moving away. His interpretation was that "some people just perceive more responsibility than others." I relayed this to Stacy, who replied, "We should wait until Jeremy perceives less responsibility." In retrospect, I was misled by that "empathetic" interpretation. Think about it: what kind of people tend to perceive more responsibility than what is actually given to them?

Julian was kind and benevolent, and as an ethnic minority in the Midwest, he had to deal with a lot of stress himself. By the way, he was the person who taught me the word "Xenophobia" — something he had faced after he moved to Ohio from the South. I wasn't an English major in college, which objectively set a limit to my vocabulary outside my technical field before entering the US.

Regarding Jeremy's stress with med school, I once asked Stacy why she didn't look as stressed as him. She explained that Jeremy felt threatened when surrounded by other competitive classmates, especially those with higher intelligence. Like many other achievers, he grew up being the smart kid in his class, even in college, but med school suddenly made him feel average among the elites. He wasn't the only person to feel that way. His personality played a role in it and his muscles didn't bring him any advantage.

I felt even worse knowing Jeremy was back in Columbus for the new semester. That morning, under extreme pain, I finished a new song whose title was named after Jeremy. The melody had been in my mind for a long time, and the constant pain motivated me to finish the lyrics, which contained signs of attachment throughout the text. It was the first of the three songs I wrote to seal the pain caused by him. Understandably, some people would use that as "evidence" for their suspicion of my romantic fantasy toward Jeremy, and I had no control over that. In fact, the lyrics didn't sound romantic at all. The way he treated me facilitated my writing. The song was special because it described my perception of rejection by America as a whole. How did this obvious overgeneralization happen? The primacy effect, I guess. In my mind, Jeremy, my first White male American housemate, rejected me by playing me, and that was a massive blow to my ego. Bad omens, so to speak. It didn't mean he, as an ordinary person, was that special to me. However, he, a typical American professional student deemed as the "elite," presumably represented a whole category of Caucasian males who would unanimously reject or even discriminate against me. It was my feeling at that time, something many other international fellows could easily relate to.

Almost out of instinct, I posted on his Facebook timeline, "Sorry, I have finished writing the song called *Jeremiah*." Previously, I had notified him of my plan to write this song, but I guess he would rather not know the content— he knew it wouldn't be in his favor. I didn't like him as much as his girl imagined. For songwriters, the process of songwriting can be very therapeutic but also exhausting. Though not a fan of her music style in the slightest sense, I gradually came to understand why Taylor Swift would have so much passion for writing about her exes. She had no control. It's her method to get over it. No therapy could be as effective for her. The same mechanism applies to John Klein in the pop-rock band LANY.

Ten minutes later, I received his text message, something I will never forget unless I have brain damage because every sentence was a lie, an excuse, or a defense:

"I didn't have time to respond to your email, but here's a short one.

I think you're giving me too much emotional responsibility, and it isn't fair.

I don't have the tools to help you.

I think what you need is more than a friend. I know it is not what you want to hear.

I can only afford this type of friendship with limited time and energy.

I do not feel comfortable being a strong validation of your life. It should be something from within, not from other people."

I spotted his lies from the very first sentence because he was on Facebook all the time during the winter break. He was previously trying so hard to maintain a glorified image in front of me and then told me I shouldn't try to align myself with such a "decent" person. **I was enraged by his hypocrisy, his evasion from admitting his deception, and his pattern of redirecting attention to my limitations and making everything sound like my problem.** He surely reminded me of Doug, my Y chromosome provider. Notice in that text message almost every sentence started with the word "I." Months later, when I met with several international grad students from different institutions, they all shared the feeling that so many American students had a sense of self-righteousness written on their faces. And sadly, nowadays, it has become America's public image when it comes to international affairs. Based on a course I took in college, International Business Culture, American society has a very high masculinity index, but now it seems more like toxic masculinity. If only it were only exhibited in American males. Ms. Foster, the senior professor who purportedly plagiarized the work of Mr. Osman and bullied several other junior researchers, was also said to be a narcissistic person by my former colleagues at OSU. It is well-known in psychology that narcissism (not narcissistic personality disorder) is merely a crust around one's inner insecurity. Unfortunately, Jeremy, who had a minor in psychology back in college, had learned to counter-analyze and gaslight me in order to avoid being accused by me.

Immediately after receiving his reply, I was intoxicated by the phrase "this level of friendship," which gave me a transient sense of delight. Did he just say he recognizes me as a friend? Even if it is just an entry-level friendship, it's better than nothing, isn't it? On the other hand, my rational cynicism warned me that his wording could just be due to the presence of Stacy at that moment. They discussed almost everything, while I had to face the world alone with my limited intelligence and experience. What was worse, they "thought" they were helping me because I looked pathetic in that lonely situation. Still, by my standard, his behavior directly caused my depression, so he owed me a huge deal despite his denial of liability. Hit and run.

However, I didn't have the gut to tear up his lies because his girl was supposedly beside him or for fear of losing the last hope. Instead, I replied softly, in self-deception:

"Thank you, Jeremy. This is what I need. I feel so much better now. I wanted to stay in touch with you because I didn't want to cope with my problem with self-pity or alcohol." In reality, I am never a big fan of alcohol or any substance.

I felt disgusted with myself because I still couldn't speak my mind freely, knowing he would never "apologize" anymore since he no longer needed to confront me face-to-face. In a nutshell, I was no longer useful to him.

To be frank, I totally disagreed with his seemingly thoughtful analyses. He only vaguely commented that what I needed was more than a friend, but he did not say what it should be. Was he talking about a romantic relationship or a group of people I should be a part of? He always stayed elusive like this, making himself seemingly thoughtful. I told him my attempt to ask a Japanese girl out at that time couldn't work out, but the truth is, she happily married a US citizen, as Asian ladies sometimes do. Jeremy didn't respond.

It is noteworthy that his last comment was what I hated most. Anyone who only emphasizes the "within" is in denial of the objective standards and injustice in the external world. Some self-help gurus promote this kind of wishful mindset that appeals mainly to the privileged and those lacking critical thinking. If one never needs to care about what other people think of them, they are presumably privileged. As I once told someone, if your professor thinks poorly of you, you may get a low score; if your romantic partner thinks poorly of you, cheating or breaking up is on its way; if your bank thinks poorly of you, a loan is out of the question; if your insurer thinks lowly of you, every claim you file will be vetted heavily. We are all being rated constantly, and it has an undeniable impact on us. I am certain he has sought validation from other people.

As a result of this ineffective correspondence, the conflict in me was not settled but updated. Whereas I wanted to believe Jeremy finally agreed to acknowledge me as an entry-level friend, I understood he was simply giving me a temporary label to make a compromise. The friendship I wanted was a spot in his heart and his sincere concern, even if we would not spend time together. However, in his understanding, I was chasing a label, and I didn't deserve a long-term friendship because I couldn't meet his criteria: a white medical student. With such a conflict going on, my brain wasn't at peace at all. I still woke up early every morning and struggled in my head until I became hungry. In retrospect, my struggle could get me nowhere because a narcissist handles relationships differently than ordinary people and can hardly be persuaded.

Worried that my low sleep quality would affect my academic progress, I asked Dr. Clark, my primary care physician, for some sleeping pills, which was the first and last time in my life. I mentioned I probably needed counseling, but when Dr. Clark asked me if I was serious, I denied it. Because I had been reading some academic papers on emotions, I overestimated my ability to regulate my own. Did the sleeping pills called Lunesta help? Not in my case. I took one pill on Friday night and had a fever the next morning. I was worried about a possible relapse of UTI (or prostatitis, whatever) and another series of doctor's appointments. Therefore, I called Carl and Lindsay directly, and they drove me to urgent care. After some lab tests, I was told by the clinician not to worry too much. Acetaminophen, or Tylenol, was enough. From then on, when clinicians asked me whether I was allergic to any medication, my answer would be "Lunesta."

When the sun finally came out after months of snow, I felt a beast inside me start to wake up. Several days of struggle made me realize that I should no longer sacrifice my dignity and that I can no longer afford to be played by him. I then came to the conclusion that he was a villain in my life, who I must stop liking decisively. It wasn't brilliant, but I needed to save myself from the struggle. It was more pain than cognitive dissonance.

I later texted Stacy about my decision, and she, this 22-year-old girl, immediately thought I was in love with Jeremy. A dude-like girl who fell for his guitar seduction would never understand how I felt. I told her that his reply was insincere and that this person with low E.Q. didn't show any reflection on his behavior. Her subsequent response disgusted me one step further, "I don't understand why you are not (in love with him). I kind of like his style. He is so thoughtful. His grumpy face is so cute." When she realized I was resolute this time, she added, "It must be hard for you to make this decision." However, when I informed her of the chronic dysphoria I was going through, she was still defending him, "Yes, he is a hard person, but have you ever thought maybe we are the wrong people? We open ourselves to other people too easily." I was confused by her standpoint. Due to her crush on him from the very start of med school, she not only lost her ego for him but also assumed we were comparable. I may seem direct or blunt, but I only say about 25 percent of the things that cross my mind. More than average, of course, but I'm by no means a transparent person. My life turned out to be miserable because I hadn't had access to accurate information about this country, nor a rational partner to discuss things with; because I was an outlier in multiple dimensions, consistent with the concept of intersectionality. All that glitters isn't gold, but this young lady liked whatever glittered the most.

Months later, Mandy warned me that I should never speak ill of a man in front of his woman and never let a colleague know that I dislike them. But as I see it, it was precisely the wrong belief in the virtue of self-censorship that prevented me from telling Stacy all the terrible things Jeremy had done to me at that time. Maybe she would not believe my words; she would not change her infatuation for him after he finally acknowledged her as a girlfriend. Still, it was stupid of me to swallow the pain and eventually implode. I cared about this couple's feelings but got nothing in return. Ironically, according to Jeremy, "I think you're giving me too much emotional responsibility."

I didn't really like Stacy as a person. She was blindly devoted to him and even told me what kind of protein bar he liked when I was buying one in 7-ELEVEN. But why the hell would I care about his taste in protein bars? That's when I realized she couldn't differentiate her own romantic relationship from the ordinary friendship between guys. To my disgust, she was treating me as some sort of "bestie" for ladies. Unlike Jeremy, who liked to take advantage of innocent girls, I have tried to stay away from them for my entire life.

I remember that night she told me she didn't like math but statistics. I was thinking, "Statistics is the easiest branch of math. You simply like something that doesn't baffle you too much." This was a student graduating from a private college? I once asked her, "Do you think those white girls would be interested in me?" She answered, in a sarcastic rising tone, "May… be…?" Since she was from California, a place with supposedly more demographic diversity, I guess her response implied the answer was negative in general. Not to pour cold water on Asian lads; life is never fair. Although miraculous eventualities are not impossible, the chance is low. A successful case entails so many hidden factors, such as wealth.

As many Asian women covertly fantasize about Caucasian men for their genetic advantages, Asian men secretly do the same for Caucasian women, not for cross-cultural communication. To someone like me, an Asian who has largely lost Darwinian feelings with other Asians, after seeing people from all over the world, the harshest thing one can say is the Chinese metaphor, "A toad that wants to eat the flesh of a swan." Yet who is to determine whether an Asian male is naturally inferior to a Caucasian male or female? During one therapy session, when I mentioned I was attracted to ginger hair and blue eyes, Layla, an Arabic American, told me to downplay the importance of appearance while seeking a potential partner because personality and values are more important. That's theoretically valid. However, I don't want to be pedantic to myself anymore or cater to the virtue signaling of these experts. I was lonely and unhappy throughout my life partially because I always listened to the don'ts announced by the "authorities." Unsurprisingly, if you follow all of the directions in this world, you will end up nowhere.

8.4 Kevin and Kelly: the Songwriters

During the winter break, Charlotte, who attended Ohio State for college, suggested that I look into some student clubs so that I could find a group I belong to outside my work. I never thought that was an option for me, considering I was already a grad student. I had been to several events and house parties organized by the Japanese Student Organization at OSU and had great fun with people from a variety of Asian countries. However, based on the neuroscience of emotions, happiness and sadness have separate neural mechanisms; one cannot cancel the other out, although people tend to visualize them as two opposite ends on one dimension. Moreover, I didn't want my friendships to be tied to ethnicity or race. When in America, if I failed to connect with mainstream Americans, I would still consider my life abroad as a failure in essence. Easterners can judge me for that, but some welcoming Westerners understood my rationale.

To my disappointment, the Objectivist Student Club at OSU was no longer in operation in 2013. I emailed the original president of the club and got no response. What then attracted my attention instead was a songwriting club. I had written and recorded several songs in English since 2012, so I had this motive to connect with other individuals with the same brain function. Once I picked up the term "singer-songwriter" in English, I no longer needed to struggle between whether or not to label myself as a musician. A songwriter is different from a professional instrumentalist or vocalist. I knew I was pretty amateurish in terms of singing and playing instruments, but for non-commercial songwriting, there is no professional scale.

One night, I emailed Kevin, the president of the student club. He invited me to meet him in a bar on North High Street, where he and his then-girlfriend Kelly hosted the open mic. That email was life-changing for me, as this talented and sophisticated undergrad later became one of my buddies in America. Several months later, he finally introduced me to a bunch of his friends in the Columbus Songwriter Association during their monthly showcase event. His thrilling guitar skills and nostalgic Irish voice made him a rising star in the local music scene. Meanwhile, his wisdom and profundity manifested in his projects inspired me deeply at that time. His characteristic blues style was refreshing to me before I was deeply acclimated to Western genres through the years. Also, in contrast with some pretentious "elites" in those "helping profession" programs, he, a CS major, was super chill and humble. He attested to my belief that people from various parts of the world could actually communicate heart-to-heart thanks to the medium of music— notice that we didn't even have much overlap in terms of music styles. By the way, Kelly, originally from California, was also a seasoned singer-songwriter. She had a strong fan base in Columbus.

My first meeting with Kevin was postponed for weeks due to my struggle in the elongated snowstorm. When I finally met him in the bar, we discussed music, and I told him about my depressive story with Jeremy. He told me, "You should just let him leave your life if he is such a **jerk**. There's nothing you can do about it." Hence he taught me a new word to describe Jeremy after Stacy taught me, "American guys are **wimps**."

The second time I met with Kevin was in Ohio Union for his show. After his performance, we four lads went to Hound Dog Pizza. As I later found out, all three of them had some level of Irish heritage, but Kevin was the only redhead. As I sat on the table and let the grilled cheese flow down my slice, at that moment, I felt accepted by a group of Americans based on my identity as a music lover, without resorting to academic papers, the Bible, geographic adjacency, or race. I was thankful that they didn't consider me too old to join them. Those happy weekend nights spent with the local musicians made me feel included again. They helped me through the most challenging times in Ohio, though I wasn't capable of performing on stage in the way they did. However, the enjoyment of music and alcohol still couldn't write off the emotional pain I was going through that semester. It shouldn't be surprising, as explained already. My brain was malfunctioning at that time, technically speaking.

8.5 The Snowy Ordeal

During the first quarter of 2014, several issues attacked me in series around the start of the new semester, which collectively aggravated my situation and my psyche until my eventual explosion.

First, I have already mentioned how the cancellation of my TA duties for the "bioacoustics" course affected me. Suddenly, I lost my chance to meet new people after the lonely winter break, though many of those students would probably hate me still. The truth is, I did not apply to TA for this course at the end of the first school year because I did not think I was ready to teach in front of native speakers. However, it turned out that language wasn't the main problem.

Second, in February, the snow was still falling. One Saturday morning, I had to drive from home to the Eye and Ear Hospital to run the experiment on one participant. If I remember correctly, I drove from West Lane Avenue to Northwest Boulevard, which cuts diagonally, to save time. However, the heavy snow on the ground had turned into ice, and the next moment, my car started to swerve and spin. Then I lost control of it. The rear bumper hit a snowdrift and nearly fell off. I drove to the hospital with the bumper hanging in the air. Our research assistant Joe also arrived. But the research participant called to cancel the appointment because they didn't want to drive in the snow—another depressive moment for me to repress.

Why wasn't I smart enough to cancel it preemptively? Work ethics? Because I was never aware of this option or the danger of snow!

Joe helped me fasten the bumper with his bungee cord, a tool I had never seen before, and we drove to the nearest auto repair shop in the Grandview area. Finding the store took us some trouble because my sedan was stuck in the snowdrift across the street. The shop owner offered to use his truck to pull it out. According to him, the bumper had to be replaced with a new one, and some paintwork needed to be done. The "friendly" owner only told me the price of the bumper and assured me I didn't need to pay anything else, which sounded suspicious. I drove a car with no rear bumper for a week until the new one arrived the next weekend. The final bill came as a shock to me because the astonishing labor fee was added to it. He only accepted cash. The transaction ended up making me very unhappy because, from the very start, he concealed the actual cost from me, the gullible-looking young driver. His old mechanic explained that the owner was afraid the customer would not use the service here had they known the actual cost beforehand. I wanted to give this place a bad review for its lack of transparency, but there was no way to leave one anonymously on Google Maps, as I found out. Yelp and Reddit were not installed on my phone back then. Anyway, I wasted several hundred bucks and two precious weekends for the sake of a potential participant for my thesis project, and this person, who clearly knew Ohio better than me, didn't show up to the experiment on a Saturday morning. Not worth it, considering it was a poorly designed experiment. But at least I realized Joe was a trustworthy colleague with survival skills.

As far as I know, many international students from warmer places or more urbanized areas have had a terrible experience driving in the Midwest snowstorm. My Canadian colleagues told me the climate could be worse in Canada.

The lesson I learned was to operate only on the big roads where other people also drive and forget the shortcuts in the extreme weather. Jeremy had a big SUV with tires durable for the snow because he grew up in the countryside of snowy Pennsylvania. However, I didn't even know the distinction between various types of tires. I was simply compelled to drive by that life situation in Ohio.

School was canceled for several days that month due to the snow, but the days when school was open became disastrous for the students. So many cars were stuck in the parking lots of OSU. It was not uncommon for students to miss lectures because of the weather. Meanwhile, seeing people help each other to set the cars free was heartwarming. Sadly, this little bit of touching memory associated with a sense of community could not outweigh the general tragic tone of my second year in Ohio. I knew some people whose departments were on Main Campus, and they didn't drive throughout their four or five-year-long programs at Ohio State because they didn't need to. These people typically lived near the Medical Center, the location I was longing for. Of course, they didn't get as many weird health problems as I did.

Third, one frigid evening, as I took out the key and tried to open the door to the condo, the key broke. I suspected the key became fragile under the extremely low temperature. American keys all looked so frail to people from Asian countries. The door was open, and I managed to get the piece out of the lock, but a new problem arose— I no longer had a key to use. I couldn't lock the door if I wanted to get in. I emailed my roommate Kayah, who was on her trip with poor access to the Internet, and she replied and told me the neighbor was holding the backup key. So I went to the neighbor, and we tried the other key, which turned out to be a mismatch for our door. These ladies had never validated it. Therefore, the only thing I could do was never shut the door tight.

Unfortunately, over the previous year, I had developed a habit of locking the door from the inside when leaving the house. It was my instinct to close the door when going out. Then, one Saturday morning, it happened. I locked myself out while the city was still covered with snow. I never dared to lock the door from the inside after this event. The neighbor called the landlady living in a satellite town called Powell, and the landlady refused to come to Columbus herself. "My husband will kill me if I drive in this weather," she said. I asked Charlotte if they could host me for a night or two, but she insisted that I should fetch the key as soon as possible because I had to get things on track.

There I went, with no alternative option. Against the snowstorm, I drove the car without a rear bumper to Powell. On Freeway 315, I saw many vehicles paralyzed on the road shoulder. After some searching, I finally found the landlady's home. At first, I entered her neighbor's territory and got stuck in the snow again. Luckily, I remembered the skill I learned from the owner of the auto repair shop. I accelerated backward, then forward, and successfully escaped from the snowdrift and returned to the path. She and her lawyer husband lived in a mansion in this suburban area, far from everything. City people like me never understand why these rich people like to live in the suburbs, for they have to drive an hour to work. I had known the term "de-urbanization" since high school but still couldn't appreciate their taste. Do wealthy Americans all prefer silence to infrastructure? I don't want to overgeneralize that.

THE SNOWY BATTLEFIELD OF OHIO

I stopped my car in front of her door, and she saw me through the window and yelled at me, "Don't kick the dirty snow onto my yard!" This senior lady went outside and handed me the key. "So, you locked yourself outside?"

"I lost my bumper the other day because of the weather. And now I'm almost homeless after the key broke. I don't know why my life became like this." My face looked as gloomy as the weather to her.

"Okay. Be sure to return it after you get a copy. It is my only key left." According to the neighbor, this landlady owned all four condos in that row. They rented one to their son's friend so that he could monitor the behavior of other tenants.

"Okay, I will. Sorry about the dirty snow." I said.

"Don't worry about it. I'll have someone shovel the snow later." I felt some sympathy from her at that moment. Just one tiny moment. I didn't care who she was or how rich they were. The only thing I knew was that I never wanted to live in that kind of remote area, even if I could live to that age.

With a deep breath, I drove back to Upper Arlington. On the way back, I saw even more dead cars on the road shoulder of Freeway 315. It was not my first time driving out of town, but I felt I was risking my life in order to survive in a disappointing country, and it was not worth it. In hindsight, I would rather pay much higher rent to avoid the hassle. I could comfort myself by saying that I achieved something and became stronger as I got more driving experience in adversity, but inside my brain was the cold feeling of walking on a tightrope and fighting alone every day. What didn't kill me did exhaust me.

My Japanese friend Takashi reminded me that Whole Foods was near Upper Arlington, but even one slice of pizza over there seemed so expensive to me. I felt much worse living in Upper Arlington than near the Lennox center. I was pushed far from the campus area, which was the most suitable for international students. As a graduate student, I felt less independent than some undergrads. The location per se prevented me from seeing the pleasant side of that city.

I went directly to Ace Hardware, got a duplicate for the key, and purchased a larger snow scraper before throwing away the tiny one Jeremy gave me in the past (he had a big one himself). I wanted to get rid of any trace of him from my life, including some pull-up bar he had deserted before moving out of the "Shining" House. Then I grabbed a late lunch at Chipotle, the best option for single customers. After I finally got into my home, my brain was empty. I looked at the gloomy sky and laughed to myself, "What a wonderful world."

Fourth, for several weeks, I tried to make my lonely situation less depressing, so I found a temporary co-tenant to rent Kayah's bedroom through an OSU-related email newsletter. This girl was also nice and enthusiastic at first sight, in an American way. She needed a place after she broke up with her boyfriend. Yet, she often went back to his apartment to play video games with him, and gradually, they were together again. In other words, I was living alone again. I pointed out to her one day that because she had two places to sleep, she had an excuse to leave dirty dishes in the sink, just like Jeremy did. It was my objective observation, and I was never wrong about it. After she moved out for a 3-month-long international trip with her boyfriend, she never replied to my message. Again, no friendship ever existed. It is worth mentioning that she was also disappointed I wouldn't speak Mandarin to her, as she wanted to practice and eventually open a company in China.

I was happy to communicate with her and her boyfriend, two sociology majors, while they were in the condo, but something before that interaction gave away her complex nature. One day, I was hiking with her and my Malaysian friend Ali, and she told us that she had been skiing with and dating another middle-aged man in Colorado, presumably a sugar daddy. She justified that although she occasionally spent time with other men, that loyal boyfriend would always be there for her. One month later, when I had dinner with Ali, he said to me without reservation, "She's a b*tch." I understood where that label was coming from—her boyfriend deserved more than the status of a back burner. Interestingly, she once told me to show respect to Lady J, who was labeled a "b*tch" by Charlotte.

After she discontinued the lease without notice to me personally, I was back to the lonely life. And I asked God why I always had to live with this type of person? I had witnessed several guys being deceived by their female partners that year, including my buddy by a medical student who was a classmate of Jeremy and Stacy. It was already March, but the snow came back to break our hearts. People were moaning about the weather on Facebook. I suspect that year marked the start of my seasonal affective disorder, the same time I took the Abnormal Psychology course. This label simply described a correlation between time and mood but never revealed the root cause. In my opinion, a trigger was necessary.

Spring break was approaching, which was another thing I dreaded because it would expose my loneliness when everybody was gone. Remember, Jeremy got upset after one lonely weekend with no party, but I had endured this loneliness for so long. The transient hope was usually taken away from me quickly. I asked Stacy if she had any plans for the break, and she told me they were preparing for an upcoming midterm. The medical school used a different academic calendar. That week, I also got my first cortisone shot on my left wrist and then drove back home from the hospital with only one working hand. The pain disturbed my sleep at night, so the primary care physician finally referred me to the hand specialist after two months of physical therapy. If you remember, "pain" has been one of the keywords for my life.

Fifth, the week after Jeremy's reluctant response, a Chinese friend Lily invited me to go to karaoke with her and two other Asian ladies. An Asian karaoke store was opened in Columbus, but I never followed that kind of news because I listened to Asian music less and less when surrounded by white people. I drove to pick up the girls at dusk, only to find out she lived in the same apartment complex as Stacy. While waiting in my car, I saw Jeremy's blue SUV approaching. He got out and walked toward my car with a bottle of wine in his hand. After a deep breath, I rolled down my window.

"Why are you here?" He asked with an amused look. He probably thought I was invited by Stacy for dinner as well.

I told him my plans for the evening with no facial expression.

"I'm going to cook dinner with Stacy. Have fun." Then he went upstairs.

I watched his back disappear into the stairway and felt nothing but disgust. I'd rather he'd never appear again. Anyway, after that weird encounter, the next morning, his old lies gradually popped out of my traumatized mind, which led to me searching through his old text messages and finding evidence of him breaking his own words.

Finally, the brutal Oscar night. In February 2014, I learned from some family members in China that my paternal grandfather had passed away, which signified that I no longer had any grandparents alive. I grieved for a while but didn't feel very heartbroken about his death since I was no closer to him than to Mandy or Doug. He was a respected intellectual who suffered from political persecution in his youth, so his death was a big deal for some relatives. However, I didn't love him as I loved my maternal grandpa, as he had hurt my childhood by inflicting a weird first name on me. He used to teach the ancient Chinese language, so naturally, he would capitalize on this opportunity to show off his impractical knowledge. I changed my legal first name in high school, in defiance of Mandy and Doug.

Every year on the night of the Academy Awards, my old Bible study group would hold an Oscar party to honor members in that group. I attended the party in 2013, but this time, when I asked the guy who posted this event on Facebook whether I could attend, he responded, "Sorry Slim, this party is only for people who believe in God. I'm sorry to hear about your grandpa's death, by the way." I sighed and then spent the night with myself, perhaps studying for a midterm. After I graduated, one of my religious classmates explained to me that evangelical churches were not very open to the general public, unlike some Protestant churches in the area. There was no way for me to verify that, but I knew religious denominations were very complicated. Anyway, that was the night when the fire in my heart ultimately died down. During the day, I would look like a fully functional person studying and writing my thesis in loneliness except when going to a seminar; in the evening, I would be occupied with the pain in my body and psyche.

In 2020, based on my Ohioan friend's Facebook status, this evangelical church called Xenos in Columbus, Ohio, was going through some administrative problems, and therefore, its members have become scattered all over the place. But who cares? Churches are no more than religious vessels. If you believe in God, God is everywhere, and God is within you, so you don't necessarily need to go to church to feel close to God.

8.6 Maybe I Was Wrong?

Weekends and holidays were the time I felt the worst. Meeting insensitive people like Ali made me feel worse because he kept asking me about Jeremy. I kept my mouth shut.

The snow in the city had not melted away, and the temperature was still low. As I was taking an undergrad course in Abnormal Psychology, I had to resist the negative labels every week. Now that I was still experiencing dysphoria, I couldn't help but check myself against those terms in DSM while learning through each chapter—Medical Student Syndrome. Also, after the data collection for the thesis project was finished, the remaining tasks were typing out the manuscript and analyzing the data. These tasks were completed in the basement's dark office, which had poor ventilation. However, one day I was told by the department chair, Mr. Williams, not to hold the door open with the doorstop in case the computers got stolen. That was his legit concern, but this risk factor of my poor mental health still went unnoticed.

I stupidly told Stacy how awful I was feeling. Remember, she previously told me, "Have you ever thought maybe we are the wrong people? We open ourselves to other people so easily. One can only hold on to those supportive people." That must seem to make sense to some people, and I knew why she thought I was oversharing: I told Jeremy and her that I went to the E.R. and had to meet a urologist. Outside of that, I was very selective about the things I disclosed to different types of people. Who isn't?

This time the response was different. After emphasizing how cute her boyfriend was, she said, "Just give him some time. He was just overwhelmed. He's been so affectionate lately. He even bought me wines and flowers. I believe everything will turn good eventually."

I didn't know how to respond. Nor could I understand the basis of her Pollyannaish attitude. How could she generalize his affection for her, whether temporary or long-term? What does it have to do with me, the person he hurt with zero petulance? That day, I concluded that she wasn't mature enough to understand that how A treats B can be independent of how A Treats C. I wanted to warn her that a person's true nature can only be tested in adverse situations, but I was too frustrated even to communicate with her afterward. Nowadays, I am no longer surprised that many benevolent ladies would not believe in the objective existence of vices in the population. In other words, some of them are subconsciously seeing this world through rosy lenses until they are deeply hurt.

Gradually, I started to doubt myself again in solitude. I felt like those victims in the movies, always eager to know why I deserved such deception from such a villain, in this case, a future clinician. The more I tried to understand, the more I had to struggle and ruminate. At that time, I had not watched any T.V. series about the medical profession, and therefore, I was ignorant of the complexity of the "helping" professions. Neither had I known the concept of the dark triad (narcissism, Machiavellianism, and psychopathy) in social and personality psychology because I was mainly on the cognitive side, the most technical branch of psychology. The trending concept of "vulnerable narcissism"? Not at all. I thought to myself: Did I do something wrong? Did I intrude on his privacy, which made him want to alienate me? Was he uncomfortable that I could predict his behavior? Was he jealous, as his girlfriend suspected? Was he a closeted white supremacist? What did I do that was wrong to him but not to other white people? Should I let him explain himself so I don't make it difficult for this silly but goodhearted girl? Why? Because his girlfriend wanted me to like him again. To "like" him, I had to forgive him first. To forgive the person, I had to know if he had repentance about his behavior, and the only way to know for sure was to confront him face-to-face since he would dodge other ways of contact.

Unlike us, who believe every decision should be based upon evidence, one religious friend sympathized with me and wanted me to forgive him, even when doing that was irrational. He said, "Forgiveness doesn't always need to be rational." Layla, who attempted to persuade me to forgive Mandy and Doug for what they did to my childhood, told me, "Forgiveness is like a switch that you can turn on and off by your mind." In retrospect, I suspect she didn't understand this topic deeply enough, and she might be religious herself, which is not uncommon among American therapists. If she learned that simplistic view from grad school, then her grad school was wrong.

My mind was set under torment by this desire to see hope out of hopelessness, regain something I already gave up on and forgive someone I already labeled as evil in exchange for a possible "future" friendship. My soft heart was swayed day by day by the words of Stacy. Still, I wanted to protect myself from being hurt and humiliated again, and that's why I needed proof of his self-reflection and petulance. I couldn't randomly decide whether or not to like this person, as she wanted me to, as I wanted myself to, in order to compensate for the cost of my time and energy. Suffice it to say, part of me was still clinging to that notion of elitism or the dream of networking with the future upper class in this first-world country.

Months later, Rachel, my journalist friend from Shanghai, pointed out that I was so naïve and childish to expect an apology from him. Rachel had been cheated on before, and that's why she understood that cheaters would not be genuinely apologetic. In great agony, I later realized that even if he was forced to apologize, he could still lie to me to look good in front of Stacy. The same realization applies to Doug, who has apologized to me once under Mandy's pressure but has never changed his worldview denying the human rights of the minor. Many friends told me, as for those powerful people who took away everything from you, you should not expect them to feel remorse. Truly ethical people wouldn't have done those things to hurt you relentlessly in the first place. Although we hope individuals can change for the better through intensive and benign intervention, it usually will not work for villains who know how to get away with their sins and capitalize on the imperfect system. Some experts told me the best way to deal with someone who has traumatized you is to stay away from them. The fact that they could traumatize you indicates they are more powerful than you.

However, in my particular case, I was bound by that interpersonal triangle. There was no way to delete Jeremy from my life without also deleting his girl, who seemingly wanted to befriend me in the long run, unless it was my delusion. Still, as some clear-minded people pinpointed, I was naïve and childish because she would, of course, choose him over me in a critical situation. After all, I was just some temporary sounding board to her, or at best, a co-victim. They were both first-world Caucasian elites who benefited each other directly, so she would try to persuade me to sacrifice my interest. Most people in this world don't make decisions based on publicly reinforced moral values, such as justice. Instead, they choose whoever can provide them with the most tangible short-term benefit. I admit I am sometimes like that myself.

An analogous example would be my chromosome providers, who tortured me as I was growing up. All **their** friends and relatives in **their** generation would ignore **my** suffering and keep telling me that I ought to empathize with them and love them back. In those people's memories, my chromosome providers are certainly benevolent people to **them**. In their shared worldview, torture in the name of love is not real torture. What's worse, most cultures discourage people from exposing the violent side of their family dynamics to the public, so how can you see the skeleton in another family's closet? You can't see it, so it doesn't exist?

I know it would seem even crazier for me to admit my jealousy about other people's intimacy, but the lack of intimacy has been a constant in my life. It takes its toll sometimes. I'm not alone. However, I never think intimacy is necessarily better than independence if you cannot find the other half with a commensurate cognitive capacity who can accept your weaknesses and stay honest with you (and vice versa). It's a tricky and time-consuming process, even with the aid of artificial intelligence, because it's as much science as it is art.

8.7 The Second Email

In that isolated state, one evening after dinner, I finally decided to write the second email to Jeremy. I was calm when I first started. The tone of that email was wildly different from the first one. I was ready to let it be the final correspondence, so I didn't conceal any negative attitudes. In the past, I always had to tolerate him because I wanted his friendship. Nobody likes long emails, so I felt he might not read it. I had never written such a long message to criticize a person in and out in such a stereoscopic way, not even to my chromosome providers. As you see, I had bottled up too much because I used to have no channel to express my feelings but songwriting. Unfortunately, songwriting could only do so much. Besides commenting on his appearance and accent, which were out of his control, to be fair, I pointed out his behavior caused my depression and psychosomatic symptoms this time. I sounded furious but not hysterical. When I told him I didn't care about his feeling anymore, I pointed out, "I am not inferior to you!" and "I am no longer vulnerable to your toxicity!" I know people who can't empathize would think it was all in my head, which is understandable. I was no longer begging for any friendship at face value but instead fell into a tirade mode. It was my first time realizing how much I hated him after he took away my hope. That moment, even his neutral features seemed devilish to me when I recalled his appearance: in the only photo we had taken together, he was wearing a purple long-sleeve sweater, and his eyeballs creepily reflected the red light from the phone camera. He said I "kidnapped" him as his classmates did in those med student parties. The photo was taken by the landlady upon my request when we were

PLAYED AND THEN CRUSHED

discussing the house drama at Lennox Town Center near the "Shining" house.

From some T.V. shows, I know I'm not the only deeply hurt person to unleash themselves in angry emails after long-term inhibition by the superego. The Internet made human communication easier and harder at the same time, as we millennials often preferred text over voice. In reality, a therapist will advise you against actually sending that long letter full of your spiteful emotions and thoughts because they don't want you to look like vulnerable prey for the predator in this jungle of adulthood. Therapists want you to behave in a professional manner because that's what looks safe to them, considering we all have some darkness inside of us.

I was exhausted and sleepy at that time, and somehow my id took control of my body. (In Freudian theory, the id, as opposed to the ego and the superego, refers to the impulsive and unconscious part of one's psyche, so I borrowed this concept here.) Once the beast was unbridled, the dark side of me took over. In retrospect, I would attribute my darkness at that time to how I was treated as a child: coercion through violence and humiliation. Based on psychological theories, I must have modeled that from my chromosome providers, who were the first to beat or threaten me with culturally granted rights in a society with no legislative effort to stop such tyranny. Those school teachers in urban areas would typically use verbal abuse, confinement, or extra homework as punishment and refrain from using violence on students for fear of liability. I didn't grow up in a war zone, so no Nazi or terrorist could torture me physically, although I often compared the way I was maltreated to the way Jews were persecuted by Nazis.

In the final paragraph of this long email, I used demanding language, in capital letters learned from Mr. Hoffman and Mr. McCarthy, telling him he must respond to me before the midterm and must pick a place to meet me before the finals or he will regret it. This final paragraph, which I referred to as the "ultimatum," was what scared him into self-defense according to him. The "authoritarian" tone was exacerbated by the overuse of capital letters. I never thought it would hurt him. I didn't know that saying the movie lines would get one in trouble in real life. The stupidest thing I did was put everything in an email, a "permanent record," because it was the easiest way of communication in a snowstorm, for me at least.

I offered written evidence to the other party, Jeremy, so I had no way to defend myself adequately. Before I moved to the United States, I was warned by online posts that we should ask for everything to be written down because some Americans, such as rental agents, are so good at denying what they have said. In the case of Jeremy, his character almost determined that he never intended to honor his own words, not to me, at least. He felt righteous as long as he could find a sound excuse to justify his behavior, and someone like Stacy would blindly support his "thoughtful" justification, thus reinforcing his lying habits. Someone later told me, "That's what a girlfriend is for." Does this remind you of the fanatic fans of some celebrities? Ladies in real life or on T.V. screens (e.g., John Smith's wife Helen, in *The Man in the High Castle*) are expected to trust their partner under any circumstance, and I am not sure about the rationale behind it. What I believe instead: a person who does not respect their own ego does not deserve love from another rational person.

Several days later, early Monday morning, the weather was still freezing. I was on the crowded school bus heading to the Main Campus when I realized he hadn't read that email. So I texted him, "Congratulations. You seem prepared." I felt no emotion when I texted because the neurochemicals in my brain had supposedly been drained out over time.

"Prepared for what?" He responded within 30 seconds.

"You ignored the deadline stated in my email, so you will regret it." I simply repeated the words in my email.

"Sounds like a threat."

"When you lose the most important thing in your life, you will know whether or not." I didn't know what I was referring to. All I wanted was to prompt him to read my email. What was the most important thing in his life? I had no idea. His white coat, I assume. Moreover, I didn't realize "you will regret it" could be construed as a threat of violence, which was universally illegal unless one belonged to law enforcement. If you translate "you will regret it" into Chinese, it conveys nothing concrete, and few people will take it seriously. I know this could offer some Americans an opportunity to glorify Western civilization. In the context of the American justice system, it was no doubt in my ignorance. I had no American family to teach me the rights and wrongs anyway, only American professors who taught me how to use capital letters in an email.

"What? Are you going to take my life?" When I saw his words, my first reaction was that he was so ridiculous, narcissistic, and illogical.

"Of course not," I said, "If I take your life, I'll have to take suicide. It won't give me any sense of achievement." Those were my exact words in 2014, with English being my second language and the word "suicide" never formally learned. I was simply speaking out of my logic and notion that a murderer should actively end their own life unless they are okay with jail time. However, a frail Asian man like me would no doubt fall prey to the rapists in prison, and to me, it sounds even worse than suicide— I was not merely paranoid. American jails are notorious for the prevalence of sexual assaults; if you have any doubt, ask Shawshank. The number of individuals who commit suicide after being raped each year is not negligible but underreported. How about expatriation or, say, repatriation? Expatriation is as traumatizing for hard-working international fellows from the third world: you lose everything you have worked for.

What I didn't realize was that the word "suicide," even in a negative sentence, pinched into the nerves of these mainstream Americans. Someone later explained to me that this particular word means a lot to a deeply religious culture. I, personally, hate the word "commit" being used before the word "suicide." In reality, self-execution is often a painful decision for the individual, and it takes a lot of courage. It is not necessarily a result of instant rage or long-term depression, as the media like to portray. It can be neutral, adaptive, and even ethical when life is not worth continuing due to the foreseeable deadlock of the future, as manifested in, for instance, the loss of one's dignity. Dignity shouldn't be taken for granted— once lost, it's hard to regain.

The irony is that every week, some people in Japan jump onto subway tracks to end their inner conflicts, and the public has grown numb to it. Every few months, some anti-social campus shooter in America takes the lives of innocent students, and people across the world send hollow thoughts and prayers on social media (Anthony Jeselnik, *Thoughts and Prayers*). However, only people close to the victims truly feel the pain, which reflects some irksome truth nobody wants to admit: the unaffected public has developed tolerance to the news over time, partially because they feel powerless, partially because new attacks arrive before old ones are fully processed. And for suicide, one's suffering cannot get serious attention until this startling word is put on the table. How pathetic is that? How hypocritical is that?

My former Saudi Arabian American colleague working in mental health care once said she appreciated my honesty and directness for saying inappropriate things most white people wouldn't say. My explanation is as follows:

Firstly, as a foreigner growing up outside a multicultural environment such as the US, I had no prior knowledge of what was proper or improper to say to people. Secondly, I simply refuse to sacrifice my own free speech to appeal to other people's emotions. Thirdly, I learned to understand some Americans based on what other Americans taught me. Sometimes the information was either inaccurate or laden with ethnic stereotypes. For example, an Indian American housemate once taught me a quick hack to tell if a person is Jewish: their nose. Not always correct, and it is not offensive to everybody, either.

Anyway, I got no response from Jeremy afterward. I thought he didn't care and that my previous understanding of him was correct: I was nothing to him but a tool. So for the entire day, I drowned myself in work, in the dark basement, with no notifications allowed on my smartphone. In consequence, I didn't see the text message from Stacy sent around noon, "Jeremy said he got some serious messages from you. What's going on?" There was no phone call from either of them.

I responded around 2 PM, immediately after seeing the message, "I want him to confront me directly. See? He is still using you to talk with me, just like he was using me to talk with Jessica. I don't know what I will do, but I will not hurt him." I was angry but didn't want her to get involved. But, of course, she did eventually. I didn't realize that it would become our final correspondence before the nightmare landed on me. I was still planning to return to my office that evening to finish a take-home midterm exam, which was due the following afternoon.

8.8 Confronting the Police

Around 5 PM, I was still in the dark room, drafting my thesis, when I received a phone call from an unknown number. It turned out to be some school police officer asking me to meet with them at the police station in the evening. "Mr. Jeremiah wanted us to talk with you on his behalf." I knew something was wrong, but he assured me, "No, you won't be put in jail." So I went there after grabbing some dinner, and awaiting me was some security check. Before that, Chris texted me and invited me to go to karaoke with him and his friends, but I told him I was wanted by the police.

Around 7 PM, in their office, I was seated on the bench, faced by a middle-aged white police officer. After they asked me how to pronounce my legal name, the officer asked me cogently, "Mr. Sun, what exactly are you planning to do to Mr. Jeremiah?"

"I just want to talk with him. Wait, I thought this was a personal matter." I was still confused about why the police were involved.

"But he doesn't think so. He thought he was in danger. Kid, don't you know you're in big trouble? Mr. Jeremiah and his girlfriend, they are good people. They just didn't know how to help you anymore, so they called the city police this morning before this case was forwarded to us school police."

What? Good people? Just based on their looks and their titles? I was dumbfounded. Not by any chance would I predict he would do this to me. It was the first time I'd ever talked with any cops in a police station, except for Lost and Found, ID card, or passport issues.

"The sheriff will be here in a minute. He would like to speak to you." Luckily, I had learned the word "sheriff" before, not from the textbook, though. The sheriff with a mustache came in, dressed in his heavy uniform, and started to read to me in a formidable voice, "Mr. Sun, I'm ordered to deliver this Protection Order filed by Mr. Jeremiah to you. You must abide by the terms and appear in court on the designated date. You will face serious consequences if you fail to do so." Then the sheriff left. From that day on, I hardly had any good impression of that profession for several years, despite my knowledge of their job. I couldn't help it.

He left a pack of paperwork on the table, and on the first page, the title said, "The State of Ohio Protection Order for Civil Stalking and Sexual Assault." In case you didn't know, the term "Protection Order" is only used in some states of America; "Restraining Order" is more commonly used, especially on the coasts. I will use these two terms interchangeably hereafter for the readers' convenience.

Unfortunately, at that age, I was unaware of such things. None of the few American TV shows I had ever watched by then taught me that concept. Unlike many Chinese students who had watched many American and British shows before entering America, my knowledge of the US justice system was close to zero. Documentaries, Sci-fi, and medicine-themed TV shows certainly would be less likely to mention such a term. Ironically, those students who spent considerable time watching super lengthy and addictive TV shows would probably not have enough GPA to enter America on American-sourced scholarships. It is worth noting that such kind of legal weapon did not exist in the developing country where I grew up. Like most civilians in every country, I was unfamiliar with the justice system, being a STEM major in college. By the way, I got a C in the only elective law course I took in college — Intro Antitrust Law.

What struck me most on that piece of paper were the words "stalking" and "sexual assault." I had no idea how I was associated with these words. In retrospect, no surprise to me. It was the quick solution of least resistance for a neurotic person like Jeremy, who enjoyed watching *Breaking Bad* all the time while pretending he was studying at "the girl's" place. He was using the police as his shield and weapon. Those shameful and insulting words were like a mental cross on my back, against which I was crucified in the following months. After talking with a school official and after watching many American TV shows, I realized that some Americans could be stalkers and that some can be violent, even as domestic partners. In some cases, civil stalkers won't let go of their ex-partners who unilaterally choose to end a relationship with or without a convincing explanation. However, Jeremy was not my ex. He was only my housemate, not even a true friend by our definition. In his heart, he didn't even consider me a friend. The juxtaposed term "sexual assault" looked even more stigmatizing, considering I wasn't attracted to this guy at all. I was well aware that any record of violence would jeopardize my stay in America. How could any of these make sense to me at that time? Years later, I finally understood that's the dark side of American society.

I was crying hysterically for the next hour, nonstop, apologizing to each of them as if they were present as the police officer explained what this legal form entailed. He exaggerated it by telling me I could no longer see them again in my life. Not even Stacy, although her name was not listed on the paper. Only days later, when I met a school attorney, did I realize this restraining order "ex parte" was temporary, which meant the police officer was trying to scare me to the extremity — the common practice among the task force, according to many TV shows. That partially explains why a lot of young people hold negative attitudes toward the police in general, even if both sides are innocent in general. By the way, the Latin term *ex parte* indicates that the issuance of the restraining order only requires evidence provided by one party in an attempt to protect the allegedly threatened individual. I wish I never had to learn this.

As I read what he wrote on the application form, with his childish handwriting, I felt even more visceral pain. He wrote, "Mr. Sun, my former roommate/acquaintance/friend was texting me and emailing me obsessively after we both moved out of the shared house. I am not familiar with his rambling nature. I do not know if he carries any weapon. I'm not close with him. His messages made me worry about my safety." He followed by quoting the final paragraph from my email, including "I am not vulnerable to your toxicity anymore," which certainly convinced the judge that I was delusional, or at least in a pathological state. Who in that Midwestern justice system wouldn't sympathize with a celeb-looking, hard-working Caucasian American medical student preparing for one quiz after another, accompanied by his Caucasian American medical student girlfriend? As opposed to an Asian international student whose name they couldn't even pronounce, who wrote a crazy long email full of non-native grammar and lexicon? God knows Grammarly wasn't available to me back then.

The officer explained the 500-foot restriction to me and watched me unfriend Jeremy and Stacy on social media. He asked me, "Did you write in the email that you are a psychology major? Oh, God. I was just wondering, how could a psych major act like this?" He must have read the email in which I pointed out to Jeremy that I had wanted to become a psychologist since I was a kid but could never have direct access to it in my life. Not many people in my life knew this fact; most people don't get their dreams realized anyway. I told him I wasn't a psych major but rather a Communication Disorders major because I didn't have the energy to explain how these departments were interrelated to this old man. Many outsiders in my life had mocked me for having a problematic psyche when they heard me talking about my intention to get into a psychology program. I am fairly used to that.

While I was self-loathing, He went outside to print some documents for me, which contained a list of resources or offices I should visit in the next days to minimize my loss. I overheard him talking with his colleague in the hallway, "This guy has an obsessive personality, for writing such a long email and not letting go." I wish I dared to open the door and refute that heart-wrenching comment, but of course, I wasn't that reckless. Instead, I was still sobbing to myself until I felt more visceral pain. My whole mind was f*cked. And so was my future, I thought to myself. One hour had passed.

When he returned with a pamphlet, I knew it couldn't be the first time they showed this to a traumatized international student. The first item was the phone number of the ER of OSU Medical Center, and the second was the Student Counseling Center on Main Campus. The following items included the Office of International Affairs (OIA) and Student Legal Services. They warned me Student Conduct would contact me within a week, and my department would be notified soon. Because I was a teaching assistant that year, I could also expect my position to be jeopardized. It didn't eventually happen because my original TA duty, which involved teaching lab sessions to many students directly, had already been canceled, as mentioned previously.

D*mned. I was perplexed and overwhelmed.

"Listen kid, you just made one mistake today, but it's not the end of the world. Tell me, do you need help? We all need help sometimes. I get help myself after some big cases. Just tell me, do you need help?"

I nodded.

He offered to send me to the ER for psychotherapy, but I said, "Oh no, absolutely not. I went to the ER last semester, and I can't afford the medical bill." He paused, looking anxious because he feared I might kill myself that night under a surge of pressure, even after I explained I was not suicidal at that moment. In retrospect, it was his duty to ensure I could survive that night. Otherwise, why did he need help sometimes because of his job? Likewise, mental health care clinicians would ask this question again and again, sometimes with redundancy, because it was better to err on the side of caution when it came to their client's life or death.

"You know the Student Counseling Center on the Main Campus. I can make an urgent appointment for you. You just need to show up. Someone will call you very early tomorrow morning."

"Okay, I'll go. "I then thought to myself that I should have made an appointment back in January rather than let the police do it for me.

I put all the paperwork into my backpack and was ready to leave. It was about 9:30 PM. The officer asked me if I wanted him to escort me back home, and I said in a tired voice, "No. I need to go to my office now. I have a midterm exam to finish tonight. It's due tomorrow afternoon." I was procrastinating for that take-home exam paper, like many grad students who had multiple types of duties at the same time.

When I went back into my car, the first person I called was Chris. He was still in the karaoke, but he quickly understood what was going on as he knew how I was played by Jeremy in the past. He tried to comfort me and told me to have a good night's sleep. Over the next few days, my buddies, like Antonio, Joe, and Kevin, received my bad news. Antonio said, "He sounds like a professional liar to me." Alex was very indignant and said, "I've only met this guy twice, and I already know he is a d*ck." Of course, Alex could be biased because he had my back. In contrast, Charlotte said to me directly, "Slim, You're already 24. You know you can't threaten people." She was right about it, from an American point of view, except that foreigners' definition of a threat is not quite the same as the American version. Meanwhile, I found it very hard to mention this to my religious friends like Carl and Julian, especially since Carl's wedding was approaching. I shared this with some lab mates and classmates in the seminar. Luckily, I didn't receive more judgment from any Caucasian or non-Caucasian classmates. Everybody seemed shocked and confused, but more importantly, no individual among these future scientists and clinicians had any experience with the justice system. People seemed to know very well that this system was very complicated, just like the healthcare system. Later in the summer, when I mentioned to my Vietnamese immigrant friend that I had some trouble with an American roommate, she immediately reacted, "Oh no, don't mess with those Americans! I've had some issues with a local too, and their tactics were pretty harsh."

The first thing I did back in my office that night was to write an email to the three professors/supervisors, telling them how sorry I was to bring personal trouble to the department and that I was perplexed about how things could develop to this level. At that time, my anxiety was overridden by post-traumatic depression, so I didn't even think about anything but the court. Mr. Osman, who was a first-generation immigrant, replied to the email early the next morning, telling me to stay strong during that crisis and show remorse. After discussing with Mr. Williams, Mr. Hoffman, my official academic advisor that school year, found me in the basement two days later and asked me about the situation. He told me the department would not take any action before Student Conduct because they all wanted me to finish my research project and get my degree eventually. That was the first and only time I revealed my loneliness to a faculty member. Loneliness is a serial killer for international grad and undergrad students, especially those working in a small-sized and remotely located department.

When I finally finished the exam paper and drove back to that home of loneliness, it was 2 AM. My head felt awful. I took a shower the next morning before receiving a phone call from the Student Counseling Center. They told me to arrive by 9 AM for the earliest time slot.

For the rest of the semester, I lost my balanced lifestyle and lost 5 pounds off my already slim body.

8.9 Emergency Psychotherapy

Tuesday at 8:45 AM, I arrived at the Student Counseling Center on the Main Campus and was asked to fill up some questionnaires on an iPad. Then at 9 AM, I met my first individual therapist, Teresa, who led me into her therapy room. It turned out she was on her way to getting licensed. I imagine she was carefully reading my faxed police files before 9 AM that morning, possibly discussing with her supervisor how to handle the first session.

After we sat down, she asked me how I was feeling. I burst into tears in no time and answered all her questions in my sobbing mode for that hour. I was a crier as a child because I was often coerced to do things I hated. I thought the depressive experience over the winter had drained my neurochemicals already, but I was wrong; all the sadness related to Jeremy rushed to my mind until I felt that visceral pain again.

"In one of the questionnaires, there was a question about child abuse, and you answered yes. Can you tell me more?" She asked seriously.

"My parents physically abused me. They beat me when I was young." I answered without hesitation.

Teresa told me some American parents beat their kids as well without being caught. What I didn't mention was once I entered adolescence, I started to fight back against Mandy and Doug, as many Chinese adolescents would do. The more they tried to beat me up so as to consolidate their authority, the more hatred I had accrued toward the family, the hometown, and the collectivist culture in general. Months later, on Skype, I told Mandy and Doug about what I had revealed to Teresa. Their immediate response was, "You can't speak ill of us in front of those Americans!"

When Teresa asked me about the emails I wrote to Jeremy, I gave her the same answers that I gave to the police: I didn't plan to do anything to him; I just wanted to know if he had any reflection on his previous behavior. Of course, after seeing his comment on the restraining order, I got my answer instantly: he didn't think that lying to me was wrong; he didn't think that lying to the judge was wrong, either, as long as he could maximize his own interest.

"I thought he was a good person, so I let him hurt me again and again," I said. "He told me he was pursuing his childhood dream to help the people with no easy access to healthcare. Was that all just a lie?" Back in 2014, I didn't know the term "virtue signaling" yet.

"It's possible what he said was sincere," she said. "That doesn't necessarily contradict with his personality and his behavior... Human beings are very complicated."

Due to her busy schedule, we arranged to meet each other every other week. The second appointment was days after the court meeting, which was scheduled one day after the spring break, on a Monday. In retrospect, that frequency was far from enough for crisis intervention for a traumatized person.

Then I walked to the Student Legal Services on High Street to make an urgent in-person appointment, and I was scheduled to meet with Mr. Parker on Thursday afternoon. As usual, I went to the two-hour seminar on Tuesday afternoon to hand in the exam paper. I appeared enthusiastic in the discussion, as if nothing had happened. I felt particularly safe in that seminar inside the Psychology

Building because most attendees were from psychology or healthcare programs. However, when we did our group project later in the semester, I told my difficult situation to these teammates. One afternoon, I brought two American classmates to my office in the basement for some data analysis, and they commented, "This room does seem creepy. I can't imagine myself working here. One can easily get depressed down here." Well, it was definitely a factor.

8.10 I Cannot Represent You, but Here Are Your Options…

Thursday afternoon, I arrived early at Student Legal Services. Sitting in the same lobby, I was ruminating about the three donuts while holding back my tears. Only this time, I came here alone, and the opponent was my former "comrade," who ate my third donut last time.

Mr. Parker finally called me in. It wasn't my first meeting with this white attorney. I remember that the first time he saw me, in the fall of 2012, he was amused by the fact that I, an Asian, went by an English first name in America instead of by my legal name, which he couldn't pronounce. Throughout my life in Ohio, he was the first and only person with that strong reaction. He never felt comfortable addressing me as Slim in emails. I guess he had never been to California, where many Asian faces were paired with a Caucasian-styled first name. If you remember, Jeremy from rural Pennsylvania even laughed at my hot cereal. Some people from the Midwest are sadly provincial— it was how I understood it at that time, and many other international students concurred. Mr. Parker didn't understand that for a foreigner, if the locals can't remember your complicated foreign name, they will hardly think of you for any opportunity. Once they alienate you verbally, they will also alienate you behaviorally.

As soon as he asked me what I needed the most at that moment, I answered in a sobbing mode like Ben Platt singing *Words Fail* toward the end of *Dear Evan Hansen*. "I feel so lonely." It had nothing to do with being away from my country of origin or not having people around but a result of having no cohort to belong with outside specific courses. For example, I had to figure out a lot of homework by myself, while many Chinese grad students in engineering programs or medical students, such as Jeremy, had their study groups. It made a huge difference. International students from the same country scattered in different programs across the humongous campus often have very little overlap in life. This tragic situation wasn't improved after I moved to Davis, California, as long as I was still working with Mr. Osman, who didn't like people or big cities himself.

To show his empathy, Mr. Parker shared his own poignant story, in which he was abandoned by an ex-girlfriend in college when he was hospitalized for a severe injury. Then he suggested I follow his example and read many books during that vacuum period because "you need to be adaptive." Unfortunately, at that time, the books I read were very academic; for example, one was called *The Human Amygdala*. I forced myself to read seemingly relevant things I didn't wholeheartedly enjoy in order to get into those research labs on the east coast. However, I started to watch some TV shows that month since television was available to me for the first time in years. In particular, one night, I ran into the very final episode of the final season of the show *How I Met Your Mother*. That was the first and only episode I ever watched on TV myself; a year before that, Carl and his friends introduced me to this show in his home church. Interestingly, when I visited San Francisco in 2015, some hostel roommates from Germany told me Ted in that show was from Ohio. That day I realized that American showbiz is influential worldwide, just like soft drinks.

He explained I had three options, all of which I still remember nowadays:

My first option was to leave America permanently. To my knowledge, it is not uncommon for an international student to be kicked out of America, and their near future can also be doomed in their country of origin. However, handling legal cases can be more nuanced than black and white. I didn't know it until recently, and I am still no expert on that. As I suspect, the higher integrity a person has, the more likely that person will become depressed and suicidal if not have a mental breakdown. Good people suffer greater losses in an injustice society.

My second option was to accept a five-year restraining order without appearing in court. If you Google it, you will know how inconvenient your daily life will be with that shackle on you. The psychological burden only applies to civilians with high moral standards, not those villains you see on TV shows. For a moral human being like me, who would not lose a single point on my driver's license in either Ohio or California, it would feel like a big cross galvanized on my back. I was receiving training to become a scientist in America, not an expert in dealing with every possible interpersonal disaster.

My third option, the one Mr. Parker recommended, as if I had any choice, was to go to court to face the other party. He told me per the routine procedure, there would be a pre-conference between the judge and each party before the court hearing, geared toward optimal reconciliation, so I would no longer need to interact with the other party. I should just pick the best offer available myself. Usually, as he predicted, it would be a 6-month cooling-off period before the case could be dismissed, contingent on my good behavior of staying out of the other party's life.

Unfortunately, he could not represent me in court because the other party was also a student at Ohio State. Then he gave me a piece of paper on which he circled a couple of names registered with the local Bar Association in case I couldn't handle it myself. Before I googled what the Bar Association meant in English, I subconsciously associated it with the phrase "behind bars," which sounded extra gruesome. What a relief when I found out it was talking about the elites, not the incarcerated.

At that moment, even when I was depressed, I could feel something else in my stomach: I was abandoned again, even by the Student Legal Service, due to the so-called conflict of interest. I know they had no solution but to look over from afar.

In retrospect, I should have consulted another lawyer before going to court, but I was already overwhelmed then. Like my peers in science and engineering, I had no idea what the American justice system was like, let alone finding an inexpensive lawyer to represent me. I knew an international student showed up in court because of a speeding ticket, but then the judge told them to go back to the Student Legal Services in their university instead of accepting the charge without any defense. Even today, I feel sick when I have to look at those legal terms— a similar feeling to when I was forced to memorize organic chemistry in college.

Without knowing what to expect, I couldn't even practice communication with the judge. I suppose my brain didn't function normally and exhibited difficulty retaining new information in the next few weeks on a subclinical level.

Normally, I would feel paranoid and strive to err on the side of caution, but during those months, I lost my advanced executive functions and was possessed by these traumatic feelings. I walked like a zombie on campus and chose not to think about the future if free will ever existed. What then emerged into my mind was those stories I had read: some Ph.D. girl from China became a lunatic after being kicked back to China; or, like in the movie *Dark Matter* starring Meryl Streep, the Chinese Ph.D. in astrophysics became a mass shooter after being bullied by his egomaniac professor to the extreme. Moreover, minority immigrants developed schizophrenia after years of being alienated in the US. I was afraid that mainstream American students would think of us foreigners as dangerous people. Was it the reason behind the punishment I got? Things I couldn't understand when I was an undergrad became so understandable when I was in grad school in a different country. Yet people back in China would never understand the unique pain each poor international student was going through; instead, they couldn't help but psychoanalyze us based on speculative articles published in Chinese media, without realizing the situation varies for each person. Their interpretation tended to be inaccurate most of the time, as they still projected their traditional vain values on us, such as academic scores and "honors."

Toward the end of the consultation, our conversation drifted away from the legal side of this incident.

"Last time he and I came here together to fight against Lady J. Now I'm here alone to fight against him." I said.

"Yes, I saw that on your record. My colleague was in charge of that case." He said.

"Last time we were here, I bought three donuts and saved my favorite pumpkin flavor for the last. Then he ate it. He ate my favorite flavor." I said.

"Yes, you mentioned that in the second email. But why didn't you eat your favorite flavor first?" He asked.

His question caught me off guard. "I don't know. I never thought about that." I answered.

He made a good point. Why did I have to save the best for the future instead of consuming it when I still could? Was it indicating my dogma of delayed gratification, which could be as unhelpful as the Asian dogma of humility in a fast-paced American world? Was it because I knew I would have no appetite for other flavors after eating my favorite flavor? Was it a sign that I had no gut to pursue what I truly loved? That question revealed something about me, something very maladaptive.

After that day, my behavior pattern changed. I learned to prioritize my favorite flavor instead of letting the infinitely delayed gratification take away my opportunity for happiness. Of course, it was easier said than done in real life, but I did make some effort. For example, after leaving Ohio for California, I created some good memories of traveling to the major cities in America. This change also manifested in the sense that I prioritized doing what matters most to me right now while keeping other temptations on the shelf. Life in the biological sense is short and volatile, so I have to focus. An increase in lifespan and life experiences will not necessarily add to the total joy of my life anymore if I simply live for the promised "future." It's not how I want to spend the rest of my life.

"Are you hungry? Give me a second. I'll be right back.
"He then brought me a box of four mini cupcakes and a cup

of water.

"I saved these from lunch." he said, "Now you can have them."

"Thanks," I said.

"You can stay in this room for a while, but I need to meet my next client now." He said, "By the way, let me know the outcome of the court hearing. I'm curious."

I nodded, and he left. I ate all the cupcakes, with my tears dripping like a mountain spring.

When I discussed this part of my history with Layla, she tried to convince me that if she had said the same thing I said, she would have faced the same consequence. She, a US citizen with Arabic heritage, didn't want me to associate the court ruling with my race or country of origin. I wasn't fully convinced, of course. Firstly, because my American classmate had told me that not all Americans would resort to the legal weapon so quickly in a conflict. Perhaps, Jeremy had some prior knowledge from college or even earlier life, and of course, his personality was crucial to his decision. Secondly, a highly-educated American wouldn't do such a thing from the beginning. After all, my ignorance of American law directly resulted from this variable about me: my country of origin— 23 years of living in a completely different country. Thirdly, an elite American student, white especially, is less likely to feel isolated like me in the Midwest. Now, what about bias? A good textbook on Social Psychology has a whole chapter talking about the political injustice inside the **justice** system, the jury system in particular. Human beings are biased, although the bias might not overturn the outcome in most cases. I could only imagine if I had been a black foreigner, I would have faced an even harder time. My country of origin was a tricky one for everybody involved. They normally would not want to trigger an already depressed international student to jump off the cliff, which would draw too much attention for a county court. At the same time, they might still be able to cover things up, as the government has the power to control the narrative. I was such an insignificant civilian, anyway.

Here's how a female relative in China blamed me afterward: Why didn't you tell us earlier so we could find a lawyer for you? As I understand it, it was another manifestation of their 20/20 vision. They had no connection at all with people in the US. I was alone on this adventure because that was what I chose, or more accurately because I had no better choice. Even when the whole thing was over and I was back in China, they didn't want their close friends and relatives to know about my traumatic and stigmatized experience, so how could I expect them to be reliable and supportive back then? I could only expect them to tell me to "come back to the motherland" and then further blame me for "messing with the Americans" because all they could see about Americans on Chinese media was negative, chaotic, and pathetic. In recent years, even worse, thanks to the Trump administration.

8.11 Student Conduct and Student Advocacy

Before the end of that week, I received an email from Mr. Frost, a Ph.D. in Education, from the Office of Student Conduct, asking me to meet with him on Main Campus. He wanted to investigate the case and listen to my side of the story. He was well-trained and sounded like an active listener, almost giving me the impression that he was on my side. As I remember, the interviewer for my Worker's Comp. claim, purportedly from a third-party company, was also in that style. As an interviewer, if you can develop some rapport with the interviewee, you will have a higher chance of obtaining more authentic information from them. As someone with experience in counseling, I understood the technique myself.

Based on the two emails, he asked many questions, including whether I was in a romantic relationship with Jeremy and why I would even write a song with his first name as the title if I weren't in love with him. People don't understand that it was precisely this type of suspicion and misunderstanding that prevented male victims from seeking help in the first place. Academically speaking, everybody's sexual orientation is on a spectrum and can be fluid throughout their lifespan. Still, I couldn't just fake some nonexistent romantic desire in order to appeal to the curious audience. No offense, but imagine if Jeremy was not a med student but a grad student in Theology, Mythology, or East Asian Literature, I certainly wouldn't be interested in networking with this person.

I told Mr. Frost all the negative comments my American friends had made about Jeremy until he got a better idea of both parties. Particularly, I pointed out that a lot of compliments I made to Jeremy in daily life were actually loaded with sarcasm; however, a narcissist wouldn't detect that. I understand that international students' perspectives seemed enigmatic to people like Mr. Frost, although he was more knowledgeable than average. He was right about one thing in particular, which very few of the people involved in my case saw through: this was a "unidirectional friendship." According to him, his acumen came from his rich experience in dealing with conflicts between students.

I was too optimistic about what Mr. Frost would do to me simply because he let me speak my mind. Remember, I was still a naïve student at that time. On the same day, I also met the lady in Student Advocacy. She worked in one of the twin towers next to the Medical Center. The lady gave me some advice and told me to focus on the court first. During my second meeting with her, instead of comforting me, she explained what I really did wrong in this process. Regardless of my intent, they only cared about the end result. She made me realize my behavior was indeed posing a menace to someone else's **free will**, despite a lack of intention to exert harm. Free will was something I didn't have access to as I grew up, but I had no right to take it away from other people, no matter how badly they treated me. It's the law. I cannot overstep into law enforcement. Not a vigilante here. Those so-called vigilantes are presumably acting out of their self-interest anyway.

As far as I remember, my free will was rarely acknowledged, let alone respected, in Smoke City. As a kid, I was coerced to take extra-curricular lessons by Mandy. I remember being dragged by her from one end of a street to the other and crying, "I don't wanna learn the keyboard! You already forced me to learn painting last year!" Then she yelled at me, "No way! You must learn it!" When she was working in a different city during my elementary school years, Doug would force me to eat the food I hated (and still hate today). He would beat me if I refused to comply, yelling, "You need nutrition! I won't spoil you as those Americans do to their kids!" So I would wipe out my tears every morning and ride my bike to school — to take on the role of one of the top students in that non-accelerated class. At that age, I was already picking up the concept of "suicide" from the newspapers and the idea of "human rights" from domestic television. Reading psychology books, I was also aware of the toxic impact of irrational parenting on a person's lifespan development. So how could I be optimistic about life in general?

During the summer break after the 7th grade, Mandy forced me to learn "go," a.k.a. "Wei-qi," an ancient Chinese board game, from an extended family member because that game was believed to increase one's IQ. "Wei-qi" is a board game in which one party uses their tokens to strategically besiege the other party's tokens. I quit learning after two weeks because I wanted to watch Pokémon in the summer and had zero interest in that black-and-white game. I knew she must have listened to some of her female coworkers and just wanted me to achieve higher test scores for her sake.

Moreover, from 1st grade through 12th grade, I was constantly required by the public school teachers to provide free labor for them. This includes designing the bulletin, collecting fees from students, distributing magazines that students have subscribed to, monitoring the behavior of fellow students as a snitch instead of a manager, ensuring that students turn in their homework assignments every morning and many more. These teachers would take it for granted that I was obliged to sacrifice my precious time for those who were NOT my friends. If I ever underperform these non-rewarding tasks, they would call me derelict or selfish. Occasionally, they would impose some virtual honor on me in exchange for free labor, without my permission, similar to numerous cryptocurrency companies giving away free coins in exchange for people's attention. The key question is: where is the intrinsic value in the "honor" that earned me nothing but subsequent requests of sacrifice?

When I asked Student Advocacy why Jeremy would not befriend me no matter what, she used an ambiguous example to convey the idea of xenophobia without mentioning that word. Simply speaking, I was alienated because I was different from white people. When asked why Jeremy would cheat me again and again, she gave me an answer that worked more effectively than any psychotherapy session: "Welcome to adulthood." That answer crucified me and then set my mind to peace. It stopped struggling. It was dead. Whereas everybody told me to take a lesson from the tragedy, the "lesson" meant different things to different people. However, the most important lesson for me was to realize that I shouldn't trust people based on their words. That universally benevolent part of me was executed at that moment, which might sound sad to some people. Such is the pain of growing up. I was past the point of no return.

When I walked out of the building of Student Conduct, their "Have a nice day" or "Enjoy the weather" sounded so pale to me. I didn't know how. That being said, I admire people who can work in this kind of place day by day and choose to believe in the value of their work.

By the way, the word "education" may sound noble to many people, but never to me, thanks to my personal experiences.

8.12 The Spring Break after the Heartbreak

During spring break, I went on a road trip to Pittsburgh with several Chinese international students I met online. We separated into two cars, and my shabby Nissan was one of the two. It was my first time visiting that city, and the driving experience inside the city was horrifying in general. It snowed at night in Pittsburgh, and my GPS directed me to some neighborhoods where I had to drive uphill and downhill. Anyway, the fun road trip turned into a scary adventure for me, while other people enjoyed themselves by telling horror stories when dining in a restaurant. We had some exciting times together, but somehow I felt I didn't belong with this group of good people, not because they only spoke Chinese to each other, but because they seemed too worry-free and too wealthy for me to hang out with.

On our way back, the girls in the group all jumped into the other car, a fancy car driven by a seasoned young driver, leaving me with another guy who didn't have a driver's license. I felt abandoned again. Besides, the Google map navigation on his phone spoke a combination of English and Mandarin, which freaked me out while I was driving. I was amazed at how I managed to drive back to Columbus from Pittsburgh by myself with just one cup of Starbucks.

When I mentioned this trip to my therapist Teresa later, I told her this getaway trip did not make me feel better. I wanted to relax and distract myself from the pain, but it worsened my panic instead. I had to pretend to be a normal person in front of a group of happy strangers and challenge myself to drive in a city with more complicated terrains and traffic signs in snowy weather. It was mid-March already.

Generally speaking, I had a very blurry long-term memory of that trip. Only in 2017, when I was attending my second Objectivist Summer Conference, did I truly enjoy the city with my fellow Objectivists in an American way. However, when I walked to the riverside and approached the bridges, I was still baffled by the forks on the roads. I knew I wouldn't be able to navigate like a local if I had to drive alone in Pittsburgh without a local guide. My brain wouldn't have enough capacity to respond to road signs while driving. It takes time to learn a city, but I was never given sufficient time.

Chapter 9
Meeting in The Courthouse

...
I lay down on the couch and closed my eyes
Trying to enter the deepest layer of my episodic memory
To retrieve and replay that scene
When I opened my eyes again
My face was covered with tears
...

9.1 The Long Wait

That Monday morning, my buddy Antonio, a grad student in cognitive psychology, picked me up from my department and drove me to the address printed on the court order, "200 S. Street". We put this address into the GPS, and it directed us to some weird alley. After 20 minutes, I suspected the address was wrong, so I Googled the courthouse address on my smartphone. The correct address should be "200 S. High Street". Then we drove off again to the Court of Common Pleas.

When we finally arrived at the courthouse, Jeremy and Stacy were sitting on the bench, studying for their quiz and discussing problems. To keep a distance from them, we chose to sit on the floor and took out our own course materials to study. Besides the two Caucasian med students and the two minority grad students (one Asian and one half-Latino), who were studying their asses off, all the others we saw outside the courtroom were African Americans. This courtroom was dedicated to restraining orders, at least on that specific day. During those hours, I tried to avoid eye contact with the other party, and vice versa. They already looked like strangers to me and, honestly, worse than strangers. There were moments I felt I was about to lose it, but I had to hold back tears and walk to the restroom instead.

Not sure who decided the order, and by noon, our names were still not called. Then a guard in his uniform came out of the courtroom and told the rest of us to take a lunch break and come back before 2 PM. At that moment, Stacy and I both opened our mouths in awe while Jeremy looked solemn as usual in public. We were to miss what we were planning to do in the afternoon. For the other party, it could be their quiz. For me, a scheduled meeting with Mr. Osman in the Eye and Ear Hospital. Antonio told me he couldn't stay with me for the afternoon because he had a mock test in the computer room in his department. So he drove us back to West Campus, and we picked up some Mexican food on West Lane Avenue. Then, we drove separate cars toward the city center, and I followed his lead all the way — another breathtaking experience for me because I wasn't familiar with the downtown section of the highway system. It was so hard to switch lanes in the traffic. By the time I arrived, Antonio had already secured a parking spot for me, and then we did our routine fist pump before saying goodbye. It was just that complicated because I would have no idea how to find parking in downtown Columbus. I had never driven to that area before by myself.

I was on my own again, facing the exotic justice system. While waiting alone, I started to write down some lyrics for a new song called "Lesson for Me," as my brain was producing music under that circumstance. Around 3 PM, when all the other people were gone, the guard finally called our names. Jeremy and Stacy were seated close to the podium, to the right, while I was far back in the center. He was dressed up and even wore a tie, like in the TV shows. The only thing he forgot to bring to the courtroom was his white coat, I thought. I was cautious enough to wear a white shirt. However, my dress code was still very casual compared to his because Mr. Parker never mentioned any of these details. Jeremy seemed very experienced with all of this, while I didn't even know how to prepare. Stacy was wearing her pink sweater, and the way she sat beside him made me realize she probably stuck to him like that every day in the classroom, like an "independent" bird perching on the big tree.

The judge was not a "judge." The Caucasian woman wearing a black robe was called a "magistrate," whose title was below the judge. When I was back home, I had to look up the word printed on that piece of paper. Apparently, the judge didn't even think we were worth his time. And this magistrate, throughout that day, her job was to mediate between two parties on restraining order cases, mostly for black people. And case after case, week after week, year after year, as I imagine. I don't remember what she looked like except the way she walked in that black robe, in resemblance to Angelina Jolie's character Maleficent in the movie posters. No, I haven't watched that movie or its sequel. Considering her status, I'll just refer to her as Magistrate Turner in my story instead of Maleficent.

9.2 What? No Pre-conference?!

"Since this case is our last case today, let's do it in a slightly different way and bring the two parties together to have some discussion." This was her opening line, and I was shocked.

"Sorry, but my lawyer said there would be a pre-conference, so I shouldn't need to see the other party?" After this incident, I learned to use the phrase "the other party" frequently in my daily life.

"So, do you want to reschedule the meeting?" She raised her eyebrows. In retrospect, that was a calibrated question aiming for a negation. An orthodontic surgeon once used that on me as well.

"No, definitely not. I want to get it done today." I said.

"Okay. Did you say you have a lawyer?"

"Yes and no. His name is Mr. Parker, but he couldn't represent me due to the conflict of interest."

"Yes, I know Mr. Parker. He's a good guy. So you're here all by yourself today? No friends or families?"

"My buddy was here with me this morning, but he needs to prepare for an exam this afternoon," I answered.

"Okay. Mr. Sun, uh… How do you pronounce your first name?" This is a routine question for me.

I wish I could just tell her that I go by Slim, but I pronounced my legal first name for her.

"Okay. Mr. Sun, let me ask you, do you have any romantic feelings toward Mr. Jeremiah?" That was a surprising question for me, considering we were in the courtroom, but it might be normal in America, not a totalitarian country.

"Not at all," I answered peacefully. I withheld some thoughts to avoid overcomplicating things, such as "He doesn't even have blue eyes" and "This kind of question will make him more narcissistic." Both Jeremy and Stacy were aware that I, like many other Asians, found blue eyes attractive; unfortunately, this phenotype isn't available in the majority of Asian countries.

Then Jeremy explained, "That was because my girlfriend couldn't understand why he made such a big deal of it at that time." Then I realized Stacy even mentioned her suspicion to him and to the police, and I immediately felt disgusted.

Magistrate Turner put aside her confusion and turned to look at the guy with a movie-star face sitting beside the blonde. "So Mr. Jeremiah, what kind of students are you guys?"

"I'm a first-year med student. My life is very stressful." Notice he only talked about himself when the question was about "you guys."

"Yeah, I was in law school. So I understand how stressful med school is. What about him?"

"He's a second-year grad student." He answered.

"I'm graduating this semester. And I'm writing my thesis now. I'm stressed too." I quickly followed.

Magistrate Turner had a glimpse of me and said, "You will have your chance to speak, Mr. Sun. Now, Mr. Jeremiah, can you tell Mr. Sun which part of his email scared you that day?" Said Magistrate Turner.

"He said, you **must** choose a place to talk with me… Or you will regret it… And all in capital letters." With intonation and cadence, he answered like a typical approval-seeking good student asked to read in class.

"But I didn't intend any **harm** to him!" I immediately responded.

"But that's what he **perceived**!" She emphasized, "And you mentioned '**suicide**,' which really concerned me!"

I lowered my head and knew it wasn't a good time to argue because everything was written very clearly on paper. I meant something different, but she didn't care about the context. What I had in mind was still argumentative: the way she showed her concern about me was to grant a restraining order against me. Seriously?

She then continued to ask him, "Now, Mr. Jeremiah, tell me, when you guys moved out of the original house, did you tell him you didn't want him to contact you anymore?"

He paused and spoke very slowly, in his low-pitched voice, like a self-reflective good student. "I... did not. But **later**, I told him I could not afford the friendship he wanted from me." He then looked at Magistrate Turner like an innocent child.

I sneered, in pain, because I sensed he must have had his parents rehearse with him during the spring break. His parents looked very kind, unlike him, and months ago, his mom even gave me a piece of homemade brownie to thank me for helping him move his furniture upstairs.

What does "later" mean? Without specifying the time, he was trying to blur things up. More importantly, I spotted his gimmick in his use of language at that moment. Because what he texted me in January was "this level of friendship I can offer" instead of "I cannot afford the friendship you want from me." They look synonymous, but after he flipped the tone, the connotation became the opposite: the latter signified a rejection while the former signified a deal. He used this trick to make himself sound thoughtful in front of the female listeners, but I wasn't able to pinpoint the subtlety in the courtroom. I was totally caught off guard.

"Now Mr. Jeremiah, can you tell Mr. Sun in clear language, do you want him to contact you in the future?"

She said.

"I do not want him to contact me anymore." He said slowly.

"Did you hear that, Mr. Sun?" She asked.

"Yes." At that moment, within a second, I felt frozen and then relieved. After taking a deep breath, I started to speak in my sobbing mode, "I just wanted him to speak to me directly. After she told me he had changed, I thought maybe I was **wrong**. Because I don't want to **wrong** anybody. I knew he was busy, so I didn't want to disturb him. I tried." When I was in elementary school, a female teacher named Mei taught Chinese language and literature. Due to her menacing character, she was dubbed "The Tiger with a Smiling Face" by the students. She **wronged** me twice in public in an excruciating way and wouldn't listen to students' defense, so I never liked this teacher, despite Mandy's futile argument— "She liked you." A typical teacher in China likes a student primarily because the student pulls the average score higher; in other words, because the student brings momentum to the teacher's promotion. These awful teachers in my hometown made me dread the teaching profession from an early age.

"Mr. Sun, I understand that for an international student, it takes a long time to learn how to navigate in a different culture. In this city, I have some friends from Southeast Asia too, but I just don't understand why friendship would mean so much to you."

When I heard her shift the discussion to the cultural difference, I suspected she was fooled by him, a white med student dressed up like an innocent gentleman with a young celebrity face. I raised my hand and wanted to tell her it was not about friendship at all but about cheating because there never truly existed any bilaterally recognized friendship between us. Jeremy acknowledged some temporary comradeship when we had a common enemy called Jessica, but that provided no long-term gain for him. I guess one has to accept the brutal viewpoint that "there are no permanent enemies, no permanent friends, only permanent interests."

She motioned for me to put my hand down so she could wrap up the case. For many years, I chose to convince myself that she did this intentionally because the emphasis on the intercultural factor would make my behavior look less insane from a legal point of view. Yet because I wasn't allowed to speak, what I had to repress in that courtroom that day became endless rumination in the next few months — I perceived bias in the justice system. Why did she ask a question and then silence me? Maybe I shouldn't have even raised my hand for permission to speak; instead, I should have just told her that friendship means a lot to me because I don't have a beloved family that I can rely on, not to mention we are the generation of "one-child policy" in China— a historic policy with its objective merits for the Chinese society, and the human race in general. Also, she should understand that China, or East Asia, is quite different from Southeast Asia. But what could I say? It's the Midwest, a place even coastal Americans don't like.

"Sometimes, friends just don't fit." She continued, "I propose we use this meeting as an opportunity to educate young people. From now on, you guys just stop interacting with each other and develop separately. Based on the common practice, Mr. Sun, in the next 6 months, you need to stay 500 feet away from him as you did in the past 2 weeks. I know it is tricky, but as an international student, if you are not careful, life will change rapidly for you in the next few months. Do you have any questions, Mr. Sun?"

Based on what Mr. Parker told me previously, "Your life will change rapidly" literally meant that my case could be escalated into a criminal case and that I would be kicked out of the United States with no grace period. Understandably, this menace also became the content of my rumination and nightmare.

"What about the Ohio State Medical Center? I have a lot of healthcare appointments these days. They both know that." I said.

"Okay. I'll add to the terms that you can go to the Medical Center for healthcare purposes, since he is not going to treat you. Also, as far as I know, Ohio State has very good psychotherapy services for the students. I suggest you take advantage of that."

"I've already been there," I said. The irony here was obvious: the "justice" system had dealt me a blow and then told me I needed psychotherapy to recover from it. Similarly, the lady in Student Advocacy told me that to recover from emotional distress, I should have talked to my friends or a therapist instead of messing with the person who had hurt me. Surely I could tell myself that everybody was simply doing their job and that I had better take ownership of my wrongdoings. Still, as an inevitable byproduct, I would lose trust in the so-called justice system, like everyone who had been treated unfairly in major conflicts.

"Okay. Anything else?" Said Magistrate Turner.

I wanted to ask about the gym, but I figured she would just tell me to use another gym to avoid him, so I asked another hypothetical question.

"After the six-months cooling-off period, I still cannot make contact with him? Is that correct?"

"You shouldn't. Because if you do, he may file another

protection order against you. After 6 months, your case will be dismissed, and you should come here to sign the paperwork. Not you, Mr. Jeremiah. Now Mr. Sun, do you agree you will never contact Mr. Jeremiah anymore?"

"I have no desire to contact him anymore," I said.

"I want you to answer me directly." She said.

"I agree," I said.

"Do you also agree with the terms, Mr. Jeremiah?" She asked.

"I agree." He said.

"Also, Mr. Jeremiah, it seems your girlfriend and Mr. Sun have developed a friendship somehow?" Asked Magistrate Turner. She was well-prepared and meticulous.

"Yeah, but when they were together, their conversation was mostly about me." Said, Jeremy. He was correct in the sense that his ears would filter out anything that was **not** about himself. But sure, for the most part, the bond between Stacy and me was based on our common complaints about him and our common fear of him losing his temper and rejecting us, these lonely people. Now that he had become so affectionate to her while I became useless to him, the foundation of this bond naturally vanished.

"Since you guys are a couple, I think it's a good idea for Miss Anastasia to stop communicating with Mr. Sun as well." Said Magistrate Turner.

"I agree this is the best solution." Stacy said in her low-pitched voice, which I never felt comfortable with.

"Did you hear that, Mr. Sun?"

"I agree. But I have a friend who lives in the same apartment complex as she does. So I can't even visit my friend?" I asked this because I thought of the night I went to

MEETING IN THE COURTHOUSE

karaoke with my Asian friends.

"Considering your current situation, maybe you should ask your friend to visit you instead." Said Magistrate Turner.

"Okay. No problem." I knew there was no point in continuing the bargain. That friend of mine wouldn't really visit me, because she didn't have a car. I wouldn't want to see Stacy anyway. All these years, although I've been telling people that Jeremy, this grandiose medical student, was the heartless person that took away my health, I never had any doubt deep in my heart that her stimulation was what drove me into my ultimate insanity. Unfortunately, people all thought she was a benevolent person in the story. I tried not to involve this innocent lady in the battle or to taint her boyfriend's image in front of her. This seemingly considerate and ethical inhibition, based on the maladaptive education I had received from the softy Chinese culture, was the pitfall I dug for myself. Stacy never knew why I was in so much pain because I had never shown her the evidence of Jeremy cheating me. Instead, I let myself drown in frustration and shut myself down. I wished for her understanding, but my action had the opposite effect. Now, if you think I am overthinking, I am not. I had to regurgitate the whole conflict myself in order to unravel it, and no one else could do this on my behalf.

I remember seeing her Facebook status the night I wrote the second email, "I don't care how long this happiness can last. I just wanna enjoy the present." It was clearly a message for him, and it directly revealed to me how insecure she was. I felt almost no loss about being cut off from her as she reminded me why I never liked these innocent young girls in the first place. If you have ever read the Chinese science fiction trilogy *The Three-Body Problem*, you might remember that the earth was eventually destroyed because of the weak personality of the young lady character. This type of role always overcomplicates things, if not screws things up.

Stacy, in real life, was devoting herself to a man several years older than her— a flippant bird needs a tree to perch on, a big and muscular tree. In contrast, vertically challenged people like me will never become a tree for other people, perhaps a cactus at best, not the ones in Arizona.

"Since both parties agree on the terms, I'll bring you both the paperwork to sign." Said Magistrate Turner as she disappeared into her office.

9.3 The Outcome

Magistrate Turner came back after a minute. As I looked at this new piece of paper, bewildered by the terminology as always, she explained further, "After the case is dismissed, you'll need to hire an attorney to file a motion to seal this case for you." She did not mention this would only be possible 6 months after the dismissal, so I originally overlooked this detail printed on paper.

"What does it mean to seal a case? How much do I have to pay for that?" I asked, thinking I would be slaughtered this time. Besides the medical bills, I had to pay the legal fees out-of-pocket, all because I engaged with this person Jeremy. No surprise, my brain treated him as a jinx in the subsequent years.

"I don't know. You'll have to ask the attorney. It's a legal procedure you need to do. This kind of record will make things difficult for international students in many ways, for example, during your job application." She was correct: based on what I later learned from OSU Office of International Affairs, as an F-1 student, I needed to apply for

MEETING IN THE COURTHOUSE

the Employment Authorization Document (EAD) card Issued by Homeland Security right before graduation; after receiving this work permit, if I couldn't find a position within 3 months, I would be kicked out of America. That happens to a lot of international students every year.

"You mean employers can see it?" I began to cringe.

"I am not sure. You need to ask an attorney." She said. I was surprised that Magistrate Turner would give me that answer of uncertainty.

Then Jeremy started to talk, "I don't want this to affect his job application."

"So you want to shorten this period?" Magistrate Turner asked with interest.

"Yeah, if possible," he said.

"Mr. Sun, did you say you are graduating this semester?" Said Magistrate Turner.

"Yes, I already submitted the graduation form." It was true. If I remember correctly, they invited some celebrity to be the speaker for the spring commencement, but for the summer term, the speaker would be the new president Michael Drake, MD, who was taking over the office from Gordon Gee, the grandpa who liked to wear fancy bowties.

Magistrate Turner went back to her office and asked the clerk to look up the academic calendar of Ohio State. Then she came back with the updated form, which said the case was to be dismissed at the end of April. In retrospect, it was a much better outcome for me than the original "six months" predicted by Mr. Parker because the day after graduation, I would not have an open case on me. It would set me free in many ways. However, due to the lack of professional knowledge, I didn't even realize I could and should have bargained down the other six-month period posterior to the dismissal of the case. I didn't plan to stay in Ohio for long anyway, knowing I wasn't accepted into my desired Psychology program here for the next academic year.

Those days, my brain mixed everything, so I didn't notice the second waiting period on the form to be that long until I tried to hire an attorney to file the motion for me. Besides, Teresa warned me not to look at those forms I had hidden in my drawer because it would interfere with my therapy progress. But when I needed to hire a lawyer, I had to take out the paperwork and understand the terms thoroughly. It's the inevitable conflict of life if one wants to take ownership of their life at all. Never listen to professional advice in a dogmatic fashion. Nobody else is completely in your situation and knows what needs to be done better than you do.

After Jeremy and I signed the forms, they let the couple leave the courtroom first. I waited for another 10 minutes before I was free to go. The guard standing at the back of the room, who witnessed the mediation of every case throughout the day, said to me, "Have a nice day, sir." I tried to take a deep breath while walking slowly out of the Court of Common Pleas. I realized my breathing was super shallow, close to not breathing at all, and I was uncertain of how long I had been breathing in fear like that. For weeks? Or for months?

Anyway, I found my car and checked my phone. It was past 4 PM, and Mr. Osman had emailed me, saying he was going home early. I still drove to the Eye and Ear Hospital and worked on my research data. There was no lab manager anymore— the old one from India had quit. Some medical residents in ENT had already started to use our lab for their medical examinations. You see, my life was still intertwined with medical school, and it would always be like that, even after I moved to California.

9.4 The Psychological Trauma

The next 50 days felt like a prison for me. My prison was walking through this world all alone (*Desperado* by The Eagles), even though I was not strictly alone 24/7. I was doing everything I was supposed to do: physical therapy, psychotherapy, classes, and exams, as usual. My brain, however, was going awry.

The morning after the court, I started to hear voices hovering over my mind:

"I'm a first-year med student. My life is very stressful."

"Yeah, I was in law school, so I understand what med school is like."

"As an international student, if you are not careful, life will change rapidly for you in the next few months."

These lines in the courtroom repeated themselves again and again wherever I went, and I couldn't shut them off, even when I was driving to campus. It went on and on those days and would always reappear to haunt my mind whenever I drove on the roads near the Medical Center. The flashbacks lasted for months, even after the dismissal of the case, and the word "medical" seemed to be the cue. I realized I was having the first-hand experience of having "ghosts" in my mind, as those fictional characters often do.

When I realized I couldn't focus on work or the lectures at all, I called the Student Counseling Center and asked for an urgent appointment at Teresa's earliest availability. Fortunately, she had a cancellation that afternoon. As soon as I sat down, I explained to her that the court didn't go as Mr. Parker predicted, and I wasn't well prepared for it. Because Magistrate Turner didn't allow me to fill up my side of the story, I felt choked inside my chest and couldn't get over that scenario. In this session, I had no motive to cry. Instead, while I was recounting the scene in the courtroom, I felt terrified and alienated. Yes, I knew I was alien to America, but it still felt awful. It reminded me of the poignant complex behind my childhood dream of becoming a psychologist — nobody in my core family believed what I said. After hearing about my latest experience in court, she decided that for the next few weeks, her main goal was to help me "get over it."

"What you are experiencing is a trauma." She said. She then used a metaphor that I had to walk through a dark forest and eventually escape from the forest. However, despite my efforts, I always felt I was occasionally dragged back into the forest by some irresistible force. I had so much pain and rage after the day in court, which was unexpected. In retrospect, that's probably why the state of Ohio set the standard length of the cooling-off period to be six months. Without enough time, people can't let things go, and there can't be any substantial change in the quality of life that has been brought down by the other party.

The fact that I was taking an entry-level clinical psychology course beyond my primarily "cognitive" background was a double-edged sword. The positive side was I learned many clinical terms or symptoms, so I was able to describe my own symptoms to the clinician. I knew the intrusive thoughts I was battling against fell under the concept of rumination, which greatly facilitated my communication with Teresa. She could directly introduce effective therapeutic approaches for me to try. From my neuro-cognitive point of view, some of my brain functions were in disorder after that trauma. The auditory flashbacks were a result of "leakage" of episodic memory (a.k.a.

autobiographical memory), figuratively speaking. Besides, consistent with one chapter on "mindfulness," she raised an interesting point that all of us should reflect on: when I told myself not to think about a negative event, I was essentially thinking about that event. That's why I was advised to watch it dissipate in a non-judgmental way. When it comes to psychotherapy, more haste, less speed.

The negative side was also remarkable: Medical Student Syndrome. As we learned the symptoms and mechanisms of each major mental or behavioral disorder, I couldn't help matching my chaotic state to those specific disorders, even just on the subclinical level, because I was not only learning a new field but also going through depression, anxiety, memory loss, impaired cognitive functions, loss of appetite, insomnia, disrupted lifestyle, social withdrawal and so on. At a certain point, I wished I hadn't taken this course that semester because I was allowing myself to be triggered every week, incessantly, until the chapters on well-known major disorders were finished. Neither Teresa nor the instructor of the course knew everything about me. When the class reached the final chapters, personality disorders became the core topic. It occurred to me again that the campus police officer said behind my back that I had an obsessive personality and that the short-term condo-mate commented that I had an OCD for analyzing people. Maybe they were right: that was how I coped with the helpless situation. I also couldn't help putting the label "narcissistic personality disorder" on people I disliked in history, including Jeremy and Tao, the high school math teacher who traumatized me with verbal humiliation. It sounded like judging people, as the instructor herself pointed out when introducing this disorder, but the negative impact caused by this type of personality was significant.

After moving to California, I read some well-written articles on psychological trauma and eventually came to understand its underlying mechanism, or etiology. Figuratively speaking, an overwhelming amount of information enters the cognitive processing system all of a sudden, causing a mental clog which may take an extremely long time to dissolve. Effective intervention can help dissolve the clog and channel it into some other medium. This mental clog surely has a physiological impact. Under the model of fight-flight-freeze response, psychological trauma leads to a "frozen" state because if one were able to fight against the predator or to fly away, one wouldn't be traumatized deeply in the first place. Therefore, don't waste your energy or risk your life trying to defeat the predator by brute force.

Like the soldiers on the battlefield, I didn't just experience one attack or blow on my fragile mind (I tried to avoid using the word "brain" so that the readers would not confuse a psychological trauma with a traumatic brain injury). What I received was one bomb after another, in tandem, and each explosion could potentially crush me with its power. After the major blows, there were long-lasting aftershocks. If you think that defending myself in the courtroom alone was traumatic enough, let me be honest with you, every day before the dismissal of the case at the end of April 2013, I felt like walking on an iceberg with a gun held behind my head, or speaking with a knife held just below my chin, or sleeping on a matrix of needles, or treading with a giant iron-made cross on my back. I felt like I would be rejected once again by the young students and was worried about how many people in the department were gossiping about me. I had to swallow the pain and the fury because I had to yield to the other party who had emotionally tortured me with his charm and iron fist. I could resonate with victims who had to keep their heads down under the humiliation and persecution of the Red Guards during the Cultural Revolution and those who witnessed their egos eroded by the Japanese invaders and German Nazis during WWII. Though I had said, "I'm not inferior to you" in the first email and "I'm no longer vulnerable to your toxicity" in the second email, at the end of the day, I still had to yield to this powerful white male US citizen standing on the higher ground, and I was still vulnerable to his toxicity, under this particular circumstance.

If you think I was being melodramatic, or "it's all in your head," I can only tell that the objective disadvantages and plights for me were beyond your imagination. My life was loaded with shame, and I hated myself for remaining another male student's doormat for the sake of an educational degree in America and an extended stay in America. To sound more positive, I could only rationalize it as "to lose in order to gain." Still, deep in my heart, I knew my shame was rooted in my lack of power and my lack of an equal citizenship status relative to the other party. At that time, a green card or citizenship already seemed so out of reach for me since I didn't even know if my psyche could survive that semester.

I really couldn't tell when a breakdown was scheduled for me. My symptoms didn't qualify for a clinical diagnosis of PTSD as some of my veteran friends had, but my post-traumatic depression was visible most of the time. I couldn't even hide my low arousal and negative valence in front of the people I felt comfortable with, including Teresa, physical therapist Frankie, and the academic personnel. I simply didn't have the energy to fabricate a smile when facing the American world anymore. Unless stimulated by some comedy show, my mental state was very "flat." For the next few years, I felt nothing but pain. It worsened after I moved to Davis, California, an extremely flat and dull place, which did very little good for my healing but brought me new health problems instead. Ironically, some friends mistook my disconnection from emotions for mature calmness because they didn't know this dark history I was trying to get over.

Nowadays, when I look back, the so-called restraining order felt like a segment of duct tape that a kidnapper used to seal the victim's mouth. When you are deprived of your right to communicate with the person who hurt you, you have nowhere to direct your resentful thoughts but toward yourself, toward some abstract "system," or into your secret journal. Yet throughout history, civilians have been suffering from a fraction of the privileged like that. When civilians are bullied, they can only swallow the pain; to fight against the powerful is like digging a hole for one's own coffin to be buried in. Such tragedies abound on TV screens or in newspapers. Teresa told me time would heal everything. I doubted it at first, but it seemed at least partially true as long as one used the right methods. However, she also told me the painful episodic memories would never go away. Still, over time, the old neural circuits will close, and new connections will be generated, metaphorically speaking. One will be able to cope with the past while embracing the future. The emotional pain turns into knowledge about the human world and acceptance of injustice. Hopefully, in an ideal world.

Please note that the high cost of a face-to-face therapy session reflects the fact that psychotherapy takes hard work from both the patient and the clinician. I never doubted that psychotherapy, whether more or less effective for one's specific problem, is concrete in its nature. In my case,

Teresa's job was to clean up the mess on behalf of the justice system that traumatized me and the emotional pain Jeremy inflicted on me. Things could have gone worse without a therapist keeping track of my progress.

I know it's true also because I volunteered in a pediatric autism intervention program at UC Davis Medical Center one day per week from fall 2016 through spring 2017. As I remember, some young patients exhibited dramatic transformation through our comprehensive treatment plan. By the way, I chose to work as a trainee in that hospital because back in 2016, I was still planning to re-apply to graduate programs in clinical psychology on the East Coast. For that purpose, it was preferable to obtain a recommendation letter from the director of the clinical program, in addition to the one from the employer Mr. Osman, a pure academic researcher. Unfortunately, due to the chronic RSI endowed by Mr. Osman, I eventually gave up that new career goal.

9.5 Avoidance, Paranoia and Rise of the White Coat Devil

We did not have much overlap in our territories. Still, as long as there was a chance I could run into him on campus or any other place in the City of Columbus, I would have to escape. Sometimes I feared that he would come to me and chase after me, and I would have to run away from him to stay 500 feet away from him. That became a nightmare for me. Simply speaking, I developed some kind of phobia toward this person.

Whenever I saw a guy with short brown hair, who had the slightest resemblance to him, I would start to panic. Whenever I saw an SUV the same color as his car in the parking lot, I dreaded going into the store. If I happened to be accompanied, my overreaction would shock my friend. Whenever I saw his first name or last name in an article or saw a deceitful character in a movie, I would have to calm myself down. So many triggers in my daily life that I refer to as "aftershocks." It felt like thousands of made-in-China firecrackers exploding in my heart, so how could it not affect my nervous system?

I was being paranoid, believe it or not. His face with those eyeballs reflecting the red light became the background picture in my visual field. Every now and then, I would have very short breaths as I did in my teenage years after quarreling with Mandy. The whole Ohio State campus felt very scary and burdensome to me, and I didn't know how to develop trust toward strangers those days.

When I told my panicking issue to my Korean colleague, Ivy League Ph.D., someone who had lived in North America for over a decade, she told me to think differently, "In Korea, we have this proverb: when you see a piece of feces on the road, you walk around it, not because it's scary, but because it's disgusting." This Korean philosophy was brilliant. However, its innate bidirectional association backfired in a way because in the next few weeks, whenever I looked into my toilet, the scary face with red eyes and a bitter smile would pop up into my mind. I had no control over it.

When I emailed Mr. Parker about the update on my case, I mentioned what Magistrate Turner did and said. I also told him I was traumatized because things did not go as planned. In his reply, he said the outcome of the court meeting turned out very well for me, and I did a great job defending myself. In retrospect, Magistrate Turner was very experienced in her role of mediating between two parties and definitely less biased than I perceived immediately after the court.

Meanwhile, I didn't have the gut to put explicit blame for my escalated trauma on this school attorney, a guy who was wearing a dismissive persona most of the time but also seemed to be empathetic with my situation and standing on the side of justice—I knew I would need his expertise in the long run. His being "dismissive" was manifested differently than that of Mr. Osman: he would only say, "you're smart," as many people said to me when my life went downhill. I didn't feel flattered at all. Either they were merely trying to comfort me when they couldn't provide a solution for me, or they had no clear idea that intelligence was just a relative concept and often bundled with a frail physical constitution and an ego that's vulnerable to attack by the irrational. Simply being smart was not enough to outweigh the disadvantage of an inferior status given at birth; other contributing factors were necessary.

When I asked a senior grad student if she had ever met someone who took almost everything from her, she nodded yes. "Of course, my former supervisor in the hospital. That's why I came back to school." This colleague had clinical experience in a famous hospital for a decade before entering her Ph.D. program. Without me detailing my case to her, she already understood what I was going through. This conversation was reminiscent of what a clinical professor once told me – "when you work at a hospital, if you don't have an MD degree, you will be treated differently."

On another thread, I had previously been Facebook friends with several of Jeremy's classmates. After the day in court, I checked Facebook and found out that most of his classmates had unfriended me, including an Arabic guy who liked the young Justin Bieber, liked to jump into the Mirror Lake, and liked to call the med school "the best school in Ohio State" on social media. He was smart enough to make his profile invisible to me. As one of those who "kidnapped" Jeremy in their group photos, he always behaved like an attention seeker in my memory. In contrast, a Latino guy and a black guy didn't unfriend me, and it shouldn't be too hard to understand. I assume they were close enough with Jeremy and Stacy to know what happened, but they made their individualistic choices. They, plus other second-year or third-year medical students I knew back then, were the reason why I didn't develop an aversion against medical students as a category. Some of them were going to become successful clinicians for sure.

Then one day, the term "White Coat Devil" emerged into my mind without deliberation or notice. As I mentioned at the beginning of the story, the term "White Coat Angel" was entrenched in my brain through the education I received. I was brainwashed to believe that most clinicians were good-natured people, despite common misunderstandings between clinicians and patients. If Jeremy were a vet student, a dental student, or even a chemistry student who also wore a white coat, the term would still be suitable. When I first started to use this epithet to refer to him on Facebook, it was around the time of the shocking news of a white policeman shooting an unarmed black teenager Michael Brown in Ferguson, Missouri — the origin of the Black Lives Matter movement. As you can imagine, "White Coat Devil" looked pretty thorny to my white friends on Facebook, who actually made up the majority of my friends on Facebook. I did not know the term "white devil" used by African-Americans historically until I watched one episode of the final season of *The Man in a High Castle*. It gave me an "aha" moment. A couple of white friends couldn't tolerate that word, so they messaged me for clarification or simply unfriended me. They did not understand that this thing wasn't intended to be associated with race but with the "helping" profession of unnaturally high social status. Did I have an issue with white people in general? Hell no. In fact, a lot of young people from Asia adore the anatomical features of Caucasians as well as the mainstream American culture, either openly or covertly. Incidentally, one might argue that the word "white" in this context could be intersectional, indicating "Caucasians in the medical school are more privileged, and at the same time, more complacent," but I didn't think to that level in 2014. Come on, it was only my second year in America, and I couldn't even name the food in Chipotle accurately.

Honestly, I was mad because this legal weapon suffocated me too much, and I couldn't find any other effective outlet in my life. I feel sorry for my friends who had to tolerate me during that period. Later, more than one person recommended expressive writing, a.k.a. journaling, to me, and I adopted this approach wildly. I typed everything on my laptop. Some expert even suggested that I print out the file and burn it. Over time, my rage against Jeremy and the "justice" system subsided, but the emotional pain was everlasting. While therapeutic approaches can help one manage emotions, some problems are irreversible and/or incurable: what is done cannot be undone. In that case, it's a lifelong battle.

I didn't believe in God, but somehow, I believed in devils. How? Western movies and TV shows, of course. The word "devil" indicates how horrified I was by that individual's existence during that period. Some of my religious friends cringed at that word, but one of my atheist buddies said firmly, "Yes, he is a devil." That's what I perceived, and I couldn't find a better word to portray his image in those years. Isn't it ironic that a self-motivated first-year medical student sickened me and then traumatized me into therapy in a way most ordinary Americans wouldn't? Frankly, it wasn't so much about his character as about his tremendous impact on me. The same mechanism applies to the historical term "white devil," as I realize.

Chapter 10
Student Conduct and Student Advocacy

10.1 Jury or Not?

When I thought I could take a deep breath and thank God for not kicking me out of America immediately, I received another email from Mr. Frost several days after the court hearing. This email contained a secure message, so I had to enter my password to download the file. Based on the student code, Mr. Frost charged me with "engaging in some behavior that led to the other party's fear about their safety." He allowed me to choose whether to accept the charge and face the consequences or to appeal and have a hearing before a jury.

Another conundrum for me. Not in my entire life had I received something like this. I grew up with all kinds of prizes and recognitions for my academic endeavor and semi-voluntary work, whether I deserved them all or not, whether I desired them or not. Now, in America, I was to receive a charge for my behavior outside school because the other party involved in this conflict was also an enrolled student. I remember in college, my classmate once had a fight with some Tibetan students in the dorm building, and he got injured in his face, but none of them decided to get the school involved. Usually, school officials would ask students to settle within themselves, and they understood that people who had direct conflicts were much easier to mediate than those hypocrites with daggers hidden up their sleeves. But this is America, where the "litigation" inside the school was even harsher than the justice system in the local government, and they took pride in that— a purported **safe** place in a country without gun control. In contrast, the school system in China cared about the well-being of students in a different way. The school teachers punished students by locking them up in the office, letting them stand at the back of the classroom for hours, or assigning extra homework if they got certain answers wrong in the exams— everything I have experienced or witnessed.

But I was charged anyway, so what should I do? I consulted Mr. Hoffman and Mr. Williams since they were both very senior at this university. Mr. Williams, who had experience with such cases, told me the students on the jury tended to be harsher than school officials like Mr. Frost. I could totally understand that because when I closed my eyes, I could see the hostile faces of those undergrads I taught in the TA sessions. If the jury were purely white, which was very likely the case in Ohio State, then I would have lost to Jeremy before the trial even began. Based on my experience, some white people will have a knee-jerk reaction to deny that race plays a role in this process, especially since the offender party isn't black this time. It's in their self-interest to downplay the bias, be it explicit or implicit. What kind of self-interest? Resolution of cognitive dissonance. People tend to associate themselves with a group that elevates their self-image. When the group label is stained, they either update their group identity or undermine the credibility of the stain. This is plain social psychology.

Anxiously, I emailed Mr. Frost and asked what the outcome would be if I accepted the charge. However, he didn't respond to me over the weekend.

This email containing a charge was even more dreadful than the court letter at that moment because a serious sanction would mean a big stigma on my record. If I got suspended, would I lose my student status and thus be kicked out of America immediately? That also meant the end of my American dream and the loss of hope for this already tragic life. Come on, why didn't he respond to me?

10.2 Student Advocacy

I waited and waited and started to panic again, for fear that all my previous efforts dealing with the court order could become futile if the school decided to expel me anyway. I didn't know what to do, so I went to Student Advocacy without an appointment and asked the lady there what I could do to minimize my loss. She first pointed out that I deserved this charge for what I did because I failed to seek therapy in time, failed to understand the xenophobia from Jeremy as default human nature, and failed to stop contacting Jeremy myself after we both moved out. She also used a weird analogy: she was annoyed when her ex-boyfriend continued to call her number after she dumped him, which indicated she considered Jeremy as the victim in this story. Besides, she picked out sentences in my long emails to illustrate the faults in my motives and my personality, as the school police did. After I convinced her that Jeremy deceived me, she made a phone call to Student Conduct and received confirmation that I could provide supportive materials to be filed in my own defense.

Regarding the sanction, she assured me that in the worst case, I could still transfer to a community college that accepted international students so as not to be kicked out of America during the semester of suspension. However, I was still worried about how the transcript would look in the eyes of my future employers. I knew my life would be stigmatized anyway, which would probably mean no lofty employers would dare hire me, especially not those "noble" academics. That's what I thought at the age of 24. I also worried about how this would affect my application to grad school programs since I told everyone that I wanted to get a Ph.D. eventually. Whether or not I should be called self-motivated or naïve, this pathway was severed by Mr. Osman later on.

When I asked her whether I should appear more apologetic and remorseful to please the school official and the jury, she said not necessarily. This reflected a big difference between American culture and a self-scapegoating Asian culture. If I acted like an appeaser, they would take it as evidence that I was totally at fault. But in mainstream Chinese culture, you will be criticized even harder if you defend yourself. This impression was based on my first-hand experience with those tyrannical teachers who traumatized me in each stage of my short life. Other kids were better off than me because they were more intelligent than me, too ordinary to become the teachers' target, or lucky enough to have protective parents.

Based on a textbook on Social Psychology I have read (David G. Myers & Jean M. Twenge), the jury would naturally be biased. There was no doubt that race (with skin color as the primary marker) and country of origin would play a big role in it. It's very unlikely that they would invite a foreigner into the jury, so I should be prepared for the worst outcome on my next Judgment Day. The jury system is a very complex science that does not exist in every part of the world, unfortunately. The real question was: why did I have to face all this sh*t in my second year in America? Am I supposed to regurgitate it for the rest of my life? This abstract concept called "life" is largely unpredictable and sometimes downhill all the way to the abyss.

10.3 I Surrendered

Several days passed, and I still didn't receive any reply from Mr. Frost. In the Chinese language, there is a proverb describing one's eagerness to put the anxiety to an end: the sooner you die, the sooner you reincarnate. That's how I felt. I just wanted an answer, even if the answer was execution.

With all the information gathered, there was little doubt that I should not choose the jury hearing because that would mean a bonus trauma for me, especially if all the students on the jury were Caucasian Americans. There was a significant chance they would unanimously support Jeremy in the hearing. In that case, their images would all develop into devils in my subconscious, although I wasn't religious. People from most parts of the world don't want warfare but peace and reconciliation. Harsh punishment would only lead to deeper hatred, often repressed rather than dissolved. Well, that's different than saying we should assassinate all the dissidents to make this world look so homogeneous or harmonious, like taking an enormous amount of NSAIDs or tranquilizers.

The following Monday, I emailed the professors that I would like to accept the charge without a hearing because my body couldn't tolerate another blow. I believed I was a good person inside. However, I was also aware that good-natured people could be played and exploited in this competitive and fraudulent human society— I am simply telling the bitter truth which most people don't have the courage to acknowledge openly. In the face of this life-threatening charge, I had to numb myself once again emotionally to be able to function physically, which was exactly what I did during the final year of high school after getting depressed by the autocratic, narcissistic math teacher Tao.

Then I signed the paperwork and brought it to Student Conduct. At about the same time, I received a reply from Mr. Frost. He explained that he was out for some workshop off-campus, so he was unable to read emails. While sitting on the COTA bus from the West Campus to the Main Campus, I felt serene or, say, ready for the guillotine. "The sooner I die, the sooner I reincarnate," I murmured to myself.

When I finally met him in his office, he assured me my violation of the student codes wouldn't result in immediate suspension. What I eventually got was suspension on probation, based on his research into historical cases. This sanction would be over by the end of the semester, contingent on my good "conduct." He told me the record would not appear on my transcript and would be destroyed in 10 years. He also offered to help me with the tricky questions if I decided to apply to grad school again. Yes, everybody makes mistakes when they are young; some make even bigger mistakes when they are old, such as corruption. Right or wrong, it all depends on the standard, namely the law, the bylaw, the regulations, the hidden rules, the ruling party, and so on. Was it wise of me to accept the charge without fighting? Nobody knew the answer for sure because each case is different. I was simply exhausted, like I always have been in this life, because every few years, I would be traumatized by a parent, teacher, housemate, or employer, often in the same pattern and not allowed to fight back. Some senior people in China try to tell me it's good for young people to get some setbacks because they assume as a "good" student, I presumably have lived a smooth life.

STUDENT CONDUCT AND STUDENT ADVOCACY

They also imagine people living overseas would all have a gorgeous and cozy lifestyle, as news media portrays. Why? On the one hand, they are ignorant of things happening in other parts of the world. On the other hand, people like me are only allowed or conditioned to show their achievements on their resumes, not their plights, which often involve mistakes and shame. In fact, folks like Mandy and my elder cousin sister Lulu couldn't tolerate any true negative information in their eyes or ears.

According to some senior faculty members, The Office of Student Conduct used to handle cases very slowly. The fact that I was invited for an interview within the week since the onset of the incident was out of the expectation of the administrators. It turned out that this young and energetic Educationist with a Ph.D. was not a procrastinator but a doer. According to him, he wanted to process students' cases on time so that people could get inner peace sooner. He made a point there.

Before I turned in the signed paper, he educated me on how to use language and how not to be fooled by people's various titles or degrees in this country of America. He told me one couldn't choose who to work with, and I didn't deeply understand that until I started working full-time at UC Davis. To further "discipline" me, he required me to write some essays to show my self-reflection without pointing the finger at the other party.

Formality. I complied. No choice.

Shame? Kind of. Already numb at that point.

Remorse? To some extent, but more importantly, I had to express and exhibit that in order to be allowed to stay.

Grateful to the other party for teaching me a lesson? I'm not a masochist.

Come on, your tragic life written in the stars: 12 years a slave from elementary school through senior high school in Smoke City, and this is just a bonus year of mental slavery in your adulthood. As I remember, Dr. Li, the Whistleblower in Wuhan, was also forced to write an apology letter for disseminating the truth about Coronavirus in 2020. Therefore, in my humble opinion, it's not about any specific country or ideology but the abuse of power in a severely institutionalized society.

Months later, when I told him I graduated from OSU, he was very excited, definitely more excited than me. I wasn't excited at all, to be honest, not just because of the post-traumatic depression. Still, I knew that not everybody invited to his office could eventually get their degree. Through his sanctions, people's life trajectories would usually change drastically. I was no exception. My worldview changed quite a lot after this incident, with no turning back. One important thing I've learned was, "you shouldn't jump into the river for those who wouldn't even get their shoes wet for you." Most people, however, grew up receiving the opposite message. In my opinion, it's immoral to be blindly benevolent because if you are showing mercy to evil, you are indirectly contributing to the destruction of the world. No, I will never become Mother Teresa.

Mr. Frost told me he got a Ph.D. because he wanted such a position, and I should only get a Ph.D. if the position I desired required a doctoral degree—golden advice. I wish someone had told me that. Unfortunately, since I was a kid, I had been lured into believing that because I was smarter than average, I was supposed to get a Ph.D. to make myself superior, if not to make my family proud.

I asked him, "Why do you want a job that requires you to press charges to the students and then sanction them?"

He looked at me behind his thick glasses and said, "Well, I think in a different way. My job is not to punish people but to help them become better human beings. We want to help students get their degrees as well, just like Student Advocacy." But in a fraction of cases, his goodwill for the students simply couldn't turn into reality. Instead, their future would be turned upside down. For instance, he admitted that a student ended his life after being suspended from OSU. Unsurprisingly, Mr. Frost had a hard time getting over that case himself.

I paused momentarily and murmured slowly, "You... are... an interesting person."

He burst into laughter, "I hope you're referring to the good side of me!" His façade just cracked up in front of me, and he was as self-conscious as he claimed to be.

"You know it can't be that simple." I didn't want to dig into his personal stories because I didn't have time or interest in them. His position is one with scary power but also full of conflict, so it can't be easy. That's probably why they only allowed a man with a doctoral degree to take that burden. Whether or not his job actually makes the world a better place, I think it is subjective. From my perspective, despite knowing he was just doing his job with a high-functioning brain and good work ethic, I still couldn't make myself admire or thank such a person who sanctioned me; otherwise, it would have become another toxic relationship, such as Stockholm Syndrome.

Before I left, he asked me about the aftermath of my court order, and I told him I needed to hire a lawyer to help me seal the case after this semester. He said, "You mean to expunge the case?" Since he mentioned a new word to me, I kept it in mind and thought it was synonymous with "seal" — a less unfamiliar word. As an international student, I no longer had time to learn each new word systematically as we did in high school or college. There was no more supervision from English teachers, so there were many chances to misunderstand new words while assimilating them into my vocabulary. I didn't realize the term "expunge" he brought up overcomplicated my story later.

Back in my department in Communication Disorders, I told my professors that Mr. Frost had decided not to suspend me, and they all got a big relief. Mr. Hoffman was pleased that I could continue to write my thesis and then schedule my thesis defense. Seriously, I didn't have much time left because the series of traumas distracted me from the original course. I told him I wanted to postpone my graduation till the end of summer, knowing I would receive no stipend from the department for the next three months. Technically, the defense, revision, and submission of one's master's thesis would take several months anyway. It couldn't be as smooth as one would wish. Tuition was waived for the summer, but very few fascinating graduate-level courses were offered during that period. No celebrity was invited to the summer commencement, and considering the irrational cost of renting the regalia, I opted not to attend the ceremony for the M.A. degree. Ridiculously, without my consent, OSU sent the diploma to my permanent address in China, so I was the last person to see it.

When I met Mr. Osman to discuss my thesis the following week, he said, "I think you are misunderstood by the people here. If I were you, I would spend more time with people from my own country. I wish I could see another person from my home country in Ohio." He thought it was unusual for a Chinese international student to live with white American students. I wish there were more Chinese people in the field I studied. I wish Chinese people were all friends with each other, but it was certainly not the case. The total population of China, particularly the number of Chinese students all over the world, has already rendered it impossible. People's presumptions about foreign countries were often oversimplified. Similarly, it's precarious to assume that two random immigrants from the same Middle Eastern country would naturally befriend each other. Human nature doesn't work that way, not in practice. Admittedly, the US would open its door more easily for Christians like him, but not all immigrants from Middle Eastern countries are Christians. I could be biased, but when I look back, I find a lot of things he said to be questionable or even illogical.

At the end of our meeting, the lady in Student Advocacy told me I should notify her of the result by the end of the semester so that she could close my case, but I totally forgot about that. She was one of the characters I actually liked in the story for her enlightenment on me. For sure, her position or role gave her some advantage from the start, so she could afford to sugarcoat less. While the role of Mr. Frost is comparable to an oncologist who diagnoses me with stage II cancer and wants to wipe out my tumor cells with chemo, Student Advocacy was playing a more rehabilitative role. Thankfully, most students would never have to deal with Student Advocacy throughout their education, just like most US citizens never have to deal with the complicated justice system. The hospital seems like a place full of care and love, but it's still better to avoid getting hospitalized.

10.4 What Did I Want from Him?

Remember the question asked by Rachel, my friend from Shanghai: what did you want from Jeremy?

I simply said "his apology" back then. By giving her this

lame answer, I did make myself look overly childish. It wasn't that simple; in fact, I wanted an explanation, as every victimized individual would. It was in my instinct to investigate the mechanism behind a mystery. Although Mr. Frost and Mr. Hoffman told me sometimes one would never get the answers to many questions in life, the lady at Student Advocacy helped me understand it quickly, and I was actually convinced. Xenophobia explained most of it, med school superiority for the rest, and racism a little bit, which he would certainly deny. Stacy said he was a stubborn and hard person, but "stubborn" only describes the inertia to change, not the rationale behind the initial momentum of exclusion. We are all stubborn about certain things, and intellectuals in particular. If I allow myself to be more cynical, Jeremy may have gained some psychological reward by sending me mixed signals and keeping me hooked and tormented. I simply can't exclude that possibility.

Through my therapy sessions with Layla, my suspicion got confirmed: he was a narcissist. Had I noticed the red flags and known how to label this person in the early stage, I would have known by reading Psychology Today or even WebMD that narcissists would not feel apologetic sincerely for their wrongdoings. In other words, my second email could have been omitted. I needn't have been influenced by his infatuated girlfriend. From his deceitful writing on the court order in an effort to portray me as an obsessed lunatic, I already knew he didn't see his deception as immoral. What was worse, his lack of repentance was particularly charming to his girlfriend. Life lessons came at a price, including two bad records, but it was because I lacked practical skills in deciphering people, including myself. This kind of knowledge had always been available on the Internet or in bestseller books, but I didn't attend to the resources. I always surrounded myself with authentic folks, and when the wolf in disguise crept into the herd of sheep, I failed to spot it and was slaughtered. Therefore, here is my sincere warning: It's never too early to learn the types of people we have to cope with throughout our lives. Don't wait till the day when everything's too late.

In contrast to that kind of knowledge, the cognitive science I was studying and researching didn't help me deal with people very much because cognition doesn't treat an individual as a human being with flesh, blood, and desires. Genetics, epigenetics, and algorithms didn't help either. They all looked so remotely relevant to this matter. At that point, I was already convinced that academic neuroscience would not equip me with the desired skills, and I was probably pursuing the wrong goal. Yet I was still struggling on the wrong track. Later, two female psychology majors from Case Western Reserve and Ohio State said to me separately, "Neuroscience is the worst. Why? Because it's real science." "Yes, it is the worst." Their comments sounded insulting to me then, but their viewpoint left a mark on me. I have to acknowledge at least some validity in that after living in pain for so long. However, science, as a methodology itself, is still valuable.

In April, the weather got better, and so did my cognitive functioning. However, my depression and sadness were still drowning me every day. The radio station Sunny 95, which used to cheer me up when I was driving, sounded flat and bitter every day. It baffled Teresa. From her perspective, my symptoms didn't deserve referral to a psychiatrist yet, because the latter would entail a prescription for antidepressants. In one session, I mentioned the differences between male and female topics, which inspired her to refer me to the group therapy devoted to male grad students. Honestly, one semester of biweekly individual therapy wasn't enough for me to recover from a series of traumatic events, especially since the ongoing therapy and the traumatic events had so much overlap in time. Teresa's role was like the med unit in a war zone while the soldier was still being attacked on the battlefield.

I told my buddy Kevin about my ongoing problem. He pointed out that it was crucial to learn to handle different types of people based on his experience playing gigs at various venues in Ohio. When I couldn't tolerate the emotional pain anymore, I recorded the song named after Jeremy with my second-hand Yamaha keyboard instead of waiting for Kevin to help me with the guitar track. Luckily, the keys on the keyboard were much softer than those on the piano; otherwise, my inflamed wrist wouldn't be able to tolerate it. As some people may know, playing an instrument itself is enough to cause tendinitis. A few weeks later, I also recorded the demo for the song I wrote outside the courtroom. It was called *Lesson to Me*, available on SoundCloud (@stanthefeline).

As I have mentioned already, one afternoon, while I was waiting for the school bus to return to West Campus, Jeremy was running on the sidewalk of West Woodruff Avenue on campus. He saw me in green from head to toe that day and showed me his gruesome smile for a second. I had no expression on my face as usual because I was still depressed. I didn't know what I should do. From that moment on, I was 100% sure he was enjoying that period of being legally superior to me on American land. The vehicles on the avenue prevented him from running toward me to scare me even more; otherwise, I would have to run away from him at the expense of missing the bus. I know someone might say it was all just my projection, but that's because they didn't see that creepy smile on his face.

When I told Teresa about my fear of running into him on campus after the case was dismissed, she told me I was worrying about something that hadn't happened, as Dr. Gallagher, the sports medicine physician, once said. I could never understand that logic because prevention seemed as crucial as post hoc treatment for me— when it did happen, I might be traumatized again, and it would already be too late. In fact, my work-related injury at UC Davis and the coronavirus crisis in 2020 made me realize that this notion of "prevention" wasn't entrenched in American culture except within the healthcare community.

"What do you plan to do if you see him? Why don't you just walk away?" She asked. As I exhibited a lot of anxiety about this Jeremy, whose name I barely mentioned in therapy sessions, Teresa asked me to visualize a scenario where I would run into Jeremy on campus. When I closed my eyes, I saw his red eyes glowing below his brown hair, and I started to breathe heavily. "What do you plan to do? Take a deep breath. What you plan to do? He is just a human being." She said.

"I... I'll just walk away." When I opened my eyes again, I felt tears on my face. This phobia was real, not about his white coat but his figure, face, and haircut.

As I had absorbed so many Christian concepts before this semester, particularly from the Bible study, his image became the ambushed reincarnation of Satan in human society. A person I once tried to help became the devil who destroyed my psyche. In my dream back then, Satan said to me, "Even if you trade your soul with me, you will still fall victim to his bigotry and discrimination. Hahahaha..." Then he put on his white coat and quickly disappeared into the med school.

I didn't tell any of my therapists about the code "White Coat Devil" for fear they might label me as delusional and anti-white— I could not afford the ramifications. One crazy thing about America and the modern world, in general, is that whether you are a believer or an atheist, you use these biblical terms in your daily life in a pragmatic way. With all the TV shows about ghosts, zombies, and vampires added to our vision, it becomes easier to blur the boundary between reality and the imaginary world. "Satan" is a word I would never use in China or in academia, but that term just popped up in my brain under that circumstance. Still, I wouldn't blame you for calling me insane at that time. By the way, I was once surprised that there were a lot of religious people in American academia, including in STEM fields. Considering Mr. Osman even uttered "oh my Lord" during a casual lab meeting, I wouldn't make a fuss about it nowadays. Academics are just people.

10.5 My Support System

Before the end of the month, I received kindness from many people in my life, who were from different countries. Some knew what happened to me, while others only noticed my erratic behavior on Facebook and my unnatural face when I told them, "I'm good."

People in Communication Disorders, Psychology, and Music offered me assistance when I was writing my thesis and preparing for the defense. I managed to finish everything before Mr. Osman officially left his position in the Medical Center. As mentioned previously, the thesis defense was not smooth, but they let me pass, and both advisors helped me revise my writing before submission and forwarded job posting emails to me. Not all students have such a privilege, and not all international students can graduate without hiring a professional editor. It is noteworthy that Mr. Osman remained a positive character during my stay in Ohio. I wasn't his employee back then, just a graduate student doing research with him. I was funded by my home department, and the project was funded by his collaborator.

One day, Mr. Williams came down to the basement with a potential new faculty member. When he saw me, he asked me in his Maryland accent, "How are you?" I could only say, "Good." And he responded, "Good." That moment was very awkward, like many life situations. Unfortunately, the existence of a third person, a stranger to me, prevented me from responding otherwise.

Finally, Kevin introduced me to the monthly showcase event organized by Columbus Songwriter Association. I never went on stage myself; instead, I paid a cover fee of 5 bucks. It opened the door for me to know a community of talented songwriters in Columbus. All of a sudden, I made a group of new friends with the same brain function, except that they knew how to play the guitar while singing and often started performing at an early age.

One Sunday evening, a preteen girl performed her original song on stage while playing the keyboard. She reminded me of myself writing sad pop songs as a teenager after being pushed to learn the keyboard and to practice classical music by brute force for years, namely from kindergarten to 4th grade. I never revealed my songwriting ability to the public until I went to college in Shanghai because I didn't like the hometown or the family I grew up in. Also, I could only play the keyboard with printed music sheets. It always took an excessive amount of time to learn even one pop song because I wasn't trained on how to analyze music professionally. Without knowledge of advanced chords and chord progression, I could only digest music in the form of high-density notes instead of the Gestalt of harmonics. Through a waste of my childhood, I overused my eyesight by reading the complicated music scores and tortured my spine, pelvis, and limbs by sitting several hours a day in front of the keyboard. For what? To pass those certificate exams year after year so that Mandy, my X chromosome provider, would be satisfied. Happiness? I could only write sad songs as self-therapy, no matter how many happy songs I had listened to. What about the opportunity cost? I have been bad at sports and ignorant of sports throughout my life; athletic men and women can laugh at me for that.

During the showcase, the best thing I could do was sit there as an audience, a special member of the audience, the only Asian in the audience, and somehow I felt at home. These local band players were not maestros but my friends and fellows who shared similar struggles about school, work, and relationships. On the very last night of April, we attended a show at Brothers Drake Meadery, where Kevin and Kelly performed their fascinating new song together. When chatting about music stuff, I told Kevin it was my Emancipation Day because the next morning, I was heading to the Court of Common Pleas by bus through High Street to pick up my "emancipation paperwork." I was finally free of both the legal and disciplinary shackles on May 1st.

My friends in the Japanese Student Organization also showed great concern for me. Particularly, one Japanese buddy, Takashi, was graduating from college and moving to

California. During his farewell drinking party at Chumley's on North High Street, he asked me about the background story of my angry Facebook posts. I didn't talk much about my handful of Japanese friends in the US, but from their house parties, I realized how much Americans liked to hang with Japanese people. The Cherry Blossom Festival in San Francisco is another great example demonstrating that Japanese culture has found a solid market among mainstream Americans.

Antonio took me to hike in the mountains one weekend. Julian once dropped in at my house after work without even asking me who the "White Coat Devil" was. Alex and Charlotte continued to invite me to their social events and helped me move to my next place for the summer. Chris, the Redditor, invited me to hang out with his friends multiple times. A grad student in engineering, who'd only known me for less than a month, invited me to his birthday dinner on a table for six. My lab mate Ashley went to a music concert with me at a downtown venue called The Basement, and we got to know each other's life stories better. She tried to comfort me by saying I just had some bad luck. I wish it were that simple. However, I was 24 that year, and based on the superstition component of Chinese culture, I was supposed to experience some trouble or disaster because my age was a multiple of 12, a zodiac cycle. Ridiculous as it might sound, many people take it seriously. They even encourage men to wear red underpants and socks to avoid bad luck. Of course, I never did because I don't like that extroverted color.

I didn't intentionally conceal my experience from some people, yet for some inexplicable reason, I couldn't find a comfortable opportunity to share the story with them. Some of them were from China, while others were religious

Americans. Maybe I just didn't want to be judged or reminded of my misery. It's a matter of how to minimize the risk of confiding in the wrong person. For example, in Davis, a friend originally from Cleveland thought I was telling a joke when I told him I was traumatized by Ohio. I figured my experience was beyond his imagination, so I just laughed along.

Mandy once said, "Why do you want to be understood by people? We understand you, and that's enough." That was ridiculous to me. As analyzed previously, my childhood complex around becoming a psychologist was precisely because people around me refused to accept my credibility or respect my independent identity, even though my academic score was fueling their vanity already. Essentially, my childhood dream was subconscious overcompensation for the deficiency of approval or recognition in the environment.

They never understood me better than my American friends. Throughout my life, I had to pretend to be someone I wasn't for fear that I would receive more "re-education" from the parents and the teachers or even the authoritarian Big Brothers. While I tried to keep a low profile, they forced me to be a role model for other people and would scold me when they found out I wasn't the golden puppet they were looking for. Borrowing Jeremy's wording, I could say they "kidnapped" me into those roles. They were the cause of their own disappointments.

The day after the court, I called Carl and told him the whole incident because I was invited to attend his wedding in April. I wanted to be honest with him, one of the decent people on this earth who I could trust no matter what. "Yes," he said, "some people in this world don't care about principles." I politely declined his offer to pray for me because I believed the cause-and-effect was in the hands of the people with free will and power. On his wedding day, his family members and other friends in the home church also showed concern about me. Some of them shared their own lonely story with me and tried to persuade me to embrace the Christian God again, but I couldn't.

I was looking forward to a new community awaiting me, namely the Objectivists. I knew I was an objectivist when I read a compilation of essays written by Ayn Rand in high school. That summer of 2014, I was eager to attend the summer conference held by the Ayn Rand Institute after I finished reading the English version of *Introduction to Objectivist Epistemology*. However, I had to let it pass due to the time conflict. More importantly, I feared that traveling across the country with a legal stigma on me was too much of a hassle. Theoretically, the conference was to be held after the dismissal of my case, but my mind was still haunted. I decided to prioritize my healthcare appointments before moving on to philosophy.

If you have read *The Fountainhead,* you should know that the protagonist Howard Roark had to face the court of law in that fiction, despite his true integrity. In contrast, the justice system in that fiction was just a machine controlled by those with power and wealth. The real world we live in is probably better than that. After reading *Atlas shrugged* in 2016, I understood the world better and felt less stigmatized. That's when I thought I was ready to go to the conference to meet with other fellows. The "side effect" of attending the conference was that I could easily spot hypocrisy in my surroundings. Not surprisingly, Asians were super rare in this conference for a Western ideology, but with Objectivism as our common ground, I felt included again, at least by my peers and our intellectual leaders. Indeed, it was a life-changing experience, even if it didn't solve everyday problems for me.

It's worth mentioning that I had seriously overestimated Ayn Rand's popularity and reputation in modern America before I came to the US. How come? As a college student in Shanghai, I studied the translated version of *Introduction to Objectivist Epistemology*. The Chinese publisher claimed on its back cover that *Atlas Shrugged* had a total book sale in America only second to the Bible and that she was one of the most influential authors in 20th-century America. Both campaign slogans were seductive enough to foreign readers like me, whether or not they were accurate. Today, knowing that Objectivists are the minority in 21st-century America, I still choose to stick with these fellows. I was never converted; I simply belong with these people. As someone trained in empirical science, I never feel the need to use mainstream philosophy to make myself look sophisticated or look like a moral person.

As you can see, people in China were not my support system for this specific incident until the case was dismissed because I consciously excluded them from it. But why? Because I didn't feel close to them at all. Because they had never been spiritually supportive throughout my growth. All they wanted to do was negate me, control me, utilize me, or want me to give up my American dream. When I was in a crisis, they would habitually ask me to pacify the opposing party or push through the pain. Of course, not all families in Chinese culture are like that. Mine is particularly irrational and pathetic for some historical reasons. Even Mr. Frost told me during one meeting, "You don't have to tell them." But when I felt I had survived the traumatic period and was ready for their judgment, I progressively informed them of the case. During a Skype call, Mandy told me not to dwell on a civil case like this and prepare to graduate peacefully; Doug told me not to threaten people whatsoever— cogent advice from someone who beat me up when I wrote the Chinese equivalent of "I WANT FREEDOM!" on paper and stuck it to the front door in third grade. In another Skype call with my elder cousin Lulu, she blamed me for being stupid and gullible while trying to hide her tears. Her parents just told me to move back to China because I would always be disadvantaged in America. I didn't shed a tear over these video chats because my tears were drained out already. Now I think I have lived through the tragedy and can transcend this bizarre life story, so I have less fear about sharing this history with the civilized world. Why should I bring all the secrets with me into the morgue, after all?

10.6 Another Cortisone Shot

The pain in my left hand, which was coded as wrist pain in the electronic medical system at OSU, still hadn't disappeared completely. However, physical therapy and acupuncture helped a great deal. Because MRI didn't show any structural change in my tissues, the hand specialist had to agree with my friend in Shanghai that it was tenosynovitis. While microsurgery was an option, I chose to get a second cortisone shot, which would send the drug more pervasively across my hand. The hand specialist had a hard time determining where to put the needle, but once he decided, the needle went very deep between my hand bones, and the shot lasted for 20 seconds or so.

"Survived," he said.

"Only a specialist can do this," I said.

The second cortisone shot turned out to be more of a success. It sealed the shooting pain in its source like my songs sealed the emotional pain in my brain and gut. Acupuncture appointments ensued to help eliminate the pain in the forearm and the phalanges, but it took a year or so for my left wrist to fully recover from that fall. In retrospect, the medical system in the US played a big role in delaying the correct diagnosis of my condition, without which physical therapy would not be effective at its maximum. A similar tragedy occurred in 2015 at UC Davis, whose consequences could linger on for the rest of my life.

10.7 Summer Housing

Before Kayah, the condo-mate in Upper Arlington returned from her trip, I had already decided to move out of that deadly quiet rich neighborhood. Since I would mainly be active on the Main Campus that summer, I found a single-room sublet near South Campus through Craigslist. The available bedroom was on the upper floor of a duplex apartment. It was the buyer's market in the summer because a lot of students were working in other cities as interns. Charlotte helped me make a sound decision, which allowed me to stay 4, instead of 3 months in the college area, with easy access to downtown resources, by which I mean the music venues. I have to nag again: many students whose departments were located on the Main Campus were living near the South Campus from the beginning. They didn't need a car at all.

There was a hitch for me. What if the landlord wanted to do a background check on me? I wasn't overthinking this matter. At that time, I didn't know there was nothing for them to see. The Indian guy who rented out his room to me didn't ask much about me; he even told his co-tenants that I was a grad student in mathematics. I got in smoothly and got along with those STEM or pre-med undergrads with no difficulty. I liked that convenient neighborhood very much, except it was loud sometimes. It was my only chance to experience the lifestyle of an American college student in the US, and it healed me incrementally over time. When I was in college, I never had my own room; besides, I had no AC in the dorm, no access to a television, no kitchen, and no bathroom with a toilet. This experience counted as a redemption. These undergrads taught me lots of living skills. At a certain point, when I felt close enough with these smart lads, who were nothing like those spoiled college brats, I told them what had happened to me. I didn't expect them to fully understand its impact on an international student who had given up too much for a one-way ticket into the US. However, I was very grateful that these people were willing to listen in.

One of these co-tenants explained to me that a proportion of medical doctors and medical students in America had developed some notoriety for treating other healthcare professionals with contempt. In the meantime, they didn't always live up to their affidavits. Gosh, I wish I had known this. As a foreigner aware of the high social status of the medical profession in America, I did assume they were all admirable elites.

After living with these folks for a while, I had little doubt they would never develop into someone like Jeremy, despite their respective peculiarities. In contrast with these "innocent" and empathetic people, I sometimes worried I was the old-aged black sheep in the apartment.

Gradually, I was able to appreciate the downtown area of the city, with the company of old and new friends. Seriously, the previous lack of effective means of transportation blocked my view. My life had been too passive simply because I was stranded far from downtown. If you weren't happy as a student, how could you expect to be happy when you became an employee? If you weren't happy as a child, how could you expect to be happy when you became an adult? Remember that all hardships will not result in good outcomes as people wish.

Due to my uncertainty about the future and some miscommunication with a co-tenant, I wasn't able to keep this place for the subsequent fall semester, which forced me to look for another flexible lease. Yes, all over again. It was exhausting, and this time, the address moved to the northbound of the city, almost close to Dublin, Ohio. Did I like that area compared to downtown? Hell no. But the rent was substantially cheaper. I was like a boat on the sea, blown by a tornado here and there. Since I had learned to drive on Freeway 315 to the campus area by then, I managed to attend the songwriters' showcase every month until the snowflakes of late 2014 started to hit my face relentlessly. I mean, in October.

One day, I gave a new Ph.D. student from India a heads-up that the winter snowstorm in the Midwest would last for several months. She dropped her jaw at that moment. Clearly, she hadn't been warned about the harshness of the local climate by anybody, certainly not by any local Americans or her boss. She was planning to stay in Ohio for at least five years, like I was, with high hopes. The climate was that crucial variable we had failed to take seriously before moving to the US.

Chapter 11
Searching for An Attorney

11.1 The Horny Attorney

It was the first week of the May session, the less busy month of the summer term. I had no coursework registered for that month. In the music lab, I rehearsed the thesis defense, and people showed enthusiasm about the research topic.

On the day of the thesis defense, I wore a white Buckeye T-shirt in front of Mr. Hoffman and Mr. Osman. I got that T-shirt for free during the Homecoming parade sponsored by the Medical Center. On the back of the T-shirt was the mascot, Brutus Buckeye saying, "March for victory." The project I worked on under Mr. Osman was attacked very hard by Mr. Hoffman for its objective flaws. Within an institution, professors normally don't attack one another's work; they target the grad students instead. I felt no emotional response at all because compared to the series of traumas I went through in the previous months, it was pretty mild and fair. Pure academic discussion, for the most part.

Like my former colleague who had a baby to deliver the day after her Ph.D. dissertation defense, I had a therapy session scheduled for the afternoon following my thesis defense. Of course, it was a coincidence of scheduling, not because I expected the thesis defense to be mentally disruptive for me. When Teresa congratulated me on this "milestone," I told her this wasn't something I would personally celebrate. I didn't think a non-clinical master's degree in this clinical field could make me competitive in the job market at all. Outside academia, I didn't know what to do about it. Other people's comforting words never affected me much. As people can see, my grad school experience with academia wasn't very fruitful because so much time was used to cope with everyday life's major and minor difficulties. My friends who studied in New York City or Boston never had to deal with any of these — not that I know of.

After I passed the defense, I didn't rush to revise my thesis. Instead, I took out my old documents from the court despite Teresa's warning and embarked on the journey of searching for an attorney. At first, I called the court and asked them how to find one. One of their clerks told me to call the Bar Association. When I told the Bar Association it was about a protection order, the man on the line first responded, "Did you say your case was dismissed already? Why don't you go get the forms from the court and file a motion by yourself?"

"Because the magistrate told me to hire an attorney," I said.

The guy on the phone reluctantly recommended two names to me. I called the first one, and their paralegal answered, "Just so you know, our retainer fee for a protection order is $3000. Think about it and let us know. Have a nice day." Then he hung up.

D*mned. I took a deep breath and called the second number. An appointment was successfully made with this law firm near German Village, whose owner was a senior white man.

Since it was in the May session, with no classes, Ashley offered to go to the law firm with me in case I got ripped off.

During the initial consultation, the guy told me the hourly rates of each attorney and each paralegal in his firm. "I need money to play golf and to send my grandson to learn the violin," he said with a smile.

"Rich people," I thought to myself.

He then said he needed to do some research to make sure a protection order could be **expunged** in Ohio. At that time, I was already confusing the word "seal" with "expunge" and using them interchangeably without realizing it, after Mr. Frost brought up the latter. Besides, I forgot to bring some paperwork that day, so we decided to meet another day. In retrospect, among the documents I forgot to bring, there might be one page that mentioned the word "**seal**." Before I left, he told me to go to the courthouse to ask for a specific form while he estimated the cost for me.

"Hope next time we see each other, you can still bring this lady with you." His focus shifted from me to Ashley, who was sitting next to me. "She's more beautiful than you."

I was holding my breath at that moment. "That was so weird." I thought. Later, I told Antonio I met a horny lawyer, and he said, "Slim, are you sure you understand that word?!" I told Mr. Parker about this conversation, and he said I should report it to the Bar Association. Of course, I didn't have time for that. Nor did I bother to ask Ashley how she felt about that, but I suspected she might already be used to that kind of compliment. To be fair, she didn't have a Hollywood celebrity kind of look, no make-up; what she had was subdued composure as a musician, instead.

When I finally arrived at the courthouse by bus, I was blocked by two "mischievous" African-American guys at the security checkpoint because it was kind of late for the day. They first told me it was closed and then allowed me in. I understood they didn't see many Asian faces in this courthouse. Meanwhile, I was convinced they wouldn't play the same prank on white people in the court. They reminded me of those two middle school classmates who often tried to scare me during the breaks. These attention-seeking "tricksters" were not inherently vice but annoying.

I went upstairs and asked the only professional-looking gentleman in my sight where to collect certain forms. He was an African American, too.

"Oh no, that office is already closed for today. The attorney is supposed to collect the form for you."

Then I asked about the plausibility of filing a motion by myself.

"Who told you to file a motion by yourself? Then you'll have to study in the law library for a long time. Don't be silly. You need an attorney to represent you, and they will have access to the forms."

D*mned. He helped me realize that whoever told me to DIY probably thought my tiny dismissed case was not worth their precious time. That's particularly true for big law firms, though this case was a big deal for a man like me at that time.

The horny lawyer told me in our subsequent email correspondence that his total charge, or flat fee, was going to be $750 and asked me if I wanted to proceed. When I texted this quote to Ashley, she reminded me that it would be wise to call another attorney and compare the price. But who? Then it struck me that Mr. Parker had circled two law firms on the pamphlet he gave me. I called the first number, and it turned out to be empty. I called the second number, and the paralegal picked up the phone and delivered my request to their attorney Ms. Wilson. After a minute, he returned to the phone, "Sorry, Mr. Sun, Ms. Wilson says a protection order cannot be expunged in the state of Ohio. We are unable to help you with this case." A new heart attack just struck me.

11.2 Your Case Cannot Be Expunged...

My heart was beating fast. My future was doomed. My psyche went into a downward spiral again. I carried on for two months and then was told that the bad record would always be there for people to judge. So why did I even try so hard to get my degree in the first place? Why did I take all the trouble to collect the data for a premature project? Why did I even study English harder than most people around me? Why did I trade my freedom for a top-ranking GPA in college while many peers were cheating on the exams? If this bad record would affect me for the rest of my life, I couldn't even get into a good grad school again, not to mention become a scientist. That's the real permanent record, as Edward Snowden would call it.

I called the court and asked them why the lawyer's words contradicted Magistrate Turner's statement.

"If Magistrate Turner says you can seal it, then you should be able to." The voice on the other side said.

"But the attorney I was trying to hire said a protection order cannot be expunged," I said anxiously.

"Only a criminal case can be expunged. Yours is a civil case, so it can only get sealed."

There came my big relief. From the moment Mr. Frost brought up the word "expunge," I didn't even bother to look it up on my phone but assumed it was a fancier way to say "seal." For native speakers, especially people working in a related profession, these two words looked remarkably different, but for me, they were both just abstract concepts. Similar to medical terms, legal terms were designed to be more complicated than colloquial terms so that laypeople could not decipher them. Clearly, Mr. Frost, in his thirties or forties at that time, had rarely dealt with such a weird case as mine before; otherwise, he would have known the difference between these two words. The same probably applied to Teresa, who worked with many student clients every day. This was a typical situation where I wished I had known less. It was stupid of me to let an unfamiliar word slip into my vocabulary without fully understanding it.

Of course, I still didn't have the gut to put explicit blame on another university employee, knowing his hands had a lot of power over students' life trajectories. I mentioned it during my subsequent email update to him, and he replied, "Thank you for your clarification. I'm glad you have a lawyer to help you with the case." What came to mind was, "Dude, do you know that the school lawyer can never represent me, and I have to pay a high price for the service elsewhere?" That's how my life went. Thankfully, none of these attorneys I ever met overcharged me. One has to admit that the legal fees in Ohio were much lower than in the coastal states, just like the rent.

Anyway, I called Ms. Wilson's law firm again and told her paralegal that I had made a mistake previously— it should be "seal" instead of "expunge." At first, he responded, "Uh...What the attorney said was that your case cannot be sealed." As I insisted that he talk to Ms. Wilson again, he said, "Okay, I'll let her know when she's out of the meeting." My gut feeling told me that this paralegal was no more than a paralegal on this issue, and I didn't like his attitude of pushing things away like a bureaucrat. Interestingly, later that year, I found out Ms. Wilson replaced him with a new

SEARCHING FOR AN ATTORNEY

paralegal for whatever reason. I liked the new guy much better because he was willing to offer his personal opinions cogently for my accessory questions.

After half an hour, Ms. Wilson called me and told me she would look into my case, so we set up a time for the initial consultation. Ashley agreed to come with me again. She even arrived earlier to secure a parking spot for me. We finally met Ms. Wilson, who seemed very professional. She told me she used to work with Mr. Parker, and she would recommend an immigration lawyer to me in case I wanted to see how this record would impact my future in America. She thought a few steps ahead of me. And yes, during the summer, I did ask her for that kind of referral.

Ms. Wilson explained to me that **it's better to stay vague when one makes the first phone call to a law firm so that unnecessary miscommunication can be avoided**. She also explained that a protection order is considered **quasi-criminal**, which is why my whole experience was so horrific. I didn't go to the criminal court, but sitting in front of me was a lawyer who specialized in all sorts of criminal cases. Luckily, my case was dismissed, but my life could have been much worse if the other party had intended to torture me. I was only one step from hell and constantly walking on a wire.

"Do you watch American football? If you do, you should know that after moving forward so many yards, you are very close to a **touchdown**. So just hang in there." She then said she would go to the courthouse to get all the necessary paperwork and see if she could get the waiting period any shorter. That week, I found out I had misread the piece of paper signed by Magistrate Turner: the waiting period after the dismissal was meant to be another 6 months instead of 2 months in my false memory, and therefore, the sealing process couldn't start right away. But anyway, they quickly sent an attorney's letter to Jeremy to obtain his agreement to shorten the second waiting period. No response from him. No surprise. As I told the paralegal over the phone, "I know that guy's personality very well."

According to Ms. Wilson, most employers wouldn't be able to see my case because it wasn't listed in the public record. However, the government or those sensitive employers demanding high clearance could find a way to see it before and after the sealing. Such is what Edward Snowden would call a "permanent record," in the same sense that every entry in a database will still be available for query even after being deleted on the surface. I've understood it since college, from my engineering coursework. "Big Brother" has been and will be watching us forever.

See? This explains why Magistrate Turner couldn't give me a definite answer in that courtroom. It was complicated. I knew I wanted my case to be sealed, but even that wouldn't guarantee anything. By the way, regarding the cost, Ms. Wilson offered me a discounted rate because I was an enrolled student at OSU.

I didn't tell her how much Ohio State football I had watched in those two years, but her question did bring back some memories. I watched the home games in Ohio Stadium in 2013 and pretended to understand what was going on in the blizzard. I enjoyed watching Buckeyes defeating Penn State without effort, which made Jeremy very upset— he said on Facebook that his allegiance would never change when provoked by his friend from college. I also enjoyed eating the $6 hot pretzel sold in Ohio Stadium. After each game, when exiting the stadium, thousands of Buckeye fans were chanting, "we don't give a damn about the whole state of Michigan, the whole state of Michigan, the whole state of Michigan..." It felt like the scene after a big concert, where people would resist saying goodbye to their idol and going home. The chanting I participated in seemed like a fun exhibition of American-styled tribalism because most frantic fans were in denial of the "excellence" of Michigan Ann Arbor as a higher-ranking institution. I had never been to Michigan, but I imagined they would do something similar to OSU in revenge. End of the season, I also carpooled to Indianapolis for the final game with two strangers and watched the Buckeyes being defeated by Michigan State, not Michigan Ann Arbor. Unlike the Ohio State versus Penn State game, the final game was well worth the price.

However, in the year 2014, I didn't watch any football after graduation because I figured I was no longer obligated to care about the football team of a university that added to my suffering; besides, I am not a big fan of violent sports in general. Tailgating? Absolutely yes.

11.3 The Thesis, Let It Go, and LinkedIn

After hiring Ms. Wilson to take care of the residual matter, I started to address the revision of my thesis. First and foremost, I replaced my old HP laptop from college with a Toshiba notebook. I liked this brand so much, but in hindsight, the machine was still too heavy, considering it was already 2014. I carried it to the Science and Engineering Library every evening to work on my thesis, particularly some regression analysis graphs made with R, a programming language for statistics.

During this period, I met with Mr. Osman for the last time in a coffee shop to discuss how to revise the thesis. He no longer worked for Ohio State and was about to move back to California. I mentioned I had been seeing an acupuncturist for my wrist pain, and he told me he had used acupuncture for his arms when he was younger.

After several rounds, the thesis was approved by Mr. Hoffman and ready to be submitted to the grad school. Finally, I made it without going back to the basement on the West Campus again. When I went there one last time and took out my books and files from the office, I left a thick stack of academic papers in the recycle bin, most of which were discussed during Mr. McCarthy's seminar. "Too heavy to carry." I thought to myself, "Electronic files will do." But in retrospect, the notes I wrote on the papers were priceless. Some graduate students I knew were dedicated enough to scan their notes into PDF files, but I wasn't that patient. I just hated burdens as much as I hated the spotlight on me.

During the summer term that year, the song *Let It Go* from the movie *Frozen* went viral. I didn't resonate much with that song because I hadn't fully recovered from the trauma series. It's easier to make a good wish than to accomplish it. Nevertheless, in a specific event organized by some student club, I sent a balloon with my handwritten note "Disappear from my life, White Coat Devil!" into the sky, in the company of many other students. After that ritual, I also received a blue T-shirt which I liked very much. There was a cute yellow balloon on that shirt with the text "let it go." I once told that buddy who graduated from Case Western Reserve, "You can get a lot of free stuff if you enroll in Ohio State." And he giggled.

That summer, whenever I saw someone whose face or back resembled Jeremy from a distance, I would walk a different path without hesitation, as I had practiced in that crucial therapy session. I chose not to face the "devil"

SEARCHING FOR AN ATTORNEY

anymore for the sake of my mental health. Remember that you walk around the feces on the street not because it's scary but because it's disgusting— according to Korean wisdom.

Jeremy didn't respond to the attorney's letter, so I had to wait 6 months in full. Strangely enough, he almost entered my life again through the Internet. Back in 2013, when he first moved into the "Shining" House, I sent him a request on LinkedIn, but he never accepted it. Over time, I totally forgot about that, but then, in the fall of 2014, I got this email notifying me that "Your friend Jeremiah has just accepted your request. Start networking with him!"

I was terrified. My case was already dismissed, and I was waiting to get it sealed. I was close to a touchdown. Besides, he had said in the courtroom that he didn't want to communicate with me anymore. He probably hadn't logged on to LinkedIn since he entered med school, but why did he accept my request after I graduated? Was he trying to sympathize with me, knowing I wanted to network with the "elites"? Or was he trying to bait me so that he could gather evidence to file another restraining order against me, as Magistrate Turner conjectured? To end this terror, I forced myself to make a bold and perhaps irrational decision: considering I didn't have many connections other than with my friends in the US, I deleted my LinkedIn account and didn't reopen it until 2015. I was paranoid about being followed all this time, and I even changed my phone number for that reason.

That's what the trauma did to a person who was originally so career-oriented. "To develop separately" was just a wish. I knew he would stay in the elite group until he hit his own ceiling while I still had to search for the meaning of my life at sea.

11.4 Other People's Land

In the summer of 2014, Mandy said in an earnest tone, "You are on other people's land, and you don't know other people's laws. If you have any direct conflict with the Americans, the rule will be in their favor."

Teresa concurred. And this problem would never be solved, even if I, by the slightest chance, got a green card or citizenship in the US. Compared to people who grew up in America, I lacked so much useful knowledge and practical skills. If that fact determines I could never truly enter the mainstream American culture but instead had to stay in a small ethnic clique for the rest of my life, as game theory predicted, then what's the point of becoming an American? Of course, some immigrants came to America merely for the resources, the welfare, or the superior status, and that's understandable – no one voluntarily migrates to hell.

Here we go. Some people attributed my tragedy to "messing with the Americans." These tend to be the people who have never been to America or seen the true face of American society. This world is changing, and no country stays the same. However, the gaps between developed countries and developing countries are still remarkable. In any country, some revolutionists want to make a change, while some nationalists fool themselves into the delusion that they are superior somehow.

A senior Chinese immigrant in Los Angeles once told me in the United States, people working on their visa have to yield to those with a green card, who, in turn, have to yield to legal citizens. Therefore, I'll have to start low and be marginalized wherever I go. That's like forcing me to go through my early stage of life again. How cruel and insane is that! But life is what it is.

SEARCHING FOR AN ATTORNEY

I have read that Chinese visitors are warned not to have a direct conflict with the locals in many countries, such as Thailand, as the law enforcement of those countries will make sure to protect the locals as a priority. Strangely, the reason they mentioned was "those are capitalistic countries." I'm not sure how capitalism can be the foundation for protecting local citizens, but this comment did imply that the alternative type of country does not bias in favor of its own citizens. It might sound ridiculous to you, but it's true in many ways. To me, it's consistent with their culture. My personal experience of growing up in such a culture allowed me to realize that a lot of parents in collectivist countries, including my own, would never protect their offspring from bullies. How can one love their guardians when the latter fails to do their job for the sake of diplomacy? Similarly, if an administration doesn't prioritize the interest of its citizens, why should people vote for them?

In one session with Teresa, I cried so hard while telling her how irresponsible Mandy and Doug were in terms of protecting my rights. Whenever I was bullied or humiliated by my classmates or depressed by the teachers, they would never speak up for me but either blamed me for my fragility or just rationalized that a student with high academic scores deserves more plights in life in order to be successful later in life— the hollow belief in "future." Praising other people's kids as a strategy to shame one's own child into submission was another innate fatal disease in modern Chinese culture. However, people like me learned to counterattack tyranny. I tended to compare my chromosome providers with other successful parents who were bosses, engineers, intellectuals, or celebs. It wouldn't always be effective, as it is human nature to get defensive when feeling dwarfed. This strategy is antithetical to the conventional

Chinese virtue, that is, to succumb to your parents no matter what, simply because they brought you into this world.

One of my classmates in elementary school once told me that her dad went to the school to argue with the mean teacher Mei, after she reported to him that Mei used some adult-level insulting words on her. She wasn't a top student back then, but her parent knew their responsibility to protect her young psyche from external savages. In contrast, when Mei or other teachers wronged me, my chromosome providers would only say, "She was strict with you because she wanted you to be better. She likes you. Don't take the criticism personally."

But as I remember, I was always targeted, particularly because I was among the high-yield ones. The top-league students have the highest potential to bring these educators benefits and honors. Those control freaks feared losing compliance from top-league students, who often exhibited the strongest desires for liberty and innovation. Unfortunately, Mandy and Doug never understood that simple fact, as they craved the teachers' attention when they were little kids. The consequence? My classmate loved her dad when she grew up. Me? Estranged.

A truly rational man ought to know that one shouldn't waste time trying to find positive-looking solutions for all the feuds simply to satisfy the public expectation for reconciliation and positivity.

11.5 Why I Don't Hate America

If you wonder, after a series of traumas with some Americans, why didn't I turn my back on America?

First, the word "America" as a conglomerate means nothing to me anymore. I interacted with each individual

SEARCHING FOR AN ATTORNEY

separately. I was deeply hurt by a couple of individuals and punished by two "justice" systems in the same city, but I was helped by more American friends and colleagues. Some people viewed me as crazy, but that was because I had to keep this stigma from the public, fearing it would be used against me wherever I went. That was my legitimate concern. They only saw my emotion, but not my reason. Since I no longer share the same values with those academics, I have no desire to hide that shadow inside me and bring it to the morgue with me. Yesterday was a dirty page, and I tried not to tear it up.

Second, I hit the curb myself out of ignorance and lack of prior knowledge. From this life experience, I realized that people like me who act upon justice and respect for human rights are often outliers in society, independent of culture. I didn't want to be the nail to be hammered. I was simply exploited too much when I was a powerless student.

Third, there was nothing illegal for the other party to protect himself using any quick-and-dirty resource he knew. He was who he was, and you shouldn't expect him to handle things differently. Meanwhile, the court system and the school officials were just doing their jobs based on their perceptions and biases. They had no control over the law or student codes. The weapon of a restraining order was harsh and prone to abuse, but it was invented for a reason and can benefit some victimized individuals. It's just how human society works. In my particular case, I had zero prior knowledge of such an ex-parte weapon, which is how I got traumatized. As I stated earlier, the fact that I didn't receive basic education in a country like America was the fundamental cause of the loophole. Since I interacted with US citizens deeper than most Asian international students would, I naturally suffered more than average. By the way, my extremely high level of stress and distress could be attributed to my lack of a decent "home" to return to in a crisis, unlike those rich kids growing up in major cities in China.

People from various countries agree that Americans like to abuse litigation in solving problems, rigidly and religiously. Welcome to modern America. It's not a paradise for ordinary immigrants but a place full of risks. Contrary to your intuition, I think the brutal way they treated me demonstrated their willingness to protect their own middle-class citizens, especially since the other party was a medical student. They're not supposed to prioritize a foreigner's well-being over their own citizen's safety. Protection of the citizens' rights is what makes America attractive to refugees. In contrast, some Asian developing country condones a series of inhumane behavior, such as parents beating their kids, teachers punishing the students physically or verbally, a chauvinistic husband beating his wife in the name of traditional values, or men being sexually harassed or assaulted by both genders — media coverage used to be largely suppressed due to the sensitivity of these topics.

This next issue to bring to your awareness is a controversial one. In an online Chinese article I've read, the author claims that America has a system that bullies you and makes you feel it's your own fault. This viewpoint sounded appealing to me initially because it is consistent with the inferiority complex often embodied in people with a minority status or some inherent disadvantages. It fit me and made me feel "understood."

However, I no longer buy the "inferiority complex" theory that is often used as a scapegoat for sensitive root causes. In my eyes, disadvantages or maladaptive characteristics have objective impacts; they make one's life harder in a world full of bloody competition, whether or not one feels inferior to those with advantages. The psychological factors here are only derivative or secondary. Therefore, the attempt to get rid of or hide your disadvantageous attributes can be seen as adaptive. It is rational but will inevitably hurt some people's feelings. No, not everybody wants to associate themselves with their ethnicity of birth, especially if the conventional ethnic values clash with their personal values, if specific ethnic behavior is viewed as annoying, cultish, or barbaric in a more civilized society, or if this ethnic identity brings them discrimination or even danger. Among the immigrants and expats across the world, I wasn't alone in trying to dissociate myself from the label imposed on me. However, it's their human nature to assume my behavior pattern based on my appearance unless they disdained my appearance per se.

From the podcast *Jeselnik & Rosenthal Vanity Project*, I learned from Gregg Rosenthal that some Jews aren't proud of the Jewish label because this collective identity makes them prone to hostility and victimization. They aren't hiding something; they simply want to belong with the mainstream and the ordinary. I hear them; I feel them.

Despite my partial background in academic psychology, I hate to see psychological effects being magnified or over-emphasized in the modern world in an attempt to cover up actual medical or societal problems. However, there is no marginal cost to blame everything on one's mental health or weaknesses in one's personality. That's what makes the victims suffer more. I am telling you based on my first-hand experience. One simple example that many people can relate to is when a self-conceited clinician you see is unable to identify the physical root cause of your health problem. Instead of realizing their own limitations, they may throw the ball back at you, "Are you sure it's not psychogenic?" While every chronic ailment has a psychological component, eliminating that component alone can never solve the actual physical problem. In the real world, whether or not a clinician behaves in an overconfident manner largely depends on the person's temperament and horizon. If they feel like their authority can't be challenged but fail to convince you through reasoning, then you need to get out of that situation smartly.

As a former international student who only had a superficial understanding of what was happening in America back then, if I hated America simply because I was alienated or treated unfairly, that would be the same logic as "I can't have you, so I'll destroy you" — the typical criminal mindset. As many Chinese people hoped, I never fell into that kind of mental trap. America isn't perfect, but still better than most developing countries with a pure collectivist mindset.

A country that treats its citizens better than it treats foreigners is a country that deserves the patriotism of its citizens. At least for mainstream Americans, America seems to be a homeland to be proud of. For most Black, Latino, and Native Americans, I don't have a solid opinion. Asian Americans have always been marginalized, but I'm sure most of them love America better than where their ancestors migrated from.

Parents that verbally or behaviorally treat their children better than they treat other people's children deserve their children's filial love — that indicates their children are deemed as their true value, not just assets. Unfortunately, I, as well as many other Asian kids, am not fortunate enough to have parents like that. When childhood and teenage years are savaged, there is no cure for the scars, only coping strategies. Be careful not to confuse this natural consequence with the rebellious stage for every teenager. However, as I see through it now, when person A calls another person B rebellious or disobedient, it indicates A wants to exert control over B. Who gives them the right to control another individual with free will? The intrinsic inequality of human society. The asymmetry of power. I never liked the military atmosphere, as I hated to be commanded by other minds, and I knew that since I was a kid. Some folks only like the cool side of being disciplined without understanding the suffocating "chain of command," as depicted in Edward Snowden's memoir.

Do I still love America? America is more of an ideal than a reality. If you know how horrible the climate can be in different states and how inefficient the public transportation and the healthcare system are in most regions, you will think twice before moving there. Higher education? People have doubts about the true value of this concept. Also, American higher education is notoriously overpriced. I guess I didn't love America as a whole from the very beginning; only the cosmopolitan cities and some dimensions that my country of origin could never provide, such as respect for the human rights of minors and ethnocultural diversity. I can't but ask myself, nowadays, are these selling points unique to America, or are they available in every developed country?

PART THREE

At the end of life, I smile to you
On the back of my face, tears falling down
Before I can jump out of the plane
I don't know what to expect
What the f*ck am I gonna do?
What if I can't meet you again?
There were a million words I planned to say...

— *Parachute*, original song written in 2014

Chapter 12
The Last Summer and the Group Therapy

12.1 Group Therapy

In the first week of the summer term of 2014, I was invited to an initial meeting with Jacob (T2), the group therapy leader for male grad students, and Noah (T4), the co-facilitator during that academic year. Jacob had long, blonde hair, which was sometimes tied into a man bun. He would always speak calmly, giving people the impression that he had lived through a lot or at least seen through a lot. He was also the program director of multiple therapy groups. Noah, an Asian-Pacific American, was a final-year grad student fulfilling his clinical internship, and I only met him a few sessions before he left. I told them my concern that the existing members might see me as a dangerous person because of my stigma, but they assured me that I should be able to fit in. There I went, a two-hour group session once a week, heart-to-heart with other grad students.

It's worth mentioning that the members were all intelligent male grad students from various programs. Therefore, this group therapy didn't look like the Alcoholics Anonymous meetings or a rehab group for the incarcerated, which you sometimes see on TV screens. We had no cultish rituals to practice, either. Besides the common self-care techniques Jacob taught us, such as recognizing our own emotions, the weekly discussion occasionally went very deep and philosophical. When I first joined the group, I thought my situation was devastating enough. Then I learned that American grad students were also going through fire and water. Everyone had their professional circles outside the group, but everyone still felt lonely and helpless sometimes.

This experience in the group made me more American than before and prepared me for my voluntary work in the pediatric autism intervention program two years later in Sacramento, California — that "social skills training program" was essentially group therapy.

For the sake of confidentiality and my respect for them, I cannot name these important figures in my therapy group. However, I believe it's meaningful to list them here just to commemorate the precious mutual understanding between us. Among these gents, some were single as I was, some were married with kids, and some were divorced.

The Buddha was a student in an Occupational Therapy program who became a firm believer in Buddhism through some life events. He was sometimes agitated but very concerned for other members of the group. Stud and Mark Twain were both senior Ph.D. students studying Literature, and they sometimes spoke a literary language that I couldn't understand. Stud spoke extremely fast, despite his huge body size, while Mark Twain was a gentle and caring dad. The Alchemist was a sentimental Ph.D. student in Biochemistry, and Titan was an amazingly tall Ph.D. student in Quantum Physics. We also had Turing, a Ph.D. student in Software Engineering, who looked shy and down most of the time, despite his geeky talent. He was the only Latino guy in the group. Finally, we had Likert, an outstanding Ph.D. student in Organizational Psychology, who allegedly joined the group just to observe the group dynamics instead of by referral from an individual therapist. Not surprisingly,

I was the only Asian and probably the only international student in a predominantly white male group. This experience consolidated my belief that whether or not two English-speaking individuals could build a deep connection had very little to do with race or ethnicity. Sometimes politics and history can become barriers, especially if the individuals involved have a strong sense of tribal affiliation or allegiance, but my story didn't delve into that dimension. However, I couldn't speak for other international students because some of them couldn't care less to interact with people outside their ethnic groups at all— it simply wasn't in their plan to get assimilated from the very beginning, just like many first-generation immigrants in California nowadays. It's a matter of personal choice. Whatever route one chooses, life won't be easy.

We discussed several important issues during my stay, and I prefer to mention only a few that benefited me profoundly, as I am not in a position to teach anybody about the art and science of group therapy.

Firstly, **shame**. Unsurprisingly, I experienced a lot of shame in those years. What did I feel ashamed of? The fact that I brought a horrendous case upon myself, which jeopardized my career? Certainly, an outsider might think that way if they see me as an innocent child instead of a human being with flesh and blood. But that's not the deepest layer of my shame. I was ashamed of being cheated and played by another male student and further traumatized by the same person. I was ashamed of ignoring my gut feelings and losing my judgment to a silly girl. I was ashamed of having to force myself to yield to the person who hurt me, knowing he was in a legally superior position. I was ashamed of choosing to secure my stay in America and my so-called academic reputation over my fragile dignity. I was ashamed of being traumatized by the "justice" system and freezing like a coward, just like when I was a student in China under the tyranny of those teachers who choked me with their ill-deserved power. I was ashamed of surrendering to the ruthless world against my instinct to fight. I wasn't sure if it was all worth it when I got a master's degree, a degree I wasn't proud of — when one gives up A for the sake of B and then loses both A and B, the level of shame is enough to put one in depression. However, had I chosen my dignity over my legal status in America, I would have felt a great loss after leaving America and would have quickly fallen into a mental breakdown or a suicidal state. The shame of being kicked out of America would haunt me for the rest of my shortened life span unless I knew how to rationalize the entire matter. When I had to pick my poison, I picked the one that was less lethal, less shameful and reserved more hope for me in that situation, even though the decision might seem vane and irrational to people outside my inner circle.

Shame was a common problem for men in this group because we all made mistakes out of ignorance and sometimes fell into the pitfalls of the jungle. After all, we were still students in the ivory tower, with little power and little defense. When you are ashamed, you have to accept it and accept that it will take a long time to process the shame engendered by each of your major errors.

Secondly, **personal values**. I had already learned about the importance of values from Ayn Rand's non-fiction books. However, in this group therapy the Buddha recommended a practical way to sort out our internal values. We had a stack of cards with tangible or abstract values. Each person was told to pick the top five and share them with other group members. From that process, I realized why we were so similar and so different. I personally consider the hierarchy of values to be one's privacy, and one shouldn't share it with others easily because each of your values can be viewed as your weakness. For instance, a kidnapper can hold your child hostage because your child is your value.

As I remember, after the "gambler" Mr. Osman daunted me in a three-party lab meeting at UC Davis in 2015, I had a painful conversation with Mr. Shapiro, where he kept defending Mr. Osman's irrationality— Mr. Shapiro had only been Mr. Osman's employee for 2 weeks. When I mentioned that tolerating the irrationality of Mr. Osman posed harm to my personal values, he asked me slowly, "what are your values?" I didn't know how to answer this blunt question, so I walked out of the office with a sigh. He might have thought I didn't have an answer and just used the word figuratively. Of course, most human beings on this earth have never identified their values explicitly in the way we did. However, they could still function or even prosper better than us. Intellectuality does not guarantee a better life, depending on how you define "better."

Thirdly, **trust**. If I say I couldn't trust anyone after being played by Jeremy, you shouldn't believe that. I still trusted a lot of friends, in addition to my undergrad housemates and those members of the group therapy. Jeremy was peculiar in that he embodied chaos— similar to the chaos in quantum physics. He lied to me several times, always with malevolent intentions or, say, irrational selfishness because he knew he could afford to cheat me with no ramifications. Of course, not all medical or law students were like that, although many were also labeled as arrogant, which wasn't essentially an ethical issue. Incidentally, the future Ph.D.s in my group are technically elites too, but they just don't get the social status they deserve in America. How come? It's easy for an ordinary person to understand what problems a doctor or lawyer is solving, but what a scientist or engineer does backstage is unfathomable to most people— it's a matter of visibility.

Likert, who was about to get his Ph.D., reminded me, "Usually if a person has cheated you twice, you should stay away from that person." It didn't sound like rocket science, but I just couldn't implement it on this particular person, Jeremy, who had fooled me with his glorified title of a med student, which trumped everything questionable about him. I felt as if I would receive public shaming if I accused an elite American student in a "helping" profession of being a hypocrite and betrayer, just like not a single relative of mine would stand on my side when I pointed out the despicable things Mandy and Doug had done to me. Understandably, I wouldn't have been so gullible and vulnerable in China, but in America, the old prediction model broke down.

The word "twice" also rang a bell to me. Outside the group therapy, Mr. Frost from Student Conduct told me, "If a person has made you sick twice, you should definitely stay away from that person." However, once the **attachment** was formed, it was hard to sever it. It would have been easier if we had no overlap in our fields of study. It is common sense that MDs only play certain roles in the broad healthcare industry, but how come they are perceived to be the best, not just by themselves?

Now, as I look back in time, who taught me to use the word "elite" on the med students in America? The Chinese media and educators who wanted to push us to study harder by pointing to foreign students from a distance. "See? Those are people you should align yourself with." These tend to be the people who have never had first-hand interaction with the medical profession in America. The difference in treatment is remarkable. While American educators tend to tell their students, "You are great," even when they aren't prominent, Chinese educators tend to say, "No, you're not, because there are always people better than you." Their justification would be, "Humility is a traditional virtue while complacency is dangerous." Therefore, do I trust these Chinese educators nowadays? Rarely.

To your disappointment, no "trust fall" ceremony was involved in my group therapy. We were a mature group but not a team, in its essence. I, personally, am not a fan of the trust fall, either. I don't think it can prove anything. Meanwhile, does everybody in a group deserve the benefit of the doubt? My answer would no longer be positive as I grow older and realize the world is full of scams and gimmicks. Remember what the Student Advocacy lady said? "Welcome to adulthood." In my opinion, just like respect, trust has to be earned through practice. There shouldn't be a default state of trust. Major banks would agree with me on that when they issue credit cards and loans.

Fourthly, **masculinity**. In 2014, the term "toxic masculinity" wasn't trending on the Internet yet, so we didn't touch that. Most of the group members were moral, sensitive, and self-conscious guys, which partially explained why we ended up in therapy. Douchebags or psychopaths usually drive other people crazy, but they are too macho or self-conceited to seek help. Tears tend to be socially unacceptable for guys, and this therapy group became our safe place to express ourselves. However, I won't talk about other people's crying or the secrets they revealed. All I can say is, I did cry twice in front of these folks. The first time was when I recounted my traumatic experience to these guys during my self-introduction. I had no choice but to open up so early because I consciously knew that the earlier I told people why I came to this group, the earlier I could get help from this group of intelligent brains. In other words, I wanted to make the most of my sessions covered by the insurance company. Life sometimes requires us to take "educated" risks, especially when the potential benefit outweighs the risk.

The second time I lost it was when I saw The Alchemist giving farewell hugs to other guys. This scene was heart-wrenching because it reminded me of the hugs between Jeremy and me— even his hugging was deceitful. That was the last time I cried so hard in the group. Nobody judged each other in the group; instead, people showed empathy naturally and brainstormed about each other's difficulties. There were clashes of ideas and emotions in the room every week, but Jacob and Noah were able to induce the flow in a positive direction and only intervene when necessary. That was their expertise, similar to conducting an orchestra.

In the end, masculinity versus femininity became less of a topic of interest in our group. Everybody recognized that the deliberate separation of Yin and Yang was meaningless. The matter of gender identity might be crucial for another therapy group, but not in this particular one.

Finally, **suicidal ideation**. I have to bring it up again because Turing opened up to us about his despair during one session. Once he started to talk about it, things became easier because, after several seconds of initial silence, the group members started to brainstorm for him or share personal stories. No panic existed here. This was supposed to be a heavy topic, but it was handled differently in the group session. I honestly doubt that most counselors out there today are competent enough to coach a severely suicidal individual, as this would require specialized intervention training and years of experience— not something to expect from a volunteer on a hotline. Besides, even a specialist can't guarantee 100% success simply because there are cases of rational suicide. In those cases, they probably wouldn't even make the call— please, talk to me and help change my mind since I can't do it myself.

I once attended a workshop for suicide intervention held by OSU Graduate School Council at the beginning of the spring semester of 2014. Remember that I had a moment of suicidal ideation immediately after Jeremy cut me off on that snowy day. I was locked up in a lonely condo, isolated, when I came to understand Kayah's rationale to quit her job and travel in Asia for the entire winter, as well as my professor Mr. Anderson's rationale to work in California part-time as a visiting scholar every winter and spring. I also learned that many Ohioans move to warmer states to spend their winter break. In contrast, I found myself tragically stupid to have stayed there and to live alone. But where was my home that I could return to? I have no home in New York City, Los Angeles, or any other major city in the world.

From that workshop, I learned that some students in America also suffered joint pressure from their parents and teachers, and life could be suffocating for them. My personal experience in the last year of high school could attest to that. My experience was actually far worse than average because the tragedy was all rooted in that excessive amount of art courses in elementary school, which Mandy imposed on me in the name of "love." Fortunately, in chronic despair, I realized that the two highly correlated suffocating forces could be mentally combined as one. Therefore, there was still some hope of escape for me.

Ironically, I also learned in the workshop that international male grad students had the highest rate of suicide attempts. I belonged to that highly vulnerable group, but nobody worried about me, definitely not those med students I was entangled with. One might ask, why "suicide attempt" instead of suicidal ideation? Because self-report of any kind of "ideation" isn't reliable data to me. How can one prove that they have thought about something or not? Through the workshop, I realized people like me were so helpless and didn't know when and where to seek help. Think about it: in Ohio State, what percentage of international students knew about the ten free sessions of counseling covered in their mandated Aetna PPO health insurance? No one really reminded grad students who were new to Ohio State and unfamiliar with the resources, especially those students in tiny departments. They would only remind us to buy their football tickets every year.

During the discussion that day, I shared some personal tips with Turing because I knew it always worked for me. As a teenager, whenever I thought about suicide after some triggering event, I would also remind myself that I had never been to my favorite artists' concerts yet, so I must carry on until I could go to college in Shanghai and experience everything I had missed simply because of my birthplace. I asked Turing if he had any person or dream place to use as an anchor of hope, but he said he couldn't think of any.

Unfortunately, this "anchor of hope" method no longer works for me at this age because I listen to totally different music nowadays, and these indie rock artists I like usually live in NYC, LA, London, or Dublin, not Shanghai, not Taipei. More importantly, I have stopped idolizing any human being in this world because I have become aware that the stars I used to idolize tended to be more privileged than me. They were born with advantages I didn't have, such as citizenship in a democracy, genetics for a tall body, an English-speaking environment, a well-educated family, and a happy childhood in which they could begin learning their own favorite musical instrument rather than what their parents imposed on them. I simply had no legitimate way to catch up in those dimensions.

Besides, a geographical anchor sounds unrealistic nowadays, with the advent of Instagram and Virtual Reality, on which you can see other people traveling around the world. This kind of "window shopping" is good enough for someone with subpar mobility. My bad leg has determined that a backpacker's adventure to Yosemite or other spectacular landscapes is out of the question at this stage of life, for the most part. In fact, both of my essential hobbies, namely playing music and traveling, were largely destroyed due to the musculoskeletal issues.

As you might have noticed, the "anchor of hope" is basically some kind of extrinsic motivation to live on. It can work for a while. For example, one can get hooked on a TV series or comic series that gets updated very slowly. In order to see the ending of the story, one has to carry on, and maybe slowly, the suicidal urge will subside and be replaced with some new passion. But so can the person's morale in general: living a long yet hopeless life is no fun. So where do you find the intrinsic motivation to live in this complicated and somewhat f*cked-up human world? From the perspective of Anti-natalism, you have to perform some rational evaluation of any prospect of your life. Ask yourself, is your own life worth continuing? An answer of "yes" requires you to make the rest of your life meaningful by capitalizing on your skills, talents, and social network. Without this contemplation, any kind of superficial comfort or intervention would be no more than temporary relief. A deeply rational person can't be easily hoaxed into pursuing a meaningless life expectancy simply to please other human beings or for the sake of going to heaven.

To be or not to be, that should be a conscious decision. If someone is suicidal under depression, then depression should be treated with some effort, first and foremost, to see if the suicidal ideation could vanish by itself. On the contrary, if depression does not exist, then I consider it unethical to force a person to live an elongated life with excruciating pain because every single day would be suffering for this body and soul. Unfortunately, the concept of "rational suicide" has often been neglected because those positivity cultists cannot tolerate rational people telling non-encouraging truth based on their real-life experiences.

In Turing's case, because he was apparently depressed, his suicidal ideation could not be labeled as rational. One week, Turing's depressive case had a dramatic turnaround, to our surprise and delight. After he brought home a kitten, he became a very different person. He started to share happy moments in his life, such as receiving good feedback on his TA work. It was a huge relief for all the group members. I don't know who came up with this pet idea for him, but that person must know his needs.

Many other sensitive issues were addressed when I was there, but interestingly, any discussion about the tension in a student-mentor relationship had no place in this group. The only new member who wanted to talk about it withdrew from the group after he sensed most topics discussed here were much heavier than his own. However, this should be a common topic for male grad students because only a small fraction truly has no complaints about their advisors or supervisors, especially in a gigantic public school like Ohio State. According to my memory, people tend to assume by default that for a Ph.D. student, if you often talk negatively of a person, using a third-person pronoun, that person is very likely to be your boss in grad school. For instance, hearing me mentioning the term "White Coat Devil" a lot, a Ph.D. student from India tried to counsel me, "Don't take it personally, Slim. You won't have to stomach your professor forever." I was amused, so I had to clarify it to her.

Although I felt less lonely living with many open-minded urban undergrads, the intrusive thoughts still came back to me occasionally when I was alone in my room, especially since my physical pain wasn't gone. In other words, moving from Upper Arlington to a college neighborhood didn't flush out the bad memories completely. The environment changed, but my brain remained somewhat dysfunctional. I learned to live with it and manage it, but it was clear to me that whoever hurt me would go unpunished, according to the hidden rules of human society. Mr. Parker once said to me during a follow-up appointment when I told him about my endless rumination, "If I were you, I would move to a different city." He was right because even the city center, where the courthouses were located, was tainted with my traumatic memories. I never saw his comment as unsolicited advice because I had never planned to stay in Ohio beyond grad school.

Before the end of the summer term, Noah graduated with a Ph.D. and left the group for a different clinic. Seeing I had regained some self-esteem and learned enough coping skills for the near future, my individual therapist Teresa closed my file, but I was allowed to stay with the group for another semester after graduation, with a small co-pay. This was possible because the Aetna student insurance was allowed to be extended for a couple of months after my graduation in August, with limited services available. For example, optometry services were still covered, but immunity shots at the Student Clinic were no longer free to me.

Then the following semester, fall of 2014, a new co-facilitator, Maria (T5), appeared in the group therapy. Maria was a licensed social worker. We were surprised to see a nice lady joining this group, the first time in history since the program was founded. I joked that day, "It's very brave of you to enter the men's lair." For me, it was wonderful to have her in this group since I no longer met with Teresa after graduation. I had another female clinician check on me sometimes, "Slim, do you feel suicidal this week?"

"I am fine this month, but I was definitely suicidal for a moment last winter," I said. I was hit by loneliness, betrayal, and shame right before the New Year.

12.2 Lactose Intolerance and the Bad Leg

Still, it was the summer of 2014, when you could hear Justin Timberlake's song *Mirrors* played everywhere, including from those college students' cars.

While I was observing how my American roommates solved their meal problems every day during the summer, I also noticed that my bowel could no longer tolerate the dairy milk from Kroger, not even the 2% skim milk. Similarly, several types of cheese were making my bowel upset easily. After eating the ice cream from Jeni's on North High Street once, my digestive system collapsed several hours later. Very oily and spicy food, which many Chinese people couldn't live without, would kill my colon and rectum the next morning. When I first arrived in Ohio, I could still grab a cold beer with my American fellows, although I disliked cold drinks. From that summer on, I couldn't even drink any carbonated beverages at room temperature without getting diarrhea afterward.

I didn't know what caused it. To sum it up, I couldn't intake dairy, icy or carbonated drinks, or oily or spicy food. Ice cream or icy beers were double disastrous. When I asked Dr. Clark at the Student Clinic, he thought maybe I had developed an allergy to beer because I could still tolerate mead or wine at a moderate dosage. I also believed a bio major's interpretation that I had lactose intolerance. Some online articles said that one might develop that condition in one's twenties. Considering my physical body was Asian, I had no reason to doubt the validity of this explanation: maybe I had just reached that age. Yet no family history?

This change in my bowel forced me to restrict my diet every day, making my life more miserable because I couldn't socialize with people at ease. When someone offered me a free beer, I had to say thanks and sorry at the same time. After moving to California, I got to know some Asian Americans and found out a lot of them had lactose intolerance. I also noticed that many Asian immigrants also felt uncomfortable with the ice-cold American beer. Over time, I developed the habit of telling the waiter or waitress, "no ice," before they brought me any water. You may call that a cultural difference (because many authentic Chinese restaurants serve hot water by default, and you have to ask them for room temperature specifically), but I also see it as a genetic difference. As I told Carl and Lindsay once, I thought Caucasians might have thicker bowels; otherwise, why would anyone use cold liquid to cause muscle contractions in their stomach? Even those med students in America who have studied physiology would do the same while laughing at people who cannot.

Anyway, this was increasingly frustrating to me, even when I socialized with Chinese folks because a lot of them wanted to "enjoy" spicy food or liquor during a collective meal. This was even worse in mainland of China. Only years later, the Kaiser G.I. doctor diagnosed me with irritable bowel syndrome. I firmly believed that the winter depression and subsequent series of traumatic events added tremendous stress to my psyche and my bowel, the so-called second brain in my body. Under constant baseline stress, my bowel finally acquired this irritable trait as a physical "defense mechanism." Years later, a fitness professional recommended taking fish oil and multivitamin to help maintain a steady intake of necessary nutrients. Will I recommend those supplements to other people? Sorry, I'm not qualified to counsel other people about what they should put into their mouths.

What I want to bring your attention to: in 2018, a TCM (traditional Chinese medicine) doctor in private practice used individualized prescriptions to treat my body as a whole, and after several weeks, my anxiety and IBS were gone. Surprisingly, my lactose intolerance also disappeared, and I only noticed that when I accidentally ate dairy products other than yogurt. Therefore, I can confidently conclude that my lactose intolerance in those years was a functional change in my digestive system under tremendous stress. Yes, the misery Jeremy brought to me lingered around even after I moved out of Ohio.

By the way, according to some online articles, even when I couldn't tolerate lactose in general, there were still a few types of cheese I could eat, such as cheddar, Swiss, and Parmesan. But cream? I have never liked the dairy flavor since weaning. During that period, something that would delight me was realizing that a small percentage of white people also had this condition. Some of them were smart enough to take lactase pills or go for Lactaid milk, but I chose to stay on soy, rice, or coconut milk. Meanwhile, something that would frustrate me further was meeting other Asians who had never experienced lactose intolerance. Glad I was finally out of that minority struggle, and no more fear. The rest was just a matter of personal choice: I stuck to quasi-Paleo whenever possible, which eliminates dairy anyway; no cream for my coffee; no sour cream for my burrito either.

Here comes the unfortunate medical case of my lower extremities. While living in the neighborhood near the South Campus, I started to walk more toward the Main campus and carried more weight on my back. All of this happened when I was wearing the customized orthotic inserts to compensate for the overpronation in my feet. However, because Dr. Gallagher, the sports medicine clinician, wasn't trained to notice the leg length discrepancy, some necessary adjustment wasn't taken into account when, Melissa, the physical therapist ordered those inserts from the biotech company. Hence a lot of waste of money and time for physical therapy sessions. Later I knew most sports medicine doctors wouldn't investigate in that direction unless they had been trained in foot and ankle issues.

The outburst of spasms in my right calf muscles came like a lightning bolt and haunted me daily while walking. Eventually, I used a small luggage bag to carry the laptop on my behalf, which was understandably inconvenient as I hated attention. In addition, I didn't know what shoes to wear to reduce the overreaction of my calf muscles. In one appointment with Dr. Gallagher, I brought several pairs of shoes to the clinic, which stunned her, but she still couldn't figure out what was wrong with my calf. I seemed overreacting, but I wasn't. This empathetic physician recommended that I take out the hard inserts. On the worst

THE LAST SUMMER AND THE GROUP THERAPY

days, I felt pain in both knees and feet and dreaded walking out of my apartment on the third floor with no elevator. Appointments with different alternative medicine practitioners didn't solve the problem. Instead, they caused me more frustration, especially since a chiropractor thought I was just scared. Maybe some clinicians in the Ohio State health network were able to scrutinize my case, but I didn't know who or in which department of which hospitals. The word "podiatry" was unfamiliar and not yet in my vocabulary back then because the Chinese equivalent was rarely seen in public hospitals. Ironically, I could spell the word "otolaryngology" with my eyes closed due to my field of research.

Anyway, I was feeling miserable most of the time due to the debilitating pain coming back and forth on an irregular basis, which in turn generated fear. In one session with Jacob and Noah, during the check-in, when every group member was asked to talk about how they were doing in the past week, I labeled my feeling as being hypochondriac inaccurately. The word "hypochondria" can mean that someone worries about their health when they have no detectable physical symptoms. I learned this word from a course I was taking called Medical Terminology, another course that can easily elicit the "medical student syndrome" in students. I put this label on myself because that chiropractor said I was just scared of the pain and that there was no big problem in me. Years later, in Smoke City, an acupuncturist who couldn't eliminate my pain also used this word on me, making me feel worse about Smoke City, from very bad to worse.

During that summer, I could even feel empathetic pain in my foot when I saw a soccer player kicking a soccer ball on television — one of my undergrad roommates, an astrophysics major, preferred to watch soccer games instead of American football. This exposed some characteristics of my nervous system that I didn't like, and one can infer a lot about my general sensitivity based on that.

I suffered from real musculoskeletal and fascial pain, not just hypochondria, and these clinicians' dismissive comments could certainly hinder a patient's journey to recovery. I won't deny hypochondria 100% because I did worry about some serious problems in other parts of my body at that time, such as my heart. I suspect it was affected by the poor condition of my bowel and the uncertainty about life in general. After I restricted my diet in Davis, California, and the IBS was confirmed, the hypochondria was gone. I just assumed that I had some chronic bowel issue that I had to bear with by eating Paleo or some other diet. Even today, I am convinced of the global health benefit of Paleo as well as the philosophy of eating natural foods. Admittedly, it's difficult to commit to any strict diet when living in a human society that doesn't promote such individualistic behavior at a reasonable cost, but I try to stick to the essence, at least. That's why even after my IBS was treated 80~90%, I still stay away from irritating food.

I have never gained a lot of expertise in nutrition, even after reading *The Paleo Solution*, because my brain refuses to remember any biochemistry terms. I don't know if I should believe anything advertised to me, either. All I can do is prevent future injuries and protect myself from the intake of irritants. But, you know, easier said than done.

12.3 A Wedding and a Funeral

I've been to two weddings in Ohio, and I wrote a song for each pair of newlyweds. This particular wedding for Carl and Lindsay was held in 2014. A few weeks before the wedding, I purchased a toaster on their wedding registry at Macy's in Upper Arlington. It was a sunny weekend in May, and somehow there was no traffic inside.

The American wedding registry was an interesting concept to me, and their wish list can reveal a lot about the financial background of each family. For the same type of product, such as a microwave, one couple might choose brand A at $X, while another couple might choose brand B at $Y. If X is far less than Y, then you can make the speculation yourself. I like how the American culture links the couple with their friends and families because they can always think of me when they use the product I purchased for them. Also, if they hate me someday, they can simply sell the item on Craigslist or Facebook. It's good when they clearly state what they want since I don't like imposing some arbitrary gift with no practical use on them. In case you're curious, the wedding registry concept doesn't exist in Chinese culture. A lot of people still use red packets containing cash as a wedding gift, and I have never liked the idea of red packets in general, stemming from my childhood. Every Spring Festival, I was compelled to wish everybody to live 100 years in exchange for their red packets containing cash. I didn't believe any of that.

By the day the wedding was held in the church of their choice, my legal case had already been dismissed. But the trauma lingered for a long time. Carl always cared about my condition those years, and even when he was stepping into the ballroom hand in hand with Lindsay, with joy on his face, he gave me a glimpse. There were more than 100 people in the room, and he noticed me sitting at the same table with those old friends in the Bible Study. What made me stand out again was the fact that I was the only Asian in a white crowd. He had befriended many other international students in history, but I was the only one attending his wedding that summer. I hadn't seen these evangelical folks for almost a year, and I still enjoyed chatting with them, as long as the topic didn't involve religion. But given the whole community was associated with the church, and considering those groomsmen were all his childhood friends in the church, it was no surprise that the word "God" was mentioned frequently.

During the wedding, Carl's younger brother pointed out that the sapphires on their wedding rings were the same color as their blue eyes. And I believe their holy hearts were pure and shiny as those diamonds on her earrings.

During the banquet and afterward, I told some of them about my tragic experience with my old housemates, and someone started to commiserate with me and invited me to go back to the evangelical church and accept the love of Jesus. Back then, I was thinking about going to Las Vegas for the Objectivist Summer Conference. It didn't actually happen, but I started my initial contact with their staff that summer. The week following the wedding, when I returned to group therapy, where Jacob was teaching me alternative skills I could use to take care of my psyche, I told the group members about my new struggle. It was definitely tempting because the church community would be full of kind-hearted people who cared about me regardless of my race, ethnicity, country of origin, not even my stigma— since Jesus would forgive my sin as long as I stayed faithful to him. I liked these people, but I knew we were different. Some of them had rejected me from their Christian-exclusive Oscar party before I went insane.

Then The Buddha started to speak, "You should hang with people who can respect your boundaries. If you already told them you don't believe in God, then they should stop trying to persuade you back onto that old path. You've never told them not to believe in God, have you?" The Buddha had his wisdom. Nobody in the group disagreed with what he just said, and I had a feeling that most guys in this group were atheists, or at least not evangelical. I choose not to talk about these evangelists I met in my first semester in Columbus because they were just ordinary good people one could see all over America. I also chose not to talk much about that phase when I thought I was more of a Deist because it no longer matters. It's more important to know who I am nowadays than to associate myself with some historical figures I admire. Ben Franklin, a Deist, was one of them.

Before the summer ended, some tragedy occurred to another friend I knew from their home church. I saw the news on someone else's Facebook status and immediately contacted Carl. He told me our common friend Caleb was hit by a car while riding his bike in the neighborhood east of the Main Campus at night. His head hit the back of a bus in front of him, and his life was GAME OVER. Caleb was a nice guy who always carried a special water bottle with him. The last time I saw him was on the campus bus (CABS), running across the Medical Campus of Ohio State. According to Carl, the killer driver ran away. There was no surveillance camera on that street, so the culprit was still at large when the funeral service was held in the black church. I went to the service with Carl and Lindsay that weekday morning and stayed till the late afternoon. Due to the time conflict, I skipped that week's therapy session.

In the black church, again, as the only Asian attendee among the black and white people, I saw his family and community and was told that his African-American parents had adopted him from Southeast Asia. However, I wasn't sure how he ended up going to the home church full of Caucasian Americans from the suburb. Years later, when I brought it up in a chat, Carl explained that Caleb was introduced to this group by a co-worker who was also a member of the group.

According to a speaker, he developed a phobia toward cars because of a car accident during his pre-teen years, which is why he never took the driving test. In the Midwest and the majority of spread-out America, living without a car means being confined to a small territory— my first-hand tragic experience. You basically cannot go anywhere far in the snowstorm, which usually lasts several months. The fact that his death happened in the summer in a quiet neighborhood was extra heart-wrenching to me. The lack of bike lanes in Columbus also made it dangerous to bike on the road, considering how fast Americans drive compared to the rest of the world. I remember it was a horrifying experience riding a bike across West Lane Avenue before I got my driver's license in Columbus. Most roads outside the downtown area in that city had no sidewalks, let alone bike lanes.

The speaker was crying and blaming the culprit on the podium. That scene deepened my realization that the life of ordinary Americans wasn't easy, despite the title of "the first world." Another male speaker sounded like Martin Luther King. When Caleb's family members all stepped up to the front, I felt like I was in the movie scene of *The Pursuit of Happyness* starring Will Smith. That afternoon, when I told Carl and Lindsay about this feeling in Panera, they smiled, "Ain't all black churches like that?" He was right. That was my first and only experience inside a black church, and the reverberation of emotions sincerely touched me.

What stunned me was the luncheon after the commiseration. Throughout that day, I only saw several people cry, while most of his friends were very calm and even shared some funny stories about Caleb. People started to chat freely during lunch about all kinds of issues, and at a certain point, I couldn't believe I was still in a funeral service. I pointed out this cultural difference to Carl and Lindsay when they debriefed me later. Here's the contrast: earlier that year, my paternal grandfather passed away, and I had no doubt that most attendees were shedding tears throughout the service, whether genuinely or faking it. I wasn't there, but I could imagine the contagious scene. It's hard to stay dry when everybody around you is crying hysterically. I would at least pretend to cry as well, though I had little true love for my paternal grandpa even before I went to the US, as mentioned before.

As an international student back then, I was inspired by how American people handled a person's death. People consciously chose not to send him off to Heaven in tears, which was heartwarming in a way. I know Christianity plays a big role in it, and atheists might instead call that style hypocritical and passive because death is a severe loss of values, and there is no such redemption as a pass to Heaven. Still, one has to admit that they're not bothering anybody else. By comparison, I felt very uncomfortable about the primitive style of funeral services in several Asian countries, especially in underdeveloped regions like Smoke City— smoke, carbon monoxide, sulfur dioxide, real food for the deceased, fake money, and cacophonic music. I have no sense of belonging to this culture, even when facing someone's death. Solemnity, peace, and respect are what I adore, rather than showing off. A line in the movie *Manchester by the Sea* inspired me: a funeral is for the survivors. It makes so much sense to me.

Even today, I still don't know if they have found the killer. When I did the check-in during the following week's group session, nobody knew how to respond to my feelings. A friend died in a traffic accident, and it was real life. Because my brain felt very flat most of the time after the traumatic events, I couldn't feel worse about someone else's death than I felt about my own tragedy. However, the death of a friend, although not a buddy-level friend, was another blow to my psyche that year. In deadly honest comparison, I felt nothing about the deaths of those celebs on the news unless I was a big fan of their works.

Because of Caleb's death, I didn't hesitate to buy an expensive helmet after moving to Davis, California, since I had to bike around the so-called bicycle town in 2015. Unfortunately, that college town wasn't as bike-friendly as advertised, especially when you needed to cross the bridges over the freeway I-80. Some bike lanes and sidewalks were uneven and dilapidated; riding a generic bike on any of those would give me a headache. There is no way for a big-city personality to live a dignified life in this town without a motorized vehicle unless you only stay on campus or stay in your own bubble, but one can be easily fooled by their slogan. In general, I had no good memory of that "big farm" except for the good people I met. The wrong information I received from the Internet and from dishonest people contributed tremendously to my initial disappointment and ultimate tragedy in Davis.

12.4 The Immigration Lawyer

As mentioned before, I met one final attorney in Ohio in August 2014 because Ms. Wilson reminded me that I should ensure this case wouldn't affect my future career in America. So, instead of calling the local Bar Association again, I called the number she gave me and made an appointment with this law firm specializing in immigration affairs. The 30-minute consultation would cost 50 bucks. This time I prepared a list of questions in advance, following the guidelines I found online. I started this formal style from that day, which was later to be judged by a G.I. doctor in Smoke City, who ironically misdiagnosed me.

The law firm was on the north side of the city. I drove there and met the attorney in charge, Mr. Ivanovski. He looked experienced and established. I told him briefly about my interaction with the legal system in America and explained to him why I would probably bypass any immigration attorney from China if they had existed in Columbus at all — I was afraid to be judged with such questions as "Why did you mess with the white people" or "Why don't you continue to live with Chinese roommates?" I was certain some of them would be judgmental, like the guy I went to NYC with, even if that was unprofessional. They probably wouldn't judge me to my face, but who knows what they would say when the door was closed? In retrospect, outliers like me were uncommon but not as rare as I thought. But anyway, I was in the white-dominant city of Columbus, Ohio, and because the school attorneys were almost all white people, their recommended attorneys through the chain of networking were typically white too. If I were living in SF or LA in California or NYC, things would be quite different. Different ethnic groups usually just play their own games, and I perhaps would follow the rules too.

Mr. Ivanovski was surprised to hear that there were Chinese immigrant lawyers giving lectures on H-1B visas to Chinese international students on the OSU campus. I'd been to one of those lectures, so I knew how competitive and unfair the H-1B lottery was, especially for Chinese and Indian immigrants. When we were living together in the "Shining" House, I even received some good wishes from Jeremy, "Hope you will be able to stay in this country." Thank goodness, because we were not in the same field, he didn't see me as someone who could steal his job. In fact, most of my American friends and colleagues were highly educated people, and my eccentric major made my existence unlikely to pose any direct threat to anybody's career.

"Since you said your case is already dismissed, it should have no effect on your employment in this country. Just be honest if they ask you about it. Tell them you got a protection order from your roommate, and it was dismissed in court. Then you learned a lesson from it. Most likely, employers will not know about it."

I took a deep breath. In retrospect, Mr. Ivanovski, just like most mainstream Americans, couldn't fully understand that in such a competitive market, any tiny stain on a minority immigrant could be magnified in the employment process unless the employer was also a minority immigrant. What? Academia? Don't even think about it. Academics live on their reputation. What? Model minority? Not a model minority anymore after I carried a restraining order on me for two months.

"Now, let's practice. If you are coming to a job interview, I'll ask you: have you had any criminal record in history?"

"Uh… No." I thought that I was technically dealing with a civil case.

"Why did you hesitate?" He looked at me seriously.

Then I realized I needed to be more assertive, as if nothing had ever happened.

"What exactly did you say that made him feel threatened?" He asked. This was a routine question for me because how could he not be curious?

"I said 'you will regret it' in the email, and in capital letters," I answered.

"I see. You need to be careful with your language then." He said.

"But in those Hollywood movies, those actors say it all the time, and those movies never mentioned anything about a restraining order."

"Stop watching those movies!" He burst into laughter the same way Mr. Hoffman used to laugh at my serious words. Clearly, the America I knew from the movie screens was no authentic reflection of real life in most of America. The only exceptions might be sad movies like *Manchester by the Sea*, which only appeared in 2017.

"My friend told me that in this country, a lot of people have some kind of record on them. Is that true?" I asked, without specifying the meaning of "a lot of people."

"Some may, but not everybody," he explained, "I can't have any record myself, if I want to practice law in this country." That made a lot of sense, but even that wasn't absolute truth under every circumstance, as I later found out from Pete Nowalk's TV show *How to Get Away With Murder*. After all, the bar association comprises a bunch of human beings, and even the Attorney General might be a flawed public figure.

When he tried to search for my name in the public database of the Ohio court, mostly out of curiosity, my case didn't show up, which was consistent with what Ms. Wilson said. However, when using my last name alone in the query, he saw hundreds of entries in the past decade, which surprised me, considering my last name wasn't popular in China at all. I suspected similar last names were also provided in the results. "Are these people all your cousins?" He asked.

"No. There aren't as many popular surnames for Chinese people as for Americans, which means a million people may have to share the same last name sometimes." When you have a million people in your giant family, it's probably not a good idea to dig into your ancestry. I have never cared about the so-called heritage because those already deceased people have no impact on my current life, bitter or sweet.

Before I left his office, I remembered to ask him, "Was our conversation being recorded?"

He answered, looking amused, "Nope, I won't have time to listen to it a second time. Don't worry. Now, Mr. Sun, how do you plan to make your payment?"

I wish I had known back then that legal fees are tax-deductible in some conditions. However, my status as an international student required me to use a website called GLACIER to prepare my federal tax, which allowed us little flexibility in our tax returns. Remember, I paid far more to Ms. Wilson. Similarly, the large amount of co-pay in healthcare might qualify for some deduction, but I never became tax-savvy during those years. The final number might not change much, even with adjustments, but it's good to be aware of the advantages one can take. By the way, if one never has formal employment in America, they are exempted from the hassle of tax returns every year. That applies to a significant proportion of those rich college kids from other countries.

Chapter 13
The Last Fall and a Love Song for Myself

13.1 Skydiving

Right after graduation, I allowed myself to perform a thrilling activity with my buddy Julian, which I had been dreaming of for two years. I once told Stacy about my wish the previous winter, and she thought I was crazy. She told me she'd done bungee in California before, but skydiving was too much for her. Understandable. During the spring semester, the female instructor of the Abnormal Psychology course referred to skydiving as risk-taking behavior when she introduced certain types of personality disorders. That's why I originally didn't expect such a sensitive person as Julian to be also interested in this type of risky activity. Only later did I realize that skydiving is considered a popular sport by a fraction of Americans as well as adventurous people from all over the world.

I only booked one jump with a company called StartSkydiving located in Middletown, Ohio, but he booked two jumps, and the second time was half-price only, reserved for a later date. If you've heard the academic proverb "neurons that fire together wire together," you might also believe this, "friends that jump out of the same plane together love each other forever." Additionally, neither of us was planning to notify our families before we took action. Julian even reminded me not to tag him on social media if I decided to post any picture, so his mom wouldn't see it. People in China wouldn't know about it anyway since I only posted personal stuff on Facebook, the American platform. In case you didn't know, The Chinese diaspora uses a different social media app called WeChat, just like Indian people prefer WhatsApp.

We each registered on their website one week in advance and read and signed the electronic paperwork, namely liability waivers, for an hour. Once again, I was overwhelmed by the legal terms. The paperwork basically told me they wouldn't be held accountable if I lost my life during this activity. If I died, it was my choice and God's choice.

During the summer term, after submitting the final version of my thesis, I felt obliged to do something before heading out with my buddy to the flying zone. I made an appointment with Mr. Parker at Student Legal Services, and when the website required me to reveal the purpose of my appointment, I typed "leave a will." You might think I was making a mountain out of a molehill, but that's because you are not alone in a foreign country. Ohio State does offer an undergrad course on skydiving, but those students who enroll would have to get the signature of their advisor, so it is kind of a big deal. Nobody wants to be liable for any tragic accident in this world.

Two days later, I showed up at Student Legal Services. Mr. Parker, who was less busy during the summer, brought a stack of forms into the consultation room and asked me anxiously, "What happened?"

"I'm planning to go skydiving. I figured I'd better draft a will before I go since I don't have any family in this country. You guys' website says you can provide this kind of service." I explained calmly.

"Skydiving? I've done that several times in my life. Are you going to do the tandem?"

"Yeah. It's my first time. So that's my only option." I said.

"Well, okay. You see, you are doing the tandem. So what kind of assets do you have?" He asked.

"An old car, a laptop, and some money in my bank account," I said.

"That's it? Are you married? Do you have kids?" He asked.

"No and no."

"If you die in this country, your family in China will be notified, and according to the law, they will take over your personal belongings. So you don't need to worry about anything."

"Uh… I'm okay with that, since they paid for some of the stuff. But how about my body? I wanna donate my corpse to Massachusetts General Hospital for scientific research, definitely not Ohio State Medical Center, and you know why." In front of a lawyer, surely, I wouldn't say fantasized things like, "I want people to pour my ashes into the five Great Lakes after I die." Although, that was truly desirable, kind of poetic, and legendary. Yes, I know, this desire to donate my body reflected my preference for the private schools on the East Coast, even after I failed to be accepted into the programs on the East Coast. What I didn't realize back then was that top hospitals would never lack cadavers. Also, they are probably more interested in particular organs than the entire body. I am not that special to them; Boston doesn't lack Asian residents.

"That's fine. You can do whatever you want. If you want to donate your body, you will have to contact the hospital yourself. They will ask you to fill out the paperwork and pay a variety of fees in advance. For example, you'll have to pay for the shipping of your corpse to Boston."

"What? I have to pay if I want to donate my body for science?" I was shocked.

"Yeah. I'm afraid that's how it works. Do you still want the forms for the will? But like I said, it's redundant." I sensed I might look like an over-contemplative idiot to him at that moment.

"So... You really don't think there's any danger in skydiving? But it took me an hour to sign those online waivers."

He lowered his head. "I know, they always make those forms look so scary so that the scared people will back off early on. Just go and enjoy yourself. You will be fine."

I sighed, "Okay, if you say so. You know, I paid for the legal service, so I ought to consult an expert."

Then I told him I hired Ms. Wilson to clean up the dismissed case for me, and he looked super-duper thrilled, making me wonder if they were truly only co-workers in the past. He totally forgot that he was the person recommending her to me a while ago.

"And how have you been these days?" He asked.

I gave him some updates and mentioned my chronically dysfunctional brain. We both agreed that Columbus, Ohio wasn't the right place for me to stay in the long run.

Then came the fall semester. That God-blessed Saturday, Julian drove me to the site in Middletown, Ohio, and we checked in. We were scheduled for the afternoon when the wind up in the sky was expected to be weaker. Honestly, the previous night, I couldn't fall asleep. I didn't feel nervous or

THE LAST FALL AND A LOVE SONG FOR MYSELF

scared consciously, but the subconscious excitement occupied my body. Without any coffee, I was still very awake throughout the day.

We went to lunch at some burger place. While waiting for the food, I started to share with my buddy my newest realization, which I referred to as the "co-insurance theory" — not to be confused with the coinsurance one needs to pay in a PPO plan.

"Slim, are you nervous about the jump? I'm nervous. But there's no turning back. I have been waiting for this day for so long." He said earnestly.

"I hear you. I was nervous too, until a few hours ago. Why? Because I realized there's not too much to worry about. Think about this. We're both doing the tandem, which means we'll each be attached to the harness of a coach. From a coach's perspective, they certainly will make sure of their own survival after they jump, and simultaneously, our safety will be **co-insured**. If we die, they will die too. They'll do everything they can to prevent that from happening, won't they?" I just revealed to him a big secret about human nature, which Edward Snowden would call a "hack."

He started to belly-laugh. "Oh my God, Slim. I thought I was already so cynical, but it turned out you're far more cynical than I am."

"Are you still nervous?" I asked.

"Haha, not really. I'm ready for the adventure." He said. Apparently, without any superficial affirmation like "We'll be fine," "God bless America," or "Fortune favors the brave," I could still resolve the mental block.

Back in the flying zone, we waited for another 2 hours after getting dressed in the jumpsuit. My coach was a tall white guy from California, and he got baffled by reading my legal name aloud. No surprise. While waiting, I used my smartphone to shoot video clips for my next song, *Parachute*. It was a great pleasure to see other people falling from the sky with their parachutes in different colors. I could watch that for a whole day without getting bored. When it was finally our turn, we six clients, accompanied by the six coaches, went on board a tiny plane, and the plane just skyrocketed without notice— I know it couldn't really be like that, but that was my impression. In the sky, when I looked down, Ohio was just fields, flat fields. Honestly, I don't understand why GOP would stick to Ohio for their Convention. Maybe Cleveland was much better than the rest of Ohio? According to Carl, a Columbus native, Mariah Carey would most likely give a concert in Cleveland, and not in Columbus.

Unlike independent parachutists, we had no moment to struggle near the door. To jump or not to jump, that wasn't a question. I was buckled up, with the coach sitting right behind my back. When he decided to jump, I was pushed out of the door, and then I started yelling like crazy — we were past the point of no return. Those giant goggles covering my eyeglasses were super helpful during the free fall. After the parachute was opened, everything was controlled in his hands until we reached some height. He then let me control the swirling direction for some "experience" — as in today's "Airbnb experience." Before we reached the ground, I also requested to play a little bit so that I could enjoy the scenery in different directions — bang for the buck. Julian had already removed his jumpsuit when we finally glided onto the ground. The whole skydiving experience was no different from what you can see in those exciting YouTube videos, but one has to experience that near-zero-gravity state in person to understand that thrill.

This unforgettable risk-taking experience had a long-term effect on me; normal excitement has become trivial to my standard. Years later, I tried paragliding on the beach outside UC San Diego, and it felt very mild to me, simply because the threshold had been raised too high. I wouldn't say this tandem experience has made me mentally stronger since it was widely considered a sport or some kind of entertainment. Sorry, not even any placebo effect. After I came up with my "co-insurance theory," whether or not I was the first person on the earth to come to this realization, the suspense about safety was no longer there. In other words, I didn't consciously overcome any barrier; I simply **consumed** other people's training efforts. It is sad to see through everything, yet it is what it is. As you know already, I still have been vulnerable to depression and suicidal ideation in recent years, as life has posed new threats to me. The mechanisms haven't changed much for me or anybody else.

On returning to my apartment shared with the college students that Saturday evening, I added one life event on Facebook: "looking down on a White Coat Devil from 13000 ft above." In fact, through that summer, my attitude toward Jeremy had gradually turned from fear to despise. In one individual therapy session with Teresa, when I said, "I don't give a sh*t about him," she affirmed the positive value of this transition. As for skydiving, yes, one can legitimately see it as an atypical form of therapeutic intervention whose cost was only slightly above one psychotherapy session without insurance. As far as I have read, some celebrities use it as an idiosyncratic method to release tension caused by early-age traumatic experiences. Still, I don't believe in any substitute for rigorous psychotherapy, as a thrilling or transcending experience won't address the mental problem per se. By the way, the statement "I don't give a sh*t about someone" implies "someone is occupying my consciousness field, and therefore, I do give a sh*t."

The week after that, coincidentally, my professor, Mr. Anderson, mentioned in the lab meeting that he took a full parachuting course when he was in college. "The survival rate is higher when you jump with a parachute." When he uttered this fact enthusiastically yet seriously, the young girls in the lab dropped their jaws, aghast. That was my professor, the trailblazer for his field of research, and his brevity back in his twenties could predict his subsequent success in his field of study. And yes, I still showed up in the music lab sometimes between my graduation date and the subsequent departure date because that big lab was de facto my home within Ohio State.

Although I have explained to you why tandem skydiving is not as scary as you imagine, using my personal-flavored cynicism, most of the population won't have the courage to try it, not even once in their lives. If you have been living a peaceful and happy life in a small town, why force yourself to face your fear in the sky? Mr. Osman, a person who treated his "prestige" in academia so meticulously like many others, said he would be too scared to do that. Jeremy and Stacy, these future upper-class who value physical well-being above anything else, wouldn't do that. Frankie, a nice guy with a decent job in health care, said he could never imagine something like that.

On the contrary, attorney Mr. Parker and cognitive psychologist Mr. Shapiro have both done that. I also know a heterosexual couple who went skydiving together after getting engaged. Of course, I don't encourage people to try something they can't appreciate, but I do encourage those with serious interest to try it when they're still young and free of serious health concerns or other baggage. Time and tide wait for no man.

13.2 The Final Move in Ohio

Before graduating in August, I applied for a working permit, a.k.a. EAD card, for F-1 students. This application cost several hundred bucks and took the US government several months to process. Think about it, this governmental bureau called US Citizenship and Immigration Services (USCIS) needs to process all sorts of applications from all over the country every month.

Upon obtaining my degree in August, I emailed Mr. Osman to thank him. He revealed that he got a new NIH grant and was negotiating a new position on the West Coast. He offered to hire me as a full-time research assistant as soon as possible. I said yes because we shared some research interests, and I wanted to move to the coasts. Of course, I was looking for other possibilities at the same time.

Before I could relax a bit, there were several things I needed to take care of. First, housing. Yes, I had no choice but to hunt again. Because I knew I was going to leave Ohio, I was only willing to look for a flexible lease from various sources, including some email newsletters. Craigslist was the least reliable option for this purpose, but I had to try it. I remember one day, I checked out three different places, and one offered me the living room without a real bed. This accommodation wasn't an uncommon practice for self-funded international students. While driving on High Street, there was a moment when my anxiety was triggered—I only had ten days left before moving out of the college neighborhood, and I didn't want to end up homeless. Fortunately, I had learned to take deep breaths by then, so my anxiety was down-regulated very quickly. In case you wonder, "Why did you procrastinate?" Well, I didn't. Previously, the older guy who went to NYC with me in 2013 said he could let me rent a spare room in his basement. However, he notified me in mid-August that he had decided to quit his Ph.D. program and leave America for good, so I was all on my own again. Bummer.

Another heartbreaking event occurred in this hunting process, giving me no break. One day, on Craigslist, I got an invitation from a potential landlord living in German Village, south of downtown Columbus, which was distant from the OSU campus. I checked out the place with a young roommate, who would accompany me as a "white tag." The landlord in this newly revamped house turned out to be a firefighter. After filling out my application form with detailed rental history in the past year, it was approved very quickly. However, before I decided to sign the lease, Ashley warned me the neighborhood across the street from the house was shady. Coincidentally, an African-American lady who worked at OSU confirmed that information and even told me she grew up in that neighborhood. I panicked and told Charlotte on Facebook that I couldn't move into that place as she encouraged me to, over other options, because of the black neighborhood across the street— if someone robbed the house or came to attack me, the rare Asian in the unfamiliar neighborhood, I wouldn't even be able to run with my leg problem. Simply speaking, I couldn't protect myself in the way some locals were able to.

"What? How dare you say that?! You are a racist, even though that word mainly refers to something between white people and black people in this country." She got outraged when I tried to justify my concern and unfriended me on Facebook immediately. "I don't give a f*ck! You've been horrible in the majority of this relationship. Alex and I, we knew you had a hard time, so we didn't say anything. That's enough. No more advice. Don't include us in your life."

While still in shock, for the first time in my life, I Googled the live update of criminal activity in the city and was scared by the result. Indeed there was a higher density of red dots in the neighborhood east of German Village, while German Village itself was pretty clear on the map. However, when I took a closer look at the demographics of the criminals in that area, I found out some of them were actually white, unlike what I'd expected. I texted her to apologize for my assumption, but she told me not to contact her again. "It's good you are reading the facts to educate yourself, but enough is enough. Please don't text me again."

I texted Alex for help, and he told me his interpretation: it wasn't really about racism. "It was the last straw on the camel back." It turned out they felt I was simply using them to do sh*t for myself but didn't intend to maintain a long-term friendship with them after moving away.

"We had hoped you would come back to hang with us more often," he said.

"Not sure if I can. Last time I came back for Infinity's party, I saw my old housemate Lady J, and I felt awful for several days," I said.

"I understand. I'm sorry. We didn't invite her. She just showed up at our door," he said. Alex was the person who warned me about Jessica's appearance at the party that day. Her motive was unknown, and I didn't want to know.

"I know. You guys have always been so kind to me. I even put you two in the acknowledgment part of my thesis." I told him. In my memory, Alex always considered himself not as bright as Charlotte, but he actually had a master's degree in health care and was quite reliable.

I explained to him I was still struggling with multiple facets of everyday life, and my life wasn't as cheerful as my social media posts displayed. For example, I would never post any photo of me in a healthcare appointment with lots of needles in my hand to stun or scare white people. However, as I told him, I did realize what I did wrong in the past few months and how grateful I was to this couple, who exhibited a great sense of justice.

Despite the mutual understanding between Alex and me, I collapsed again in my tiny bedroom. While my lacrimal glands were open, some musical motif suddenly floated into my mind to fill up the bridge section of my new song, *Parachute*, which had been vacant by then. The melody of a new song was thus finished on my second-hand Yamaha keyboard. Afterward, I ate a banana to lift my mood — a trick I learned from a Behavioral Neuroscience course. No, not a grapefruit, as Stacy once suggested on Facebook.

When I regained myself, I concluded that I should no longer rely on Charlotte or anyone else as a free sounding board. Eventually, I must learn to make my own decision based on my complicated reality. Yes, black lives matter, but how about the lives of Asian folks being bullied? For certain issues, only minorities easily understand other minorities; only immigrants easily understand other immigrants. Since Charlotte couldn't be objective about or wasn't aware of the difficulties people like me faced in America, I had to let her go. In retrospect, her advice, such as encouraging me to move out like Jeremy, wasn't always effective for me. This type of escapism typically would make my life no better than before. It was based on unfounded assumptions about my viability in a different environment. By the way, it was sad to admit that most human beings in this world like to discuss other people behind their backs and never feel comfortable speaking out directly to address issues. It was true even when no one was in a dictator's or a knave's position.

On my next appointment with Teresa, I told her about this fresh tragedy. I said, "Since Charlotte told me to stay away from them from now on, I dare not contact them anymore, because I'm afraid of getting another restraining order."

She looked confused, "Why will this bring you another restraining order?"

I couldn't answer that. Maybe just my gut feeling that Charlotte also acted on impulse sometimes. Remember, I was paranoid about everything. In retrospect, Charlotte had her reasons to be angry. I did stupid things that crossed the boundary and made myself look like an ingrate, so I deserved to be reprimanded.

During those weeks, the black-white conflict was rising in the country after a white policeman in Ferguson, MO (Missouri), shot an unarmed black teenager called Michael Brown. With her human-rights-activist personality, I could imagine how Charlotte, a girl from Washington, D.C., should react to my implicit bias. Whether or not she was too politically correct and ignorant of my risky situation, it was presumptuous for me to make irresponsible assumptions about an area of low social-economic status. But, again, if it was a ghetto district, it had little to do with race per se. I did lack cultural sensitivity back then, as I still do today. Of course, some people never get into trouble because they simply never deal with people outside their ethnic community. That's also a valid option, just not for me.

Social psychologists would tell us that when performing certain psychological tasks, we are all racists to some extent, largely due to media exposure. In Davis, CA, a grad student in social psychology confirmed to me that Asians exhibited this type of unconscious bias in her experiments, just like other races. I wasn't surprised by that statement: simply look at the data in cross-cultural dating apps. Despite my casual friendships with some African-American students since college, despite my good feeling for one smart black girl in grad school, despite my adoration for Will Smith (before Oscar 2022), Viola Davis, Jessica Williams, and a bunch of jazz and blues artists like Miles Davis and Diane Reeves, I still cringed when a gang of African-American guys passed through me down the escalator and robbed a lightly dressed white girl of her iPhone in a San Francisco Metro Station, in 2017. That scene scared the sh*t out of me because we the passengers inside the train, were afraid that one of the gangsters whose right hand was reaching into his pocket might pull out a gun. I know that juxtaposition was silly as it could ever be, considering the total population of African-Americans. Oh please, individualism. Some might even say the gang just happened to be black, and there are Asian gangs in SF and LA as well. Technically, I can't refute that. Consider this: why do we fear suspicious-looking African-Americans on the street but not adorable black celebrities on stage? I'm sure social psychologists have developed some theories to explain that: for example, maybe the context shapes your expectation.

A Chinese student I met on a trip once told me explicitly that he didn't like black people in general when we entered a Walmart in Baltimore, surrounded by African-Americans. That context was so rare for us, so we walked very fast. In contrast, I took the Greyhound from D.C. to Philadelphia by myself the next morning, and my co-passengers were mostly black folks. I actually felt very comfortable on the bus. I guess the bus provided the context where everybody was decent and had equal rights to take the bus.

In recent years, I've also overheard an Asian American teenager from a middle-class family saying she would only consider an Asian or a Caucasian man as her future partner when asked by her relative from Asia. In contrast, I have seen some white female friends willing to date black men with no problem. Upon hearing this, one may conclude that Asian Americans carry stronger racism. However, I suspect a better interpretation is that many Asians lack a sense of security on the international market and do perceive or believe in some genetic advantages of Caucasians, at least in some dimensions, as beauty is in the eyes of the beholder. Phenotypes like skin color and nose bridge might sound neutral scientifically, but not under the aesthetic standards of human attraction. The truth is always bitter, and Tinder statistics probably can tell you that. Besides, pragmatically speaking, some minorities might intentionally choose to connect with the mainstream to reduce further discrimination against themselves. Whether you like it or not, this is an adaptive move on an individual level. This was also the rationale behind my "white tag" practice in Ohio when looking for housing. Thank goodness, this practice was no longer necessary after I moved to California.

What I want to re-emphasize is that the mainstream American culture has been overlooking the racism that Asians have to face from other races, especially in the regions where Asians and Latinos are absolute minorities. The stereotypes of Asians are associated with some notable vulnerability to alienation, manipulation, exploitation, or condescension. If you think I am talking nonsense, the Covid-19 pandemic in 2020 has revealed so much. People knew bat-eaters were rare in Asia, but they sought scapegoats to vent their anger and fear.

While I was sad enough to finish composing a new song, I knew I couldn't afford to be bogged down by this additional cut-off from another white couple. After all, I had to figure out my shelter still. One night, I saw a strange post on my OSU mailing list for Chinese international students and scholars. This post contained the number "18" and a phone number at the end, which were the only parts of the message that didn't look like gibberish— the sender must have typed in Chinese characters, which couldn't be displayed correctly in that newsletter. I guessed 18 stood for the COTA bus line, so I called the number, and the guy who answered the phone later became my last housemate in Ohio.

Over the phone, I told him I had just freshly graduated from Ohio State, and he told me he was new to Ohio for a new position and would be moving into the condo next week. One of his Chinese friends, who lived in a different city, owned this condo. Interestingly, he also told me that based on his observation, the best graduate program for Chinese international students in the US should be Statistics. Of course, he was a statistician himself. His point was legit, in retrospect, because quantitative skills would always be in high demand in the American job market. By the way, these days, a sexier term is "data science."

The next evening, I drove to the address he provided and met him in person. He introduced himself as Mr. Li. The location of this condo was very far from campus, good for people who didn't drive to campus often, and the rent was fair. However, the living room could be very cold when winter comes. The heating system in the US is not eco-friendly because you have to warm up the entire space, even if you are alone. The waste of energy gets worse when there's a stairway connecting downstairs and upstairs. For that reason, whoever turns on the heat before the snowstorm season arrives will surely make other co-tenants unhappy. It's a matter of money, ultimately, and some people tend to save money at the cost of getting sick. I told Carl about my dilemma, and he told me I should buy a space heater. Problem solved. I purchased a ceramic one from Walmart and used it before going to bed and after getting up.

Nowadays, I have realized that sleeping in a cold environment, where cold air is inhaled into the nasal cavity every night, contributed to my rhinitis. I think it's unfair to blame everything on the weakness of one's immune system or genetics. While people in developed countries have used a thermostat to maintain a healthy interior temperature for decades, many people from underdeveloped societies still wouldn't raise that room temperature at night in the winter, just like they wouldn't use dryers for damp laundry. They believe sensitivity is a crime and insensitivity is an honor; they believe the air is clean simply because the dirt particles are invisible to them. This brings my focus to the other contributing factor to my seasonal rhinitis: the bad air quality in Smoke City. When I was growing up, the local farmers in the rural area would burn straw and let the toxic gas haunt the entire city for a week, year after year. The teachers suffered even more than the students, as they talked a lot in the smoke. However, to be fair, the damage was easily dwarfed by the annual forest fire in California.

In that couple of months, Mr. Li and I were sharing a place in peace. The tension wasn't so common between two sociable and highly-educated Chinese men, who both had their own businesses to focus on. Over time, he started to share with me some poignant stories. As an immigrant who had fought in the US for over a decade, he certainly had learned his lesson regarding the American legal system in the early years. He told me he had received prosecution from a local for a small matter ("small" under the standard commonly adopted by people outside the US, small enough to be handled privately) and had to hire a lawyer to defend him in court. Then he learned to protect his own rights in the American way by hiring a lawyer to sue a reckless driver who posed a threat to his family's safety. The American way of using litigation to solve most problems is dreadful for immigrants, but immigrants have to accept it and learn it. I learned a big lesson myself, though I was much younger than him back then. I didn't tell him my own court experience in return because I didn't want to expose the entire sad story to a new and short-term housemate. Besides, I was very tired.

In September, Mr. Osman informed me that he would start working for UC Davis in January 2015, and I could move there after his appointment officially began. It would take some time for a new P.I. to create a research assistant position.

The challenge for me was to fill up the gap between the arrival of my working permit and the subsequent employment at UC Davis, in case I used up the 90-day grace period too early and had to leave America in tears. I found a temporary position in a lab whose members I knew very well and learned something by myself during that period as well, just to keep my neural circuits active all the time. However, nothing compares to what I learned through the group therapy sessions during those weeks. The relationships in the group were reciprocal: after I received courtesy, generosity, and even fraternity from the senior members, I learned how to think effectively in a group, and then I was able to contribute to the organized discussion on the practical topics and to facilitate other group members in overcoming the difficulties in life. No offense, but compared to that male grad student group, the basic and sporadic training I received in college in the Student Counseling Center seemed superficial. Most peers in the Student Association had no intention of advancing to the professional level or learning the scientific side of psychology, and therefore I was never satiated. Besides, as college students, we never really knew what a challenging life felt like.

13.3 D.C., Philly, and the Penitentiary

While I was still attending the lab meeting every now and then, I technically had some time at my disposal. One day, I noticed someone looking for travel mates to Washington, D.C., on the forum used by Chinese students at OSU. I signed up for it and met those guys in advance. Including me, two lads and two ladies, and four master's degrees in total. Based on the 4-way conversation, I learned that people studying in nearby institutions also used this comprehensive forum. These were all students who had graduated from grad school recently. Unlike me, they all grew up in famous major cities in China, so they knew better how to drive in big city traffic. Although everybody had a different personality, we generally got along on the trip and shared the burden of driving. One small gap between us was that they were planning to go to a live concert played by some indie band from China, which I had never heard of, while I decided to go to a local bar for some jazz by myself. I didn't want to spend money on music I wasn't interested in. In fact, I had begun to dive completely into Western music and was beginning to find Asian music somewhat unfathomable as a result of enculturation, a phenomenon well-studied by ethnomusicologists, and as a result of spending too much time socializing with Midwestern singer-songwriters.

Like most D.C. tourists, we visited famous attractions, including the White House. Then we split and explored different museums based on personal interests. Those two nights, we stayed at an Airbnb apartment. That was my first time with Airbnb, and it made me realize how old-fashioned and ill-informed I was. While I was struggling inside my neighborhood in Ohio, some smart kids were already traveling around different states of America like a pro. They even knew Popeyes was a decent place to grab fast food on a road trip. It was an eye-opening experience for me, I had to admit. I was glad my first aid kit always turned out to be useful on a group trip, which made me feel like the medic ninja in Naruto.

On that evening of their concert, I parted with the other three and went to a restaurant called Sticky Rice, which I had found on Yelp. There I had the most delicious noodles I'd had in the past two years, even better than Noodles & Company in Ohio. I felt bad that I couldn't communicate with their waiter in American sign language, and in the end, their manager had to come to take my order. The manager told me it was very common for people in D.C. to learn sign language because the city was very inclusive. What a sweet place to live in, I thought to myself.

Then my travel mates texted me that their concert was over and that they decided to forgo the nightclub. However, I had already arrived at the jazz bar recommended by a former lab mate while holding the keys to the Airbnb apartment. My three travel companions had expected me to return before them because of their nightclub plan. So I asked them to come and pick up the keys. Sitting in the bar,

THE LAST FALL AND A LOVE SONG FOR MYSELF

I ordered a glass of Riesling for the first time. I knew little about alcohol but suspected my bowel could tolerate wine better than beer. For sure, the word "sparkling" in "sparkling wine" might bring "tiny explosives" into my bowel, but I decided to enjoy myself in this special capital city of America. However, when the music started, I was disappointed because there was no jazz at all, just an open mic for pop music on a weekday evening. I came to the bar after reading their descriptions on Yelp and their website. Come on, a jazz bar... Where's the jazz? For a moment, I thought I had come to the wrong address.

While listening to these pop songs, a middle-aged white man wearing a suit and glasses came close to my table to chat with me. There were not too many people in the rectangular space, and I had been to many music bars in Ohio, so I didn't sense anything unusual in this person. He asked me where I was from, and I told him I was a grad student studying at Ohio State, now visiting D.C. with some friends. I also told him I was disappointed this venue didn't provide the vibe I wanted. He laughed.

"China? I was in China last month. I do business there on a regular basis." I figured that was how a business person would try to start a conversation with a stranger.

Then I talked about what kind of insignificant research I was conducting as a grad student, under the supervision of my professor, because that was what I normally talked about in grad school. He apparently couldn't care less about academic research. Then he threw me a question that made me hold my breath.

"Did your professor tell you you're very cute?" He asked in a soft voice. The last person who had given me such an awkward moment was that horny lawyer in the German Village of Columbus, Ohio.

I sensed something was wrong, and the word "cute" disgusted me because the last time I heard it was when Stacy was trying to persuade me to like her boyfriend again—"He's so cute. I don't understand why you are not (in love with him)." In general, I hate this word to be used on guys unless their gender identity says the opposite. Of course, under this particular circumstance, I became more vigilant.

"Uh... I should probably leave now." I murmured in a nervous tone.

"Do you have any plans tonight? I mean, do you want some sex?" He said in a gentle and serious tone, which was really creepy.

"What's going on here?" I thought to myself, "Is he a Mr. Robinson?" I was never prepared for such a scenario in real life, and I didn't know that American LGBT folks would ask for a one-night stand in such an unabashed way in such an ordinary music bar. But perhaps I was being narrow-minded: people can do anything when they are desperate. In retrospect, it was probably unusual for such a middle-aged businessman to be inside such a small and low-key bar on a weekday evening unless he was hunting on purpose. It also turned out to be a bad idea for me to check out a bar in an unfamiliar city when the person who recommended this place had already moved to a different state. Of course, he didn't tell me whether or not this was a gay bar. I couldn't help but question myself, did I just make myself look like someone sending out a hookup signal? Because the model minority folks don't normally appear in bars in D.C.? I wasn't sure. Perhaps I just went to the wrong place? Anyway, a sugar daddy soliciting a one-night stand from a stranger in a bar seemed outlandish to me. However, I had no doubt that he could get his "deal" with no difficulty when doing business in China.

"Sorry I really have to leave. It's getting late, and I don't want my friends to worry about me. Bye." I finished my Riesling quickly and stood up.

Then he said, "Goodbye. Tell your professor I think you're very cute."

I left in a hurry and didn't look back. Out of the bar, I walked quickly to the Metro station and made sure I wasn't followed. That was quite a weird experience, and my planned music night was ruined. Honestly, it didn't make me feel good to come across a person like that. Instead, it reminded me of the annoying experience of being harassed by some scoundrel I tried to avoid in middle school. Regardless of their gender identity or sexual orientation, their manner was a major problem to me.

My HTC phone died before I reached the apartment building, and I stayed outside for 2 hours before I was able to enter the building. Finally, a local resident came back after midnight and opened the gate for us. Luckily for me, on hearing my voice, my male travel mate opened the door for me, and I felt so bad about waking him up from sleep.

After three days of traveling together, they dropped me off at the Greyhound station in Washington D.C. While they drove back to Ohio, I hopped on the bus heading toward my holy city of Philadelphia. I stayed at the Apple Hostel in Philly and started my membership with Hosteling International USA. From that day, I became a dedicated hosteler and a travel enthusiast. I made good use of my membership those years and almost always stayed in HI hostels when traveling solo. For me, solo travel was rarely as lonely as it sounded because I always picked those cities where someone I knew was studying or working; it was also because I never had difficulty making new friends in hostels, especially with those roommates visiting from across the globe. Over time, my domestic and global network just got bigger and denser. Sometimes I found pals to go to scenic spots together and dine together. When no company was available, I went to some special places popping up on Google Trips, an app that is no longer supported by Google.

I had a college acquaintance studying at UPenn for his Ph.D. program, but he wasn't able to meet me during those three days due to scheduling difficulties. I couldn't blame him because we were not very close in college. As adults, we all should have an implicit ruler to estimate the depths of our relationships and develop reasonable expectations accordingly, without a sense of entitlement. Regardless, I spent a meaningful time in Philly: I went to the famous cheesesteak sub sandwich place and the Liberty Bell with a Brazilian government employee, whom I met in the hostel. I asked for "no cheese" in my sub. I went to Philadelphia's Magic Gardens by myself on a rainy afternoon and enjoyed an exclusive guided tour. Besides, the staff at Apple Hostel Philadelphia took us on memorable walking tours at night, just as many other successful HI hostels would do.

Those years of hosteling life took me closer and closer to the English-speaking world and farther and farther from the Chinese-speaking community. Understandably, only people who can speak English independently would choose solo travel in the US, and that's why during those years, I met a lot of English teachers from Germany and people studying in top-notch academic institutions, such as Cambridge and Trinity Dublin. Conversely, most East Asian international students aren't used to traveling alone. Most people from collectivist cultures tend to stick together with their compatriots when subject to the language barrier, and they often mentally translate every English phrase they see or hear into their first language. This habit prevents them from mastering a second language fully, but one should understand that everybody has their limits, just like I can never force myself to play American football, knowing the running and clashing would put my body at even more risk, if not give me a concussion immediately.

UPenn used to be my most desired institution in the US. Their campus was truly fascinating and three-dimensional, unlike Ohio State (except their Medical Center) and UC Davis, which were basically flattened out. I remember that evening, the Brazilian travel mate and I walked through the urban-styled campus of UPenn and finally stopped in front of the building hosting The Department of Psychology. This building was sacred to me, with the No.1 Clinical Psychology program in America inside. Admittedly, it didn't look as gorgeous as other buildings around it, but I knew there were tons of intelligent people working there every day.

I was doing the mundane pilgrimage thing as many people would do for their beloved fields. For example, on the 2014 road trip to Pittsburgh, a CS major studying in a community college insisted that we visit Carnegie Mellon University. At UC Davis, some visiting scholars in Agriculture and Forestry respectively told me how excited they were to be able to collect data at UC Davis, the institution with the top-ranking program in Agricultural Science. Similarly, whenever I told an optometrist in Davis that I was from Ohio, they would ask if I went to Ohio State because OSU had a big program in optometry.

But that was all: thirty seconds of pilgrimage. There was no way I would ever become part of it through the regular pathway. Not because I wasn't gifted or diligent but because life or fate isn't fair in its nature. Many of us have dreams that we can only hide in the deepest layers of our memory.

By the way, after so many years, do I still care about the ranking that much? Certainly not. The ranking was academic, research-oriented, and most probably, biased. In 2016, I had already realized that academia generally does not solve real-life problems, despite the superfluous amount of knowledge generated from it. (If you ask the academics, they'll likely deny it in front of the camera.) Therefore, it can't be a good fit for me.

On my third day in Philly, I went to the Eastern State Penitentiary alone and took a close look at this place. I was drawn to the idea itself, probably out of curiosity about how I would have ended up if I had continued to make terrible mistakes that year. The building turned out to be designed as a confusing structure. Luckily, I met a professional tour guide who explained to me every piece of it in detail. He was a history major, very composed, and serious. Unlike those tour guides in the White House who literally memorized a lot of materials, he ensured that the information delivered was re-synthesized by his own brain. When we came to the on-site clinic, I asked him who would pay for the comprehensive healthcare for the incarcerated. "The taxpayers." He said. Surely, the word "taxpayer" was used every day by Americans, but when I mentioned it once in front of my classmates back in college, it generated a dramatic reaction in some people. Surely, most senior citizens in a collectivist country wouldn't refer to themselves as taxpayers because they understand the role played by the government differently than Americans do. Sadly, even the young generation failed to be enlightened.

During the semi-personal tour, I was also impressed by the existence of a small synagogue inside the penitentiary. I knew very little about the Jewish culture back then, and even after co-working with so many Jews in the past, I still know very little about them. In D.C., I spent 2 hours in the Holocaust Museum and felt sorry for all the victims. However, it didn't affect my appreciation of certain offensive jokes told by Anthony Jeselnik and other comedians. I remember hearing some professor telling this anecdote back in college: during World War II, in Shanghai, Jewish people were confined by the Nazis and were starving. Some kind-hearted Shanghainese locals cooked some chicken legs and threw them over the wall to feed the Jews. Therefore, the Chinese and the Jewish have been in a good relationship for a long time. However, based on my own life experience, I have to remind myself to evaluate each individual separately because respect has to be earned.

The tour of the penitentiary allowed me to feel confined. Interestingly, it didn't feel that bad, as if I deserved something like that. I was exempt from jail time in Ohio, but I chose to enter the penitentiary in Pennsylvania to face my fear. In other words, I was unconsciously setting up some "exposure therapy" for myself. Throughout that year, my mind felt locked up in custody. I behaved cautiously as Magistrate Turner warned me to. Meanwhile, I had this underlying fear that I wouldn't be allowed to defend myself if I got attacked by American gangsters or racists. My brain was even simulating some affirmative voices to encourage myself, saying, "You've tried your best" or "You are a good guy." That was a form of rumination. I suppose the simulated voices belonged to people who had been critical of me in real life. Wait? Why rumination after so much therapy? The trauma had long-lasting effects on me, including the feeling of being "on exile," particularly on those overcast or drizzly days.

How did I feel after hearing the stories of the inmates? Based on those skulls and bones in the cells, I truly thought

I would have had a mental breakdown in that kind of environment; alternatively, I would have written many songs to cope with the struggle. The incarceration system in America, and human society in general, ensured that innocent people who were wrongly sentenced would lose their good nature and accumulate more darkness inside their psyche unless they were as faithful as Anthony Ray Hinton. Remember, most civilians don't want to have any association with the complicated justice system in America. I wished to be simple and clean too, but it seemed written in the stars that I would live a complicated life— all rooted in this authoritarian family environment I grew up in. To some extent, the excruciating public education in China was already some sort of confinement under a universal standard. See how I ended up? Fruitless, injured, and heartbroken. One only needs to feel confined once in life, yet for me, several periods of life already, through and through.

Standing in the atrium, I looked up to the gray sky and heard the song *Penitentiary* by Houndmouth playing in my mind. In particular, the lyrics of the chorus part made me chill. My eyes were watery for a moment.

On my final day in Philly, I visited The Franklin Institute, a science museum, in the morning and managed to pay my pilgrimage to Benjamin Franklin Museum in the afternoon, 10 minutes before it closed. Considering I'd had enough American history education that week, I went straight to the gift shop. I purchased a metal bookmark made in the shape of Ben Franklin himself, which cost me $12. Insane price for a bookmark, and that thingamajig is still with me today. If I got a second chance to return to Philly, I would visit that museum and study his life carefully, beyond what I already knew from his autobiography. However, life doesn't always allow us to fulfill every wish. I might never go back to Philly again. Also, there are no spiritual leaders for me these days, not Ben Franklin or Ayn Rand. I'd rather act out those virtues advocated by these historical figures than idolize them fanatically, as I am over that age.

13.4 A Love Song and a Pair of Socks

After I returned from skydiving with Julian, I started working on the new song, *Parachute*. On the surface, I was writing about my skydiving experience, but there was more to that. I once told Kevin that most of my songs were autobiographical songs disguised as love songs, but this particular song was exceptional. It was a real love song. Still, it sounded very sad, as Maria, the social worker from the therapy group, pointed out. Why was it sad? Because this love was unidirectional, and there would be no outcome. In the lyrics, I devised a scenario where I was thinking about the girl before I jumped out of the plane. What if this was my last chance to tell her about my feelings? I had so much to say to her, but I didn't have the courage.

So how did Maria know about my song? Here's what happened. Before I left Ohio and flew back to China that November, I had my farewell session with the graduate males' therapy group. As usual, not everybody showed up that week, not The Buddha, Likert, Turing, or Stud. Still, I made my farewell comments to everybody in the group. I had requested 10 minutes beforehand to play the new music video on my iPad in front of these guys. The music video made with Windows Movie Maker was imperfect, but the vocal tracks and the keyboard tracks were recorded more carefully than before in my new living room. Carl offered a percussion track in his basement. Not until that farewell session had I told anybody in the group about my songwriting skills. After the song was played, I ran a Q&A

session regarding this song. Titan, the extremely tall gentleman, took the initiative to ask that sensitive question: "There seems to be some romantic love expressed in your lyrics. Can you tell us about it?"

"Of course. We are in this secretive group anyway." I said, "Yes, I like one of my female colleagues. We came to Ohio State about the same time, and we weren't that close to each other until a few months ago when we went to a show together. And she volunteered to go to meet the lawyer with me. I know it's probably just my fantasy. There's almost no chance. She's older than me, and she's white." The room became silent for a few seconds. Sometimes I wonder why I tended to develop good feelings with someone before I had to leave a city. In Davis, I felt a bond with a colleague in the same department when we were about to leave that place. The same spring in 2017, I also had a crush on a girl I met at a house party. However, I was too shy in front of this glamorous girl, and our fates simply wouldn't cross, especially since I was determined to leave California for the East Coast. Maybe it was all just chance. Maybe because I never had convenient transportation during the first year in a new city, which determined I couldn't seriously socialize until the second year.

"But I really cared about her." I continued, "She's from Florida, so she likes to wear flip-flops all the time, even in the cold weather. I originally thought White people don't feel cold in their feet until she told me her feet did feel cold— she just chose to ignore it. I understand her toes don't feel like being **restrained**. They want **freedom**. So I decided to send her a Thanksgiving & Christmas gift just to show my appreciation at least. I found on Amazon a pair of long socks specially designed for flip-flops, with cherry-blossom patterns on them. The big toe is separate from the other four toes, like in those mittens. This is eye-opening for me too."

In reality, I only texted Ashley about a gift being shipped to her home address without naming it. One weekend afternoon before my departure, several musician lab mates invited me to a musical in downtown Columbus. Outside the theater, Sophie, a lab mate from Montréal, spotted some abrasion on Ashley's naked toes. She was still wearing flip-flops in November. "I tripped over a stone accidentally," She said. It seemed to me her toes wanted freedom and needed protection at the same time, but she didn't know how to resolve this conflict. I asked her if she had opened the Amazon box yet, and she answered, "No, I feel it would be more appropriate to open it after you're gone." She meant Thanksgiving. I nodded in smilence. ("Smilence" is an artificial English word invented by Chinese students, short for "smile in silence".) I could tell this box made her curious and nervous simultaneously, but I couldn't tell if she had sensed my adoration for her.

Near the end of this therapy session, when people said their farewell words to me individually, some guys applauded my creativity and musical talents, not surprisingly. And Jacob, the organizer of our group, said to me, "Slim, when you were first introduced into our group, I just knew you would bring us something unusual. When you talked about those socks a moment ago, I almost shed tears… You are a good person, and I wish you success. Safe travel."

After that, what was supposed to be the "hugging ceremony" was replaced with the "bowing ceremony" upon my request. My excuse was that mutual bows were more widely accepted in East Asian countries as a sign of high respect. It's true that in China, most guys don't have physical contact with other guys very much. But the fundamental reason was that, after the farewell session for The Alchemist last time, I realized the hugging ceremony had become an ironical trigger for me; I didn't want to tear up in front of these gentlemen again because of my historic hugs with Jeremy. End of the session, I told these guys that I would have some withdrawal effects after leaving this group therapy.

The expected withdrawal effects didn't eventually occur. An overwhelming new life was waiting for me in Davis, California, and before that, an entire month back in China was painful and thrilling enough, partially due to the manipulation of Mandy and the stupidity of Doug. The reunion was a pleasure for them, at the cost of my well-being. However, I had always been warned by Mandy that if I failed to travel back to China for a long period, the staff working for the Consulate would sense some intent of immigration in me, an intent that people on an academic visa have to conceal. I had no way to verify the validity of that warning, though. In history, she had embedded in me lots of maladaptive beliefs based on her hearsay or imagination, as many parents would do, which contributed to my erroneous decisions in many situations.

The evening before I departed from Ohio, i.e., Thanksgiving Eve of 2014, I received a text message from Ashley. "Hey Slim, I just opened the Amazon box. What a great gift! I love love these socks. Thank you so much." She typed the word "love" twice for real. It caught me off guard because it disrupted my heart even more.

"But you said you wouldn't open it until I'm gone." I added a "CRY" emoji.

"I can't wait anymore. Travel safe and good luck with

everything. We can meet up again next month when you are back in Columbus."

I didn't know what made her change her mind that evening, but this gave me some sweet hope to live on while living with pain. When I was back in China in December, except for the days when I had serious business, such as looking up the rare YouTube videos about this self-proclaimed bicycle town of Davis and searching online for a room, all I thought about was her as a wonderful human being. It was infatuation based on a deeper understanding of a person's character instead of some good feeling out of my instinct to help someone when they looked distressed. It wasn't a superficial crush, as I never had a crush on any of my former colleagues, these serious academic researchers. As mentioned before, she didn't have a Hollywood star look and never wore any heavy makeup. The latter, as an indicator of authenticity, was very important to people like me.

As I remember, the first time my lab mates went to Hounddog's Pizza together in 2012, she said to me, "Slim, you're the first person I've seen drinking a bottle of beer with a straw." It was my first time doing so, too, probably because American beer was too cold for me. Two years later, she became the first person to whom I had said, "Lady, can I buy you a drink?" In order to decline her offer to buy me a drink. I was pretending to be joking, but I wasn't, at least not completely. That was the only time we went to a band show together, and I was grateful for that opportunity to exchange information about our lives. By the way, I learned the question was commonly used in socializing after reading the books *The Male Brain* and *The Female Brain*, written by Prof. Louann Brizendine, a clinical psychologist. Before that, I didn't know what to say to a lady in an American bar.

Sometimes I couldn't help but ask myself, "Was this infatuation reflecting a natural tendency for my heart to cling to a supportive individual after a personal crisis? If I had never been traumatized, would I ever have developed this affinity for her? So was my self-labeled "love" for her just a short-term pathological phenomenon, similar to transference in the clinical setting, which should NOT be taken seriously anyway? Was it related to the "obsessive personality" brought up by the OSU policeman? However, this type of judgmental overthinking didn't stop the romantic fantasy from floating in my brain. I couldn't help it, although the aforementioned Ph.D. friend from China had told me to stop this unrealistic idea because my life was already a mess. I understood I was probably too immature and stigmatized to deserve any relationship. This stigma looked very big when I was 24, transitioning from a hard-working college student in Shanghai to a stigmatized international student mislabeled by so many people.

But really, it was my first time having deep feelings for a person in my professional circle. Those people you fantasize about from a distance may turn out to be very dull when you actually make acquaintance with them, such as those idolized celebs or your teen crushes. She was different. She fit my ideal standard: someone a bit older than me, well-educated, sociable, rational, and not controlling or narcissistic like some females in my family and extended family. To exaggerate a bit, she played the role of my Sweet Mary, as in Weezer's song *Sweet Mary* from the album *Pacific Daydream*. When I first heard this song in 2017, I immediately felt connected to the chorus part of the lyrics. I knew there was such a person once in my life, even though she might be helping me totally out of humanistic virtues. Maybe that's enough sweet memory for me to hide inside?

While staying in Smoke City in December, I had to figure out my housing in Davis remotely. As soon as I bought the one-way ticket from Shanghai to Columbus, I told Ashley about the only day I would be on the OSU campus again, and we planned to meet for lunch at Buckeye Donuts on North High Street. I planned to pick up my courage and do something I had never done to a lady in my life till that age. How come never before? I suppressed all good feelings before I could see the world through America. I never understood the logic of finding love in one's country of origin, if one has an international heart or, more specifically, an American dream. Why make a quick decision about the rest of one's life when the entire world hasn't been opened up to you yet? Is it because a foreign Asian male is always the least desired on the global market? Doesn't a foreigner like you deserve to be loved by a local? Or have you seen the depressing Tinder stats about swiping preference?

However, I forgot one fact: good ladies like her must have a lot of STEM guys dreaming about her. I had no advantage at all except being a "fungi" to her. Besides, I was leaving Ohio for good anyway, so would it still be meaningful to show her my heart? I figured I had nothing to lose if I simply gave it a try, and what if I would never meet such a great woman again in my life? Mandy had this traditional notion from patriarchal China: a man always has to be the one to take the initial step. People like Stacy were just too thirsty and aggressive by that patriarchal standard when she asked Jeremy to be her boyfriend. Well, she adored him like a fan girl at the beginning because he could play guitar.

On the day of the musical show, she brought a male friend, Owen, a final-year Ph.D. student in Nuclear Engineering. She did give me heads up, and I was fine with that. Owen was a well-educated gentleman, as I could tell. They were sitting together while watching the show. I was seated next to Sophie, the lab mate from Montréal, who later married our lab mate Edward from Santa Cruz. I didn't think much that day, being preoccupied with mixed feelings about going back to China. My common sense told me my life was overcomplicated for Ashley, who might just need a reliable partner with a stable career track. This solid friendship over the years was already a fortune for me. I knew we had a lot in common; for example, we both read a lot of science fiction when we were young, such as Robert Heinlein's books. However, she didn't know that because I didn't even open a Facebook account until I got the offer from Ohio State. (In college, we were induced to use a domestic platform, a copycat of Facebook.) Besides, reading American sci-fi was nothing special for an American kid, though it definitely made me the outlier among my peers back then, in just one extra dimension.

Chinese people have invented an exaggerated and oversimplified saying that goes, "America versus China, one has no sense of history while the other has no sense of future." I liked what American kids liked as a child, as opposed to what a typical and patriotic Chinese kid should like, but this wasn't enough to establish a strong connection between an American kid and me. It's too generic for them. That partially explains why I perceived more similarities between Jeremy and me than he could perceive. Most likely, he didn't care at all. In his eyes, these little similarities were just common American features and were easily overshadowed by cultural and racial differences: nothing special, nothing to celebrate about. It took me years to sort out this logic. What was the objective gap? I didn't grow up in a developed multicultural country, as a smaller-sized alien for him to overlook.

It's worth noting that by the time of my last lab meeting in Ohio, I had already sold my grandpa-aged Nissan at a super low price. I had no choice because it was found out that the odometer had been tampered with, indicating tremendous risk of driving it across the country. Of course, nobody could technically prove that the number shown on the odometer was false, but this was the only logical explanation for the erratic numbers on the Carfax report, according to the buyer, a seasoned driver and long-term immigrant. He told me he even tried to disassemble an old car just to understand its "Anatomy and Physiology."

I had every reason to call myself stupid, but I also had no time to dwell on that. I just wanted to leave Ohio with my hands clean after my body and soul had been contaminated. After graduation, the Student Legal Services at OSU could no longer help me with anything; fortunately, Ms. Wilson's new paralegal advised me that I should not be worried about being criminalized for having bought a bad car from that shady dealer. Again, I, the victimized consumer, was scared of the injustice of the US justice system against me, an Asian foreigner, before I even questioned the seller of their legality and morality. Besides, it was no news to me that some frauds knew how to gaslight or threaten the victims.

Several people, including my housemate Mr. Li, said I should file a small complaint against the auto dealer with the help of another attorney, but Mandy was strongly against this idea. "Don't make other people see you as someone who goes to the court a lot." This is a typical Chinese mindset among the old generation: the desire for peace and zero conflict, even when one is victimized — for sure, fighting for one's lawful rights might result in negative consequences in the dark ages; besides, she was simply a spectator on this matter. I gave up my rights again this time because I knew how time-consuming and how stressful a legal battle would be, because I wanted to leave Ohio with less mental baggage, because I was financially challenged those months, and ultimately because I had found online that the Carfax report could not be used as evidence in a court of law, at least not in 2014. If I couldn't prove the odometer had been tempered, how could I accuse the dealership of ripping me off? The other party must have known this hack, so I was doomed to lose this battle. Why even struggle? I lost another battle due to the asymmetry of information as a rookie consumer.

Dear readers, do not take my experience as legal advice. Consult an attorney if you face a similar situation, as every case is different. Your outcome might be better than mine if you have sufficient time to explore your options.

Seriously, when Antonio and I were 23 years old, the Carfax report seemed as enigmatic as the Holy Bible. He told me, "Just be more careful next time." Well, as far as I know, his first car was bought by his dad for him, and his dad knew a lot about cars. When I told this tragedy to my cousin Lulu, she was surprised, "What? This kind of fraud happens in America too?" Yeah, people in China have a lot of unrealistic expectations for American society, considering America has more established legislation and regulation on the automobile market. It's time to wake up. It's time to grow up. People from all over the world are practicing similar wrongdoings in different forms, and they can get away with it very often. Maybe we are really just one big human race, as some people like to say.

13.5 Louis Vuitton and Filial Love
Dec 2014, Shanghai & Smoke City, China

I flew back to China on Thanksgiving Day, as the air ticket was the cheapest. Carl had invited me to spend Thanksgiving with his big family for a third time, and I had to let it pass in order to meet with my biological family in China, who I didn't miss very much. But why did I have to return to China? Because I was told that not going back to one's country of origin was an indicator of the intent of immigration, which I had to conceal as an F-1 student.

After landing at Shanghai Pudong Airport (PVG), I stayed a few days in Hangzhou, a city nearby, to visit some relatives. Then, before returning to Smoke City, I spent one day in Shanghai getting my new travel documents sorted out in the US Consulate and another day meeting with several acquaintances known from college. In particular, I took a walk by the waterfront with a Shanghainese couple who both grew up listening to the Malaysian singer-songwriter Victor Wong as I did.

Interestingly, I ran into an assistant professor at my college when walking toward a metro station. She told me she had spent one year working as a visiting scholar at a famous university in North Carolina. Besides complaining about the difficulties in daily life, she commented, "those American staff members all seemed so nice when you first met them, but when you needed them to resolve some issue, they all acted like it's none of their business." I didn't know how to respond back then, but I sensed her professional experience in the US wasn't delightful. The first year without a car was always annoying, yet she only had one year in North Carolina. Also, to be fair, I think bureaucracy in higher education is a universal issue.

Then finally, I went back to Smoke City. Unsurprisingly, Mandy continued to hurt me with her hypocrisy.

I told her Mr. Osman offered me an RA position after he received a federal grant and secured a position in UC Davis. She replied, "I just knew it. You are my great son. I'm so proud of you." I always hated that kind of comment, as opposed to the simple and respectful response, "congrats!" I hated that she was using me as an indirect source of her personal pride. To me, that was stealing credit, just like my maternal grandmother used to do when she was alive — she ascribed every personal achievement we made to her donation to the Buddhist temples rather than a combination of our own efforts and environmental factors.

When I was a teen, I almost said to Mandy every week that I had no love for her as a person. However, this time, she still asked me out loud, "Can you use your first month's salary in California to buy an LV handbag for me?" I knew which model she was referring to. She already had many bags, just like most women in this world, but she wanted some credential of my filial love for her so that she could show off to her female colleagues. Unfortunately, this morbid motive is cross-cultural, based on some online videos I watched.

"No, no way. I've told you so many times that I don't love you. When can you face the fact? That superficial LV bag carried by random people on the subway? You are daydreaming. I have known your vanity since I was a kid. Your education on me has always been a failure, and the best proof is that I don't love you now. Yet you're trying to cover it up, to make your colleagues jealous. I'm fed up. Even my American therapist knows you are a horrible mom. The entire Western society knows authoritarian Chinese parents like you are harmful, but you yourselves are in constant denial! You are such a Tiger Mom, who should have been deprived of her custody!"

And her response to my "therapist" attack? "Don't listen to the B.S. of those American therapists! Therapists just say whatever you like to hear so that you will pay them! How can a psychotherapist tell the kids not to love their parents?!"

I never believed in family therapy in China, not for this family. Persuasion by any Chinese counselor wouldn't work for me because these counselors would be obliged to stand on the opposite side under the pressure of traditional Chinese culture and push me to forgive them unconditionally. To many Eastern cultures, filial love is a virtue by default; to an Objectivist, any kind of love should be earned, not enforced. The older generation rarely thought they did wrong because they had the traditional culture as their excuse. My testing on them confirmed my suspicion. After the tragedy with Jeremy and Stacy, I trusted my own judgment even more. False hope only brings more disappointment.

Our society erroneously believes that kids will start understanding their parents' perspective once they become parents themselves. And so what? Understanding is not the same as condoning or forgiving. As for the old generation, their opinions might be right sometimes, but they always resort to violence and coercion instead of reasoning. Why? They didn't understand the mechanism underlying right or wrong, or they couldn't elucidate it without revealing the dark side of humanity. The issue itself is not only psychological but also ideological. If mental health clinicians lack critical thinking and avoid pondering upon controversial issues, then counseling itself will end up a softy profession, as it currently tends to be.

Because I once worked in the autism intervention program with the kids and their parents, I could sometimes understand a parent's or a teacher's perspective. However, understanding is not the same as appreciation: the parents aren't always doing beneficial things for their offspring(s), as they also have other personal values. With finite resources, values are inevitably competing against each other.

Regarding the LV handbag Mandy solicited, I never looked into it. I will never spend my time shopping for women's apparel unless I want to spend precious time with a lady I appreciate. When I was little, I had to follow her and Lulu when they were shopping for clothes and cosmetics, and I hated that— a waste of my time and an unhealthy ambiance for a boy to grow up in. I am confident that I will never fall in love with a person full of desires for such extravagances with no outstanding functionality.

13.6 The Cockroach Powder and the Catharsis

I was stuck in Smoke City for weeks before picking up my passport from a local bank. Finally, my visa was successfully renewed. During that period, I couldn't return to Shanghai due to severe and persistent diarrhea, which was triggered after I was pressured to eat spicy and oily Szechuan food in a restaurant owned by an elder cousin brother.

My condition was first diagnosed as mild ulcerative colitis by a G.I. doctor in a local hospital after he strongly recommended a colonoscopy under anesthetics. I wouldn't say he was an incompetent doctor, but these directors in this fourth-tier city cannot compare with some renowned doctors in major cities. In a follow-up meeting with him in his office, while he was smoking a cigarette after performing a procedure, he told me that his daughter was sent to Canada for college, which indicated the wealth of his family.

"My daughter also likes to complain a lot," he said. As a heartbroken patient, I silently tolerated his unfounded accusation of me. In front of me was a middle-aged man who spoke in an androgynous tone and barely knew me.

Then he told Mandy, "If I were you, I wouldn't let my kid go abroad again."

Mandy murmured, "If I don't let him go, he'll hate me for the rest of his life."

Had I listened to his dissuasion, I would never have developed repetitive stress injury by working for Mr. Osman in Davis — a positive. Nor would I have received a second opinion in Kaiser Vacaville Hospital, which allowed me to stop taking the expensive German drug, Mesalamine — a negative. He said I should take this drug for six months, along with some protective drugs, and made me believe my condition could develop into something scarier if I didn't take it seriously. What exactly? He didn't say it aloud. I didn't ask for clarification but assumed he meant colon cancer.

However, during my appointment with her in March, the G.I. doctor at Kaiser asked me, "Do you know what ulcerative colitis entails? You'll have to stay on medication for the rest of your life. I think what you had in China was a food infection." When asked if ulcerative colitis could develop into cancer, she said, "I don't know anything about that." She ordered another colonoscopy for me, which cost me a co-pay of $100. Weeks later, I was free of the diagnosis of ulcerative colitis. There is no more Mesalamine to take, but a new label called Irritable Bowel Disease.

Several cases have informed me that there is a huge

difference between medicine in America and medicine in China. I wonder why the textbooks teach very different things on the same matter and which side to trust on which specific issue. Beware that I haven't even brought alternative medicine and various ethnicity-based medicine into this complicated equation, or, say, inequation.

If you Google this topic, you will find that having ulcerative colitis does increase the likelihood of developing colorectal cancer, but no universal causality has been established. There is no doubt that bowel health should be protected from an early age, but most of us fail to do so, and the alcohol culture is sometimes to blame.

It shouldn't be hard for you to imagine how much my hatred toward Jeremy had escalated when I believed the original diagnosis in Smoke City. Because of the trauma, I actually developed a chronic disease and had to live on medication?! So Jeremy would cost me even more money besides the E.R. visit, the legal fees, and the delayed graduation?! If not for the fact that I followed Mr. Osman to UC Davis with the false hope that he would be a good boss and mentor, I wouldn't have considered my life worth continuing in that situation. However, even back then, my biological parents didn't stand on my side.

Mandy was trying to hide my bowel issue from her friends and the cousin who owned the Szechuan restaurant. "Don't say anything. Your cousin will feel unhappy. You are leaving soon after all."

"You'd rather make me suffer than make other people unhappy," I said.

Due to her attempt to downplay my symptoms, when another family invited us to have lunch with them, they chose another Szechuan restaurant. I didn't eat anything during that meal. My heart was already dead.

"I'm sorry. We didn't know that you were having a bowel problem. Your mom never mentioned it. We thought you young people should like spicy food, because my daughter loves it." The mother said.

I didn't know this family at all, yet I was arranged to have lunch with these strangers. Had I declined to show up, Mandy would have said, "they'll be unhappy if you don't go. You can't disappoint other people. They wanna see you because you are just back from America."

As we all know, there is no free lunch in this world, so what did they expect from me? It turned out they wanted me to buy some American books for the daughter, who was a psych major in China. I didn't make any promises. Nor have I ever met this family again.

Here comes the weird part. When I was slowly recovering from my bowel dysfunction, I was told I could only eat semi-fluid food like porridge (or congee) for a couple of months. One day, Doug watched an agricultural T.V. show about a farmer who used a machine to grind dead cockroaches into medicinal powder. As Doug was assigned by the Chinese government to work in a rural area when he was young, he developed a nostalgic interest in farming and agriculture even when living in the urban area. It was claimed in the T.V. show that the "organic" powder could cure a variety of bowel diseases, with the rationale being that cockroaches never had any bowel issues themselves after ingesting all the dirty stuff one could think of. Then Doug started to advocate this miraculous treatment for me. "It's worth a try. I'll look into it and see where I can buy it."

"I am not going to eat it. Why don't you go eat fresh

cockroaches yourself? Do you want to force me to eat disgusting things again by beating me up during breakfast, like you did every morning when I was in middle school? Don't you ever think about it, unless you want me to hate you even more!" I responded.

Pharmaceutics isn't as simple as grinding some bugs into medicinal powder. If someone wants to convince me that Doug was looking for some ancient or postmodern folk remedy for my benefit, I will caution them to think twice. Here's the thing: I don't want the concern (or praise, or adoration, etc.) from people I dislike. When I mentioned this "organic" medicine to some relative of his generation, they sneered and said, "That's because he is ill-educated and has a low I.Q." I couldn't agree more. That's how I have perceived Doug since I was a kid. In elementary school, I once said I wanted suicide because I hated this miserable life under the oppression of my Chinese chromosome providers. Then he tried to push my head into the toilet and yelled, "You want death? You want death? Do you still want death? Say that again!" I struggled in full hatred, and his oppressive action proved my point. From that day, I despised him as someone who couldn't distinguish between basic concepts such as suicide versus homicide, let alone see through gimmicks and nonsense.

Everybody was speechless when I told them about the cockroach powder solution, and nobody was willing to try the cockroach powder themselves, despite them admitting that "it might make some sense." I never followed up with this astonishing idea. Suppose some active component in the powder really works for humanity; in that case, the pharmaceutical companies should preferably extract this component from the powder using biochemical methods and make it into a new drug targeted at certain diseases. Eating raw powders, instead, seemed so crude and primitive. While traditional Chinese medicine (TCM) does use some insects and worms, including cockroaches, as medicinal components in their prescriptions, one needs an individualized prescription from a certified clinician. Strangely, Doug accused us of being narrow-minded or "unwilling to listen to different opinions." You know, technically, I couldn't even preclude the minuscule possibility that he might be the only person holding the truth unbeknownst to the rest of us.

I was irritable those days because this eruption of bowel dysfunction spoiled my plan to return to Shanghai and hang out with some friends. In other words, I could only stay in Smoke City until my next flight. Mandy was happy to have me around because that was the longest time I had been stuck in Smoke City since entering college— I had avoided going back to Smoke City with every possible excuse just to not look at their faces. I told her that she was basing her happiness upon my suffering.

One day, when triggered by Doug, I had a severe cathartic episode in front of them, accusing them of contributing to a series of harmful events from my childhood to adulthood, with the length and intensity of a nuclear chain reaction. My sobbing mode was paired with dramatic body language. Yet, they looked apathetic, not because they were really "conscious," as defined by Eckhart Tolle, but because they were self-righteous, just like Jeremy— they put the blame on the Chinese examination system instead of the villainous roles they had played beyond the "system."

Samuel, the white male cat, eight years old in 2014, was affected by my behavior and started growling. He then ran behind the curtain to vomit in pain. That scene was visceral. After my catharsis subsided, Samuel walked to me and rubbed his head against my knees, something he had done since he was a kitten. People in China made it a big deal that he could still remember me when I returned from the US, but they had forgotten that he was the same cat who liked to pee into my luggage bag secretly and jump onto my lap a couple of hours before I left for college. He could always sense that I was going away and that my childhood bedroom would become his own, even when he was only three years old in 2009.

I was always reluctant to share any personal experience with Mandy because I knew the outcome wouldn't be any good. Typically, she would distort, abridge, or sugarcoat my message when forwarding it to other people and usually give unpleasant feedback, which would discourage me from sharing more. One might say the old generation simply lacks the necessary knowledge to understand us, but there was more to that.

For example, she asked this good question: "Since you are studying psychology, how could you still get depressed?" She was right that I have always been actively accumulating knowledge and skills in psychology throughout my short life span, even though I was never officially enrolled in an academic psychology program. I didn't even bother to explain to her that the cognitive science I studied was very different from the folk psychology people talk about on matchmaking-themed T.V. shows. In fact, I didn't get to take my first Abnormal Psychology course until my second year in grad school, while some Westerners could study that in high school if lucky enough. I simply didn't know how to spot the early signs. Moreover, for grad students in challenging Ph.D. programs, where success largely depends on intractable P-values and their professors' approval, the risk of depression or anxiety should be understandable. Then why are cases always underreported? Because exposing one's negativity, including victimhood, will pose a threat to their career. Last but not least, counselors and therapists also need help sometimes after absorbing the negativity from their clients — something the public barely know.

Interestingly, after I told her that Jeremy was a bodybuilder, she immediately responded, "Stay away from those bodybuilders. Those people are often mentally problematic." I didn't know what to say about this stereotype. I knew several people working on their muscles back then, and Jeremy was the only one who appeared narcissistic and emotionally unstable. Maybe a fraction of these people do have some covert issues with their hormones and self-image, but the rest still look like normal people, pretty approachable and genuine when they're outside the gym. After all, big muscles are desirable in mainstream American culture. If you look at the cover photos of Men's Health magazine, rarely do you NOT see bodybuilders.

After this exhausting adventure in Smoke City, finally, in the second week of January 2014, for a second time, I went to the Shanghai Pudong Airport (PVG) in both anger and excitement. I had packed all sorts of pills in a medicine box and carried them in my backpack. Once again, I passed the security checkpoint without looking back because my heart had always been trying to escape from the Chinese culture. Now that I would be sick and in pain in either country, why not devote my life to my "favorite" country? The forced attempt to adjust back was absurdly preposterous. Years later, Doug told me that Mandy cried for several days after I returned to the US, and I told him when I was back in China, I was the person to cry, and in fact, I'd been screaming inside for my trampled civil rights for two decades. When they accused me of being cruel, I always responded, "To show mercy to those who have relentlessly destroyed one's childhood and teenage years is to be cruel to oneself."

The trip wasn't smooth, for, in Los Angeles, I was put in a small room for investigation. I tried to remain calm in front of the officers and told myself: it's part of life, the part of life many immigrants have to face sooner or later. Then I spent my last few days in Columbus, Ohio, meeting several people. Mr. Li hosted me.

After arriving in Davis in mid-January, I smelled some cat urine inside my cameo-patterned carry-on luggage bag, so I abandoned it with no hesitation. Clorox wouldn't help much with the odor in the bag, which I purchased on Amazon for $30 to hold my heavy Toshiba due to my leg pain. I had no idea when Samuel peed in my bag. All I knew for sure was the higher temperature in California helped the evaporation of the odor.

13.7 She Has a Boyfriend

Jan 2015 (three days), Columbus, OH, move

When I returned to the US in January 2015, I went through Customs in Los Angeles. However, as previously mentioned, this time, I was called out, put in a separate room, to be surrounded by people of various ethnic backgrounds. As usual, I was the only Asian. Fortunately, I was prepared for that after going through so much humiliation in 2014. To cover my anxiety, I used that time to take my medications and probiotic supplements in a calm manner — the diagnosis of mild ulcerative colitis was no joke. After half an hour, my status was cleared by one officer, and I was released. Thanks to that delay, all the loading carts were taken, so I had to push two big and two small luggage bags with only two hands during my connection to the domestic flight. Why did they investigate me at the border? Was it because I went through the express check-in in August 2012 due to the typhoon in Shanghai? They probably saw some alert on my record and then determined I was legit enough to re-enter their country.

On the second day, Antonio happily picked me up from Columbus Airport. It was right after the New Year, and the snow wasn't too heavy. He then drove me to USPS to mail some of my personal belongings directly to my new address in Davis, California. Previously, I had purchased four big plastic containers from Walmart. The USPS staff accepted all four containers without a question.

On the third day, Ashley and I met for lunch at Buckeye Donuts. One hour before that, I went to my music lab for the last time, and there was only one person there—Natalie from New Jersey. The new semester had not yet begun, but she was already preparing for her new project. I brought a creative present to her from China, and she was delighted when she opened it up.

"I will never forget that you saved my life," I said.

"Oh no," she said with her characteristic high pitch, "Everybody gets sick." But if you have read this far, you should know that my sickness wasn't random at all, and it was exacerbated by my lack of experience in navigating the convoluted healthcare system in the US. To some extent, I picked her to help me on that day because I knew she was trustworthy and capable, based on our previous interaction. I don't know people from every state of America, but every friend I know from New Jersey is so genuine to me, just like every friend I know from Florida is so generous to me, just like every friend I know from D.C. or Maryland is so open-minded. Stereotyping and overgeneralization, I know. I don't care.

"Hey, Natalie, can I tell you a secret?"

"Yeah? Sure." She said.

"I think I'm in love with Ashley. And you know, I am meeting her in the next hour." I said peacefully.

"Oh… Wow…" Her facial expression made me think she was laughing and crying simultaneously.

"I just know it. She already has a boyfriend. Am I right?"

"Yeah… I think so." She said.

"And his name is Owen?" I asked.

"Yeah. I've only heard Ashley mentioning him once. Never met him in person." She said. The puzzle was solved.

"I think I met him last year. He seemed like a nice guy. She brought him to the musical but didn't mention they were dating. Wait, they were sitting together. Okay, I should have noticed that signal; sorry, not a signal, but a cue, like Mr. Anderson taught us. You know, ethology." I took a deep breath. "I'm so glad I came here to talk with you today so I needn't embarrass her or myself later."

"You're welcome. You'll find the right person someday. Good luck." She agreed with my vision that the demographics in California or NYC would be more diverse, which is a good thing for me, to some extent, at least.

Then I walked out of the building and met Ashley at Buckeye Donuts. I ordered my favorite chicken tender platter with Cajun sauce and a cup of French vanilla, which was super for winter. She ordered a very regular American brunch: French toast with coffee. Since I got no confession left to make, I peacefully enjoyed "the last lunch" with her as a good friend. I noticed she was wearing real shoes that

THE LAST FALL AND A LOVE SONG FOR MYSELF

day instead of flip-flops, and I was happy for her rational choice in the winter: she gave up her toes' freedom for warmth. Remember I came to America for my imagined freedom; in the end, I was **restrained** for months. It was a sunny day, and there wasn't much snow on the streets, but after I left for California, the second wave of snowstorms arrived to haunt the entire Midwest again. What a narrow escape for me!

During the conversation, I told her I was hoping to attend the Objectivist Summer Conference after I got settled in the position in California. I told her how much Ayn Rand's nonfiction had enlightened me since high school. She told me she had only read *Anthem* in high school, like many other Americans, including Mr. Shapiro. In California, I spent the next few years overcoming the obstacles of reading the English versions of *Atlas Shrugged, The Fountainhead,* and *Anthem,* until I could map the sorts of individuals I had interacted with to the vivid characters in these fictions. This reading process transformed my brain into one that felt most comfortable **reading** English text in its default mode, whether or not I could fully comprehend the material. In other words, English has become my brain's de facto official written language. A linguist might point out the different types of characters or symbols used in different written languages, but I'd rather not dig into that "visual" topic here since I lack the necessary knowledge.

Honestly, I still experienced a lot of difficulties understanding literature written by Neil Gaiman, let alone Shakespeare, who I probably would never read, but I guess it was mainly dependent on the genre. Remember, I primarily read sci-fi as a teenager, in Chinese, and nothing historical in particular. Meanwhile, I still couldn't understand some lines in Western movies and T.V. shows, especially when they contained slang and jargon. Listening might be even harder for me when some genres and accents are involved. Therefore, though my academic English skill might be better than an average American, it's not native and will never be, simply because I didn't study all the courses in English as a child. Strictly speaking, or from a linguist's perspective, I can never be truly bilingual — there are too many loopholes to fill up. The same bitter truth will hold for most gifted and dedicated Westerners studying Mandarin or Japanese as a second language. Miracles can happen, but the cost is substantial.

At a certain point in our conversation, I tried to shift the topic a bit, so I asked her, "Is your boyfriend getting his Ph.D. soon?"

"You mean Owen? Oh, we've only been seeing each other for a couple of months. We met in a Meetup group in Columbus…He said he was supposed to graduate last semester, but his professor was too busy to read his dissertation, so he has to stay for another spring. His department has agreed to offer him a research position during this period. Anyway, I guess he'll stay in Columbus for a while." She said, in her characteristic lousy tone.

"Yeah, things get out of control sometimes. Sometimes people get pushed too much, but sometimes we also feel stuck and can't make progress. They say the pace of life is slower here compared to the Coasts, but after two years, I'm already exhausted because of all sorts of trouble. Other people's orchard has become my battlefield." I sighed and took a sip of my French vanilla.

"How about you? Are you getting along with your mentor? I mean the official one, not Mr. Anderson." I asked.

"Oh, I've started to work with a different person since

last semester. The original one wasn't very available, plus he was planning to retire. There didn't seem to be any project I could work on if I stayed in his lab. So, no more neuroscience for me, I guess."

"Good for you. It's always better to do something you can grasp. I've been associated with that since college, but I wouldn't recommend it to other people, no matter how sexy it sounds." I said. This issue of switching advisors at Ohio State seemed more prevalent than I imagined. According to a senior grad student, in a large public school like OSU, professors and students are just not that close, unlike in private schools. One has to waste some time until one can find a better match. Yet life is what it is. You pay for what you get.

We hugged goodbye and went our separate ways. Of course, we were still good friends on the Internet and still cared about each other, though we rarely contacted each other outside of Facebook timelines. Gradually, many of these past lab mates I had in academia were reduced to abstract Facebook profile pictures in my eyes. Some of them chose to stay silent on social media once they entered an academic position; some allegedly decided to stay off social media completely; the rest of them rarely entered my sight, possibly because Facebook algorithms determined we were not close enough.

I don't know if I would ever meet someone as good as her in real life, I mean, outside social media. The chance is low. Grad school is where you find people you have the same depth with; once you miss that opportunity, it's even harder to locate the right person after graduation. Years later, I did meet some decent girls in the clinic but wasn't able to interact with them very much due to the time limit and legal status, not to mention most of these Californians had already had their lives sorted out in college. I wish my life could be that simple, but it has never been. I'm glad she found a reliable person and might lead a normal life like most US citizens, or an extraordinary life, as a social activist outside her regular job. I was at least a good friend, someone she cared about in life: half glass full.

After having lunch with Ashley, I went to the Student Clinic again to pay off my medical bill. Then I met the two physical therapists and told them I was ready to move to California. Their first reaction was, "That's going to be very expensive."

As I remember, during my final appointment in November 2014, Melissa still firmly believed that my foot pain resulted from a lack of arch support. Therefore, she referred me to FrontRunners again for those specialized Saucony shoes, considering my leg would overreact to customized inserts. And yes, affiliate marketing had always being around. When first moving to Davis, I wore those shoes all the time, but generally speaking, I felt these sports shoes were overly rigid, making me feel like I was in my fifties. Only months later did I realize I couldn't rely on these on formal occasions. In other words, I was never provided with a comprehensive real-life solution. As a healthcare professional, Melissa would arguably advocate those products for good biomechanics, but no, that wasn't enough.

Frankie said to me, "Slim, I know you've been through a lot of sh*t here. Some people in this region are just like that because they've never seen the outside world." I had never told him about anything I had undergone in the past year other than my physical injuries, but he could observe me over time and had access to some of my medical records.

The medical records were separate from psychotherapy, but they were indicative enough of my poor well-being.

"My opponent was a medical student, you know..." I said softly.

"Well, some med students have their complexes. You'll be making big money, man. Stay positive, and life will get better." He said in his encouraging tone, and we shook hands for the last time.

Frankie once imagined that I would be making $80 per hour someday. The truth was, I was only making $20 per hour as a research assistant under Mr. Osman, despite the computer programming, quantitative analyses, and technical writing involved in my position, with a remarkable bonus: work-related injury within half a year of employment. Then if you subtract the monthly rent and the Californian taxation from the equation, you know I wouldn't have much left.

I left Ohio with no regret, just like many other people, especially those with minority labels on them. According to an Asian friend who had worked at UCSF, the Midwest is a "white people's zone." If you feel weird about me using the word "zone," think about "the neutral zone" in the Amazon original series *The Man in the High Castle*, as opposed to "the Pacific state" and "the Reich." Truth hurts. In American history, if I remember correctly, during the westward expansion/migration, some didn't finish the journey but chose to settle in the Midwest for whatever reason. If they could turn back time, would they make the same choice? Would they decide to stay on the East Coast? Or would they carry on till they reach the West Coast? Just my speculation.

I asked Kevin for a ride to the Columbus Airport, scheduled at 6 AM the following day. I didn't need a backup plan because he was someone I could trust — an IT professional. "I have double-checked that my car can start well in the morning," he said.

The evening before my flight to Sacramento, Mr. Li had gone to Indiana to meet with his family. Carl and Lindsay came to visit me for the last time.

Then at 6 AM, Kevin arrived. He was wearing a cap that day, and his old car had a door that didn't seal very well. We laughed about the fact that the cold wind could sneak into the car when we were on the freeway. Not a big problem because I felt warm inside. He was the type of person who could cheer you up with his music and make you feel relaxed even when saying farewell. We just parted casually, as if we would meet each other again the following weekend. Neither of us initiated a hug. After all, neither of us had a personality that would make us stick to the ritual.

Did the absence of the ritual matter, though? The truth is, we have chatted now and then over the years through text and voice, thanks to modern technology. In that sense, an absolute "farewell" didn't happen between us. He will always be my Irish-American brother from Ohio, wherever I live. The same applies to my other brothers and sisters in this bittersweet story. That being said, I would no doubt hug him at the last minute before entering the gate if I could turn back time. I just couldn't do it somehow, probably because of that indescribable psychological block engendered by Jeremy. Fortunately, I relearned how to hug other guys goodbye after moving to California through the Davis Music Festival in 2015.

Seated in the plane heading to Sacramento, I wrote a sentimental poem on Facebook, which was also my last Facebook post in Ohio. Carl hit the "LIKE" button, while Kevin left a "SAD" emoji. I knew some folks were sad to

THE LAST FALL AND A LOVE SONG FOR MYSELF

see me leave, but I was destined to say goodbye to them. They understood my difficulties, and I understood their dismay. Ohio is the home sweet home to some of them, but not to me, for the most part. My emotional struggle at that moment was mirrored by what Moses sang to Rameses in the song *Make It Right* from the musical *The Prince of Egypt*. This duet song written by Mr. Stephen Schwartz has the most touching lyrics I have heard in the past few years. I wholeheartedly recommend it to anyone who cares about brotherhood or fraternity.

Chapter 14
"Sunshine" California

Jan 2015 – June 2017, Davis, CA, employee
Nov 2016 – June 2017 (weekly), Sacramento, CA, volunteer

14.1 Davis and the FBI Fingerprint

I arrived in Sacramento at noon, and Mr. Osman picked me up from the tiny airport. Then he drove me to my new apartment complex called Horizon Heights Apartments, which was within one mile from our research center. My new roommate, a UCD undergrad from Shanghai, ushered us in.

All four containers had arrived in Davis before me, but one of them had been broken and re-sealed with plastic tape. Many personal belongings were lost on the way, including my college diploma and copies of transcripts in sealed envelopes. They weren't able to retrieve the lost items after I filed my request. Thank goodness my Ohio State diploma was safe and sound because I carried it in my backpack. Later, I learned that I wasn't the only person with such a tragic experience with USPS, despite the hard work of their staff.

This accident was immediately followed by a depressive rainstorm in January. After the rain, there was a heavy-fog season, as in the movie *Silent Hill*. What else? The screen of my Toshiba notebook was broken through the international plus domestic flights, so I had to mail it to a MicroCenter branch in California to get it fixed. I paid out-of-pocket for a new screen, but their technician didn't sign the paperwork provided by the travel insurance company for the claim. From that incident, I learned so many lessons. For example, it is never easy to get reimbursement for a claim, legit or not, when multiple parties can push the liability away from themselves. And, of course, use USPS with caution for long-distance moving. Their service is economical at a serious cost. I know, I can say that again, it's all my own fault. I lacked common sense, should have used non-fragile packaging, and shouldn't have left any cushioned digital device in a checked bag. But there was another reason: I had developed a chronic tightness in my right calf, despite the intensive treatment; I simply couldn't bring too many heavy things with me in a carry-on luggage bag. Moving was truly painful.

To wash away the bad mood before starting the job, I traveled to LA for a week and met Takashi, who moved there after graduating from Ohio State. I also "met" Eminem, a white guy who surrounds himself with black folks, inside Madame Tussauds Hollywood Wax Museum. My biggest realization after visiting The Hollywood Museum was that many superstars in the film industry grew up in big cities and had family connections with the insiders. Suddenly, I grew up.

After I finally settled in, my lawyer Ms. Wilson in Columbus, started to file the motion for me. However, Magistrate Turner required my federal criminal record to be sent to her office, which sounded very weird to me. I felt baffled again by the State of Ohio, even after I moved to California. I needed to get an FBI fingerprint done to fulfill their requirement, which meant more cost and anxiety. After all, false-positive cases are where the "ecosystem" of law makes its capital gain in compensation for its losses on false-negative cases. To my dismay, in the town of Davis, the only police station didn't even open on weekends or holidays; fortunately, some officer on guard that Saturday referred me to a private agency in downtown Davis, which saved me a trip to Sacramento. I did something very similar to what Julianna Crane did in *The Man in the High Castle*—a fingerprint on a piece of hard paper when almost everything was already collected electronically in China. Thank you for giving me so much unforgettable experiences, Jeremy. Unsurprisingly, "relocation amnesia" didn't work: all the bad memories were carried over to California. Yet, I had to behave like a totally innocent person in front of these sweet Californian residents.

For a better "future," Mr. Osman, an immigrant with rich life experience in the US, said that I should make sure the case was sealed eventually. Guess what? I did everything they asked me to do. They said they would notify me when things could move on. Months later, I emailed Ms. Wilson and never got a response. I called, and her paralegal said he needed to ask her about the progress. Then, I was overwhelmed by my work, pain, psychotherapy, car purchase, driver's license, visa renewal, conference, P-values, job applications, etc., and almost forgot about this legal matter. Since my life in Davis turned out to be more and more miserable till the end, I never followed up with Ms. Wilson. Sometimes I asked myself, was it because when a case gets sealed, nobody talks about it? Or the job wasn't finished, but they decided not to waste more time on someone living in the legendary Sunshine California? If they haven't finished the job, why did I spend so much time looking for a lawyer in the first place? For psychological reassurance? If that was the primary purpose, then yes, it was effective: some burden was definitely lifted off my shoulder during that period, so I could move forward.

My friends were right: the law is a huge business in America. Civilians had better not have anything to do with it, although technically speaking, nobody can be exempt. I was involved in it, or, say, scratching the surface of it, but I still knew almost nothing about it, as it seemed like a black box to me. I'd rather not know too much as that may draw unnecessary attention to me.

Is Ms. Wilson a competent attorney beyond the positive impression she made initially? I have no way to answer or verify that as of today. Life is short, and where did my time go? If life wanted to teach me a lesson, why did it have to be this way? Am I a failure with a stigmatized image? Have my old friends all got their green cards already? Have my former colleagues got into their tenure-track positions already?

14.2 Work-related Injury

Brutal truth: no one can predict the future. When I say "future," I mean real life, not the imaginary "future" used to promote or normalize suffering— a common practice in religions. My professor Mr. Anderson once warned us that we should never say things like, "this world sees a growing number of…" in a scientific report. Instead, we can only report what has happened already. Think about this: no A.I. program as advertised online was omniscient enough to see the 2020 coronavirus pandemic coming, despite the hype making you believe that machine learning would solve all the problems for us. Fundamentally speaking, extrapolation is inferential and, in most cases, subject to indeterminacy.

After starting to work full-time as the only employee for Mr. Osman at UC Davis, I quickly realized he wasn't the solid physicist people thought him to be. For instance, he didn't write the toughest computer code for any of his previous research projects. Nor did he analyze the core data for his signature fMRI paper, despite him being the first author. Like Mr. McCarthy, he was skilled at writing compelling grant proposals. He was reasonable and pragmatic, yet softy and negligent. Because he withheld the resources from me and let me figure out everything alone in a dark booth, I was driven into anxiety and decided to seek psychotherapy again, using my family and childhood issues as a pretext. Hence I worked with Layla (T3), the only Ph.D. in my insurance network who responded to my inquiry. This relationship spanned over two years, far longer than planned. The effectiveness of therapy was visible yet contingent on my residence in America. When I started therapy, Mr. Osman was still waiting for Ph.D. candidate Mr. Shapiro, his former lab mate, to come and save him as his postdoc.

After I finished setting up the lab facilities for Mr. Osman, he asked me to use a crappy video-editing software program to cut hundreds of short segments out of a two-hour-long recording and then edit them. After several weeks of doing this tedious task on the mouse, I lost control of my index finger. That's how I knew he had secretly replaced Adobe Premiere, which he had been using since he was a postdoc in UC Davis, to save money. My condition was overlooked by the family doctor at Kaiser, who told me to rest and use warm and cold compression on the injured finger. I did, but the right arm never recovered to its original state, and I had to use my left hand to continue working. In that period, I couldn't explicitly blame Mr. Osman for fear of retaliation, and his laughing at my condition made me hesitate to file Worker's Comp — I couldn't afford to tell the world that my boss, this modern-age Mr. Scrooge, was the culprit. That was deep fear. Here's an analogy to help you understand my self-inhibition: if a janitor in a palace got assaulted by the prince in that kingdom, would they ask the king and the queen to send the prince to jail in the name of justice? By common sense, the king and queen would silence or wipe out the janitor so as to preserve their son. It has been my understanding of how a hierarchical society works, whether you like it or not. Remember, in 2013, Mr. Osman himself was fired by OSU Medical Center after exposing his superior's misconduct. It's all about money.

Notice that the phrase "repetitive strain injury" (RSI) wasn't in my vocabulary when I first got injured. Nobody ever mentioned this term until Facebook's algorithm recommended it to me in 2018. Even the concept of "workers' comp." and "work-related injury" hadn't been registered with any concrete scenarios in my knowledge back in 2015. It was my first full-time job, only a temporary position.

Despite the pain in my hand, I tried to escape from this lab by applying to similar positions in other institutions, but I was never accepted. Because Mr. Osman was only willing to sponsor the cheaper type of visa, J-1, I could only apply for academic positions or go back to school. At the end of 2016, my pain was exacerbated after using my right hand to revise a co-authored paper under tremendous mental stress. The paper had been rejected by a top-tier journal, and then returned for revision by a mid-term journal. Mr. Osman decided to add extra experiments to the project and resubmit the revamped article right before the annual review of NIH. According to him, not getting this paper published might lead to the lab losing the NIH grant, which meant I would lose my job. Besides, Mr. Osman and Mr. Shapiro had provided incompatible ideas in the manuscript, and I, as the third relay, had to resolve the conflicts in misery. Although the paper, in which I was the second author, was eventually published in 2017, other projects I had worked on yielded disappointing outcomes; in other words, those hypotheses proposed by Mr. Osman all turned out wrong. By then, Mr. Shapiro had already quit and left for data science.

Experiencing a burnout, I planned to travel back to China for the summer to see Samuel. I also filed a Workers' Comp claim, which was declined by the insurance company, as expected by a senior university employee. When I reported work-related injury to the University, Mr. Osman revealed both his hands had been overused because of computer work, too. Back in Ohio, when I told him about my accidental fall in the condo, he told me he also had got many acupuncture sessions for his hands. So, am I supposed to admire his tenacity in pursuing his tenure despite his own pain, or am I supposed to condemn him for using my body to get overuse injury on his behalf?

Hearing my travel plan, Layla took that chance to persuade me to quit my job and leave Davis. "Why are you coming back? You never liked Davis!" She told me to prepare for new GRE tests in China and apply directly to clinical programs around New York City. She had planned out everything for me with sophistication and finally admitted "Davis is a big farm." I took her abrupt advice without any suspicion, thinking leaving Mr. Osman in peace could at least ensure the recommendation from him. By the time I left, another senior university employee had suggested a teaching career for me already. They knew my condition was difficult to treat, but I didn't. I returned to China, couldn't find a cure for my pain and disability in neither Smoke City nor Shanghai, and realized I was fatally misguided by Layla. My mentality collapsed overnight. Not only did I lose my access back to the US, but I also had to behave like a patriot as if I willingly chose to return to China.

In my opinion, those darkest years, several people misled me, mildly or severely, intentionally or inadvertently, due to their limited horizon, limited freedom of speech, limited amount of caution, or other motives. Some of their advice has led to dire consequences.

In Ohio, when analyzing my condition, the sports medicine physician Dr. Gallagher and the P.T. Melissa could only see the tree, not the entire forest. The right side of my body suffered a lot in the subsequent years. To be fair, medicine is complicated and no clinician can handle every problem. We all have our biases and limits. Several clinicians in history have discouraged me from finding the root causes of specific health problems. My life experience tells me I shouldn't always listen to them. Nevertheless, I later realized it's primarily **my** responsibility to learn, investigate, and identify the possible causes in my daily life since the clinicians can't watch me 24/7.

In Ohio, attorney Mr. Parker failed to foresee the court hearing that was going to happen: Magistrate Turner wanted to process my case in an unconventional approach. It caught me off guard, and I got more traumatized afterward despite the "good" outcome on paper. Of course, one could never be too prepared, but I was pretty much unprepared for the hearing.

Still in Ohio, Mr. Frost brought up the technical jargon "expunge," which was irrelevant to my case yet added to my anxiety.

In California, Mr. Osman brought me a significant amount of pain. He destroyed my old career path with his stingy choice. He let me be his surrogate or lab rat to conduct repetitive tasks with cheap software. In the meantime, He gave me too much bad advice in my daily life, such as not buying a car when living in a suburban town like Davis. Now thanks to him, I've had rich experience with a new variety of psychological disruptions, including my old friend: suicidal ideation. I lost what I fought for over two decades, stranded in the culture I once worked so hard to escape from.

In California, my primary care physician at Kaiser Davis Clinic didn't take my injury seriously at first because, as an internist, he wasn't trained in orthopedic issues. He didn't know that the pain and immobility in my hand sourced from the forearm, and neither did I. As a result, I missed the best time window for effective treatment. In 2017, weeks after my problem worsened and I requested physical therapy, he retired. The staff at Kaiser Vacaville Hospital assigned me to a junior P.T. She also overlooked the severity of my condition, despite her caring nature. Junior clinicians are often too optimistic, based on my experience.

Still, in California, psychotherapist Layla gave me lethal advice to leave Davis for good without "realizing" that the work-related injury would not only prevent me from returning to graduate school in the US but also make it super challenging for me to seek employment anywhere on the earth. Ironically, Layla once specialized in pain management, as she revealed in my final session. I was unaware of my God d*mned rights as a university employee before I threw them all away. When I left the US, my employer, be it Mr. Osman or UC Davis, no longer needed to worry about liability. Worst of all, due to the peculiar nature of academia, I couldn't actively fight for my rights without jeopardizing my reputation and connections — everybody in academia wants to stay away from negativity and controversy.

Assuming Layla was being genuine, then she wasn't rational enough, in contrast with her "rich" professional experience. Her "assumption" that I would have a bright future simply by escaping that painful situation was fallacious. This tragedy also reflects the limitation of psychotherapy as a service, especially if the client works with only one therapist. The fact that they know you better and better over time doesn't guarantee they will eventually have a solution to your problem.

She wasn't being genuine, in hindsight. Therapists may hold back their true thoughts just to make everything look nice and smooth. I remember clearly that during the final session, she said, "Since you say you are happy now, I will not stir things up." She had her concerns but withheld them from me in order to conclude my case with a positive-looking outcome devoid of any conflict of interest — my health insurance was obtained through UC Davis, which was also her former employer before she went solo. Knowing my long-term unhappiness in Davis was NOT a result of any concrete mental disorder but life itself, she said she was going to write the report in this way, "Slim is flying back to China at the end of this month, and he's optimistic about his future." Well, I didn't feel optimistic at all; nervous and fearful instead.

As I remember, when I expressed my desire to enter a clinical psychology program on the East Coast, Layla asked me multiple times, with a confused look, "Can't you study this in China?" After working with me for two years, including re-analyzing my legal case with Jeremy through multiple sessions, she still didn't understand that immigration was my end goal. She wanted me to return to China after I had sucked up everything in Ohio just to stay in America. I could tell she knew little about Asian countries, just like I knew little about Arabic countries. Interestingly, when I mentioned the clinical psych thing to a senior hand specialist at Kaiser in 2017, her immediate response was, "Oh my god, that's another tricky field." Yes, indeed, as we see now.

I shouldn't have hastily accepted her abrupt advice, an option that had always been out of the question for me. She wasn't even an authoritative figure for me. Even my American colleagues and Chinese immigrant friends were shocked to hear about my "big" decision to return to China. I just didn't and couldn't tell them that this idea came from a psychotherapist because I was told health care was one's privacy. Only Mr. Osman was exhilarated after hearing my decision, "Oh good!" Of course, it was good for him.

- **Therapists shouldn't give advice.** A friend of mine who works in the mental health industry told me about this taboo after I shared my experience with him. Sadly, Layla didn't seem to know this taboo.
- **A client should terminate the relationship with a therapist who likes to give advice.** A friend who works in the self-help industry also shared her lesson with us. As a client, you know your values and limits better than anyone else.
- **Don't fall for the wrong advice to step out of your comfort zone without securing a way back into the comfort zone.** They will bear no liability when you fail because of their bad advice. They won't even apologize when the damage is beyond repair.
- **Just because someone can empathize with you doesn't mean they are on your side.** This applies to

every single person in your life, especially those you deal with professionally.

No rational person could guarantee any precise prediction of the future. When I was gone, the clinician-client relationship came to an end. No one else would be responsible for my subsequent suffering. Even US lawyers wouldn't represent me— although based on the information I collected, it was almost impossible to fight against a public entity like UC Davis through litigation anyway. After quitting my job, I no longer had access to first-world health care, and whoever caused my RSI didn't have to pay a penny.

The old generation wanted me to accept my fate and embrace their ideology. They wished I could just let go of the painful memories and move on. However, it didn't go as they wished because my physical injury had turned chronic: each painful episode would remind me of the deep causes of my tragedy in Davis: (1) the information asymmetry between the employer and the employee; (2) the information asymmetry between the therapist and the patient. Even more ridiculous was their enthusiasm to see the online picture of Mr. Osman when I was suffering from pain. These Chinese natives have never seen Arabic faces except in international news coverage on television. Incidentally, their manipulative actions behind my back over the years were too abundant to cover in this book.

In this human world where truth and authenticity aren't available as the default, whatever the pop culture tells you, or whatever the self-proclaimed authority tells you, you should take that with a grain of salt. For example, saints and healers may preach, "you should accept yourself as you are." But who are you exactly if you are transgender? Do you accept yourself based on your chromosomes or your gender identity? You see, their advice is too ambiguous to implement.

Chapter 15
Residues

15.1 My Relations with Jeremy and Stacy

Is Jeremy really a devil, as in "White Coat Devil"? It depends on how you define the word "devil." I am not religious, so the word means nothing more than a person that has caused deep and long-term harm to me. In that sense, the label is neither hyperbolic nor overcharged with impulsive emotions. Some of my American buddies actually agreed with my labeling. Well, one might say, that's why they are my buddies— people with shared values tend to bond together.

The term came into my mind spontaneously the day after the court hearing. I was immersed in Western culture at that time and had interacted with a group of evangelists for a while. As a result, the biblical terminology infiltrated my vocabulary. I learned to label a person as devilish if the person had overwhelming power over me to the extent that I lost my ability to defend myself. In history, all those people who had traumatized me were devilish or demonic, and they were mostly working in educational institutions.

My body sincerely treated him as a devil at that stage of life. His image was so daunting to me. At this point, I could resonate with the historic black slaves who referred to the atrocious white supremacists as "white devils." The former were aware that the latter were also humans, but they couldn't control their perception— the latter were too powerful and relentless. Again, I have to stress that the code

"White Coat Devil" bears no relevance to skin color. However, that's not equal to saying this person's skin color had nothing to do with his behavior patterns and his attitudes toward minorities within the context of the United States.

And yet, scientifically, he is a human being. He had a heart. On a snowy day, he even offered Shannon and her classmate a ride to vet school. He ate at the same cheap Asian restaurant that I did. He had no intention of kicking me out of America. He just wouldn't be sincere with me.

One might argue that my attitude toward Stacy was unfair because she didn't do bad things to me. Admittedly, I didn't hate her as much, but one has to acknowledge that humans tend to be inherently selfish toward their own values. She made her choice because it was in her best interests to remain with her boyfriend while rationalizing or condoning his cruelty. She didn't cause harm to me directly at first sight, but her words drove me crazy toward the end.

Yes, a white girl from coastal California may be naturally more inclusive than a white guy from rural Pennsylvania, even if the latter had been an exchange student to Singapore.

Considering I was torn between these two people, one might be tempted to use the Social Balance Theory or Cognitive Dissonance Theory to explain my change of attitude toward her. Partially applicable, but unnecessary. I think the change of attitude wasn't motivated by the conflict of values or thoughts but instead backed up by new evidence of her bias and self-preservation. So, what is the opposite of hypocrisy? Integrity. Let me illustrate this with an example. My college classmate was dating another classmate in the same major, and he actively broke up with her after she posted on social media her idiosyncratic rationale for cheating in a final exam. Yes, I am implying that Stacy couldn't afford to stick to integrity. She needed a man by her side. They were a couple, which meant they were "useful" to each other. After all, a romantic relationship is a Darwinian utility.

As a result of my unhealthy relations with them, I was confused and traumatized. What should one do after a traumatic experience like mine? Healthcare providers and intellectuals will tell you to stay away from the person who manipulated or traumatized you. Yet following this rationale of inaction, there will be, foreseeably, more and more victims falling prey to the culprit or mastermind. We still don't have a good solution for that because picking a ruthless fight against the villain is like attacking a nest of hornets with physical force — you are doomed to suffer more, long-term, large-scale. Additionally, let me remind you that a true mastermind doesn't have to break any law to make you suffer. They are often endowed with both intelligence and power.

15.2 Face Masks

Someone commented on Reddit that they wanted to wear face masks at the very beginning of the Covid-19 pandemic, but they were hindered by the idea that other Americans might laugh at them or even attack them in public. This is exactly the same logic as "I want to wear long sleeves and pants on chilly days in San Francisco, but I'm white, and other white people only wear shorts," which was shared on Facebook by an old acquaintance of mine. Now it is clear to me that one big obstacle to preventing a pandemic is that ordinary people simply don't want to go against the norm and become the minority.

As one can imagine, cognitive dissonance related to

group identity sets up a remarkable barrier here: most people tend to identify with a group based on race, ethnicity, or so-called culture instead of rational choices or shared values.

I remember in that extremely cold weather in Ohio, one month after I recovered from the infection that put me in the E.R., I started to wear the thick 3M face mask again, as I sensed that the freezing cold temperature would inevitably trigger my seasonal rhinitis if I went without protection. I didn't want to rely on steroidal nasal spray, as many people do. Yes, I had a car to protect me while driving. However, the distance between the parking lot and the department was enough to expose my nasal mucosa to the cold air, and therefore, I chose to take preemptive action. I always put on the mask when walking in the snow because I couldn't afford to get sick. I had nobody to take care of me if I got sick, just like I had nobody to drive me back home if I ever passed out after drinking.

One weekend, I noticed Jeremy was coughing and had a stuffy nose. So I asked him if he had "nostritis," and he denied it. Actually, I hadn't learned the word "rhinitis" by then, but when I used the wrong word to refer to that medical problem, he didn't care to correct me.

He admitted that he felt cold walking from the parking lot to the med school and even inside his car. So I said, "Why don't you wear a face mask?" He silently waved his head as usual, "I don't need that. I'm okay."

Did he not know that the face mask would effectively block cold air and wind? Did he not trust science? Most probably, he did, but he couldn't afford to look different from his peers. No one would choose to be the minority. Also, as a macho med student, he didn't want to be seen as weak, let alone to be mocked by other people.

15.3 Victimized International Students

While I was meeting with Mr. Frost for the last time to discuss graduate school re-applications hypothetically, he told me there was an increasing number of international students breaking the rules on and off campus. Admittedly, some individuals do cause trouble due to the lack of self-discipline or ignorance of local regulations, but it doesn't mean everyone should be held 100% responsible for falling into the pitfalls. Also, it is no news that the "justice" system in the US (and in many other countries, too) sometimes destroys innocent people without sufficient evidence.

I know I wasn't the only international student who had suffered from a native. Americans suffer from other Americans, too, after all. While I can blame the invisible "system," I choose to blame the dark side of human nature. People want to find an easy target to bully when they cannot defy the real bully. Generally speaking, Asian immigrants have become the easiest target partially because they never learned how to fight back in their old environment, which favors nice-looking stability over individual rights.

Just as laws can never be perfectly adaptive, the Student Code of Conduct itself can be imperfect. The "education" can be post hoc (i.e., too late) and solely toward the disadvantaged party sometimes. But the ideal wish of "prevention" is impossible because effective prevention will reveal the existence of injustice in society. What do I mean by that? They have to warn you that if you are treated unfairly by a native, you have no choice but to suck it up and consider it a toll you must pay in order to immigrate, much like joining a fraternity club—any other approach is doomed to fail because the system itself is in favor of the native. Will they say it to you directly, though? After all, the Student Code of Conduct exists to protect the interest of the institution, not just to discipline each individual.

During my final meeting with him in fall 2013, Mr. Frost used very intellectualized language to summarize my suffering because almost everyone involved in my Ohio case was White American, except for me, this international student from a rival country of America. For example, he said, "I had the advantage of growing up in this culture." He also tried to make me feel better by saying, "when I interviewed Jeremy, he admitted that he could have used a different way to handle the situation." I didn't respond, not even a bitter smile given. "Could have" means nothing to a traumatized person who needs to pay for his therapy and legal fees. We all could have made fewer mistakes in life; we all could have been hurt less in life. I hadn't learned the term "lip service" by then, but I knew he didn't essentially care. He knew how to appear self-reflective in front of a school official, just like in front of a magistrate.

Years later, while working at UC Davis, I got an alert on my newsfeed telling me that an international student from Somalia was going crazy with a weapon on OSU Main Campus and was shot to death within a minute. I was worried about the safety of those studying or working at Ohio State. Meanwhile, I understood that this 18-year-old student had come to the wrong place to study. No matter how inclusive those school officials want their institution to be, the student body and faculty body at Ohio State will never be truly inclusive, in my humble opinion. Ohio is not a desirable state for non-Caucasian immigrants, just like America is not a welcoming asylum country for Muslim refugees after 9/11. These facts will not change quickly over time. As I see it, this Somalian student's explosion was like a chemical reaction that was doomed to happen, given his unfortunate background, the unhealthy environment he lived in, and the huge amount of toxic information on the Internet nowadays.

On the one hand, I don't sympathize with the murderer, unlike an OSU school official who associated the tragedy with Black Lives Matter. I believe his death was good for American society and for himself, though not for his core family. He was already traumatized as a child, without being provided with necessary psychotherapy, and then isolated by OSU students. With this murder attempt, his jail time would be prolonged, as would his suffering. In my opinion, his life wasn't worth continuing after he pulled out his gun to shoot.

On the other hand, we sensible people know that anti-social human beings didn't develop into that morbid state overnight, as is reflected in the movie *Joker*. They were treated too badly by irresponsible parents, bullies, racists, and xenophobes without doing anything harmful in the first place. Pre-existing mental issues might be an objective factor, but a trigger is necessary for the outburst of their radical behavior.

While I didn't study his background stories thoroughly, I am certain that other "intersectional" minority human beings would easily understand how one can fall into that state without receiving enough care, guidance, and kindness. Sorry, those things are not abundantly available to minorities in the Midwest, not in Ohio State, despite the school's advocacy. I do appreciate their effort, though.

Moreover, I have to mention that it was ridiculous for that student to have access to firearms. Some people must have failed in their duties. Something should be done to protect the students from campus shootings. From a non-litigation standpoint, something extra should be done to prevent mental health problems among international students who are constantly alienated. I don't believe in thoughts and prayers.

15.4 Foreign Students into American Med Schools and Law Schools?

Remember Jeremy once blatantly said in front of me and my Redditor friends, "but it's also because it's very hard to get into the med school," after I mentioned the medical profession in America was set to be hard for international students to get in, no matter how outstanding they were in their home countries. Neither of us was wrong. People in China still believe that the so-called elitist education for American "helping professions" is a great idea to ensure that high-quality educational resources only go to the most promising students.

I once co-supervised an excellent high school intern at UC Davis who was aiming at med school. However, she told me that she would not apply to med school in the United States but in England, where med school starts at the college level, as in most countries. How? She had some family connections. In that sense, she was far luckier than most American kids. An extended period on campus doesn't make you superior to your peers.

Med schools in the United States are difficult to get into but not impossible for top-ranking Chinese or Indian students. However, as in every game we play, it's the legal status that ultimately sets endless barriers for the trailblazers among us. The summer after my freshman year, I was taking a month-long GRE prep course with the New Oriental School (a.k.a. New Oriental Education & Technology Group) in Shanghai. One may understand it as the Chinese version of Kaplan. We had four young and skillful male lecturers

RESIDUES

teaching us how to tackle problems in the standardized multiple-choice test as well as how to write essays on the computer. Three of them were STEM majors in college, while the fourth person, who was teaching the vocabulary section, had a bachelor's degree in Medicine. He told us he had been admitted to a couple of M.D. programs in the US, including the one in Michigan Ann Arbor. Unfortunately, his visa application was declined. It was the year after 9/11, and the Consulate used this as a pretext to turn him down. Anybody can see that an M.D. program shouldn't have anything to do with terrorism, but he was treated with "special care," by which I mean outright discrimination. He ended up becoming a famous lecturer in this private institution for test prep, although he'd never studied in the US, like the other three lecturers. Honestly, all of these four "ferrymen" were much more outstanding than most international students from China, but life plays tricks on us without early notice. Even today, applying to med school in the US sounds like The Bermuda Triangle to many Chinese students.

Yes, there is a tiny proportion of international students who can make it into the prestigious M.D. programs in the US, while the majority just avoided that path if their end goal was immigration. The people who could eventually get in were usually not from China, presumably for political reasons. In compensation, Chinese Americans tend to want their kids to go to med school or law school. Stacy once told me that her class had one international student from an African country. She suspected the student had financial aid from OSU because otherwise, they wouldn't be able to afford med school in the US. Nonresident aliens are not eligible for federal loans. Apparently, it's insufficient to be intelligent and hard-working; you have to have some source of funding for your education, which might or might not promise you some social ladder to climb up later on.

I can't talk about law school very much because I haven't had much interaction with law school or law students, only licensed attorneys. What I do know is that law students face very similar financial problems, so many would go where the financial aids are.

In reality, I know Chinese students who got accepted into J.D. programs, and some didn't study law at all in college when they were still in China. Years ago, I finally understood that J.D. is not the top degree in jurisprudence. There's always some milestone that requires extra effort from the "elites."

15.5 What to Do with Hatred

If I tell people that I didn't hate Jeremy, then I must be lying. Everybody can have a natural response named hatred under certain circumstances, but some people repress it when they are told they need to forgive or suck it up. Some tell other people not to be haters. They barely understand or remember what first-hand suffering feels like. The more negative experiences of injustice you've had, the more hatred you will accumulate in your body and your psyche over time. However, for the sake of your long-term mental health and safety, I highly recommend that you try to transform hatred into something else, despite its authentic nature. Hatred may function as a propelling force temporarily, like how I was propelled out of my hometown and country of origin, but it isn't oriented toward a personal value. Unless one has valid and efficient tactics to take down the evil, which the majority of us aren't capable of, hatred brewed in one's psyche is only going to erode oneself more. It is crucial not to be possessed by hatred because we still need to live in the here and now and stay civil and functional in front of innocent people.

It took me a long time to stand up again and see the "devil" from a different angle. I survived those months of darkness and regained my sanity because I didn't let hatred toward Jeremy engulf me. I had genuinely helpful people around me at that time.

Who'd have thought there would be a sequel to my ordeal? Mr. Osman turned out to be another well-disguised challenge, like a Trojan, in my life. This time I have lost more than I could afford to, including a healthy dominant hand and my legal status in the US. Should I hate the person who afflicted my hand as well as my original career path? Or should I deceive myself by saying, "thanks to those who hurt me so that I know who I don't want to be"? The damage was already done. Who can say they won't hate the culprit? Buddha? Jesus?

Should I hate the irresponsible parents who fail to protect their offspring and seek justice against evil on behalf of their offspring? In my life history, "evil" includes every creed stemming from the feudal traditions, such as revering to "God of Heaven, God of the Earth, the emperor, the parents, and the teachers" blindly and subjecting the minors to top-down infliction indifferently. Such are among the most retrogressive and maladaptive components of traditional Chinese culture under the influence of Confucianism.

I can't play the saint here, but I need to handle my emotion carefully.

This is how I understand it: without caution, one shouldn't broadcast one's hatred toward another person, let alone an organization with power. Why not? Because publicly announced hatred implies motives. If you, a victim, hate the culprit, then a lot of other victims might hate the same evil as well, although they don't say it explicitly. If someday, another victim and hater assassinate the culprit, you will be considered a remarkable suspect. In particular, if you express hatred on the Internet, law enforcement has every reason to believe you have a strong motive to engage in criminal activity. Even if you have an alibi, it still won't look good on you, not to mention some people will gossip behind your back or even stab you from the back.

The T.V. series *FBI* (2018-) has shown me that a lot of innocent people were suspected due to their relations with the murdered person. False-positive is quite normal and often traumatizing. Law enforcement will not compensate you after they profile you negatively simply because you are a vulnerable civilian. When you were little, you must have been advised by others to stay away from the controversial and stigmatized. It may sound hypocritical to you because it won't solve any social injustice, but it's not unfounded.

Moreover, despite people's efforts to hide or deny their hatred in public, their true attitude can manifest itself in a different form, such as passive aggression. You can't cheat yourself.

For that gruesome reason explained above, you'd better not let hatred possess you. Those culprits deserve nothing better, but an emotion inside YOUR body doesn't solve any problem. In a purportedly civilized society, you cannot exert punishment at will unless you ARE in law enforcement. While hatred doesn't always lead to revengeful action, law enforcement is sensitive to verbalized hatred as a precursor to harmful activity. It's calibrated that way to minimize the false-negative rate, i.e., their dereliction.

As I see it, one needs to transform hatred into some other attitude, one that doesn't pose a threat to the culprit's safety and doesn't draw attention back to you. Disdain or contempt isn't a bad option. However, most therapists probably won't encourage you out loud, as this won't make them look positive, nice, professional, or intellectual. Ideally, you will reach that transformation by yourself through the course of recovery. It isn't easy, and that's why I hesitate to preach it myself.

My viewpoint is pragmatic, and I am not ashamed of not being noble. One doesn't have to be unconditionally benevolent or universally forgiving. However, one does need to understand the consequence of uncensored speech in human society throughout history. If you find it difficult to channel your hatred into something less formidable, such as sarcasm, at least don't broadcast it without providing the context, as that will make you misunderstood by most people— my first-hand lesson.

What about Hitler or some contemporary warlord who brings chaos to their neighboring countries and the entire world? They are too powerful for you to disdain or ignore. Your hatred might be well justified and socially acceptable in this case, but still, you are incapable of defeating the evil by yourself. You can never expect reparation from them, which will bring frustration to you. In this case, I guess it's wise to funnel the hatred into doing a good cause, but the hatred will remain in some crystallized form of hatred.

15.6 The Cultural Iceberg

I once joked to Antonio that I, as a foreigner, "hit the curb" in Ohio, but later I realized I also hit something called the Cultural Iceberg and was almost drowned.

The first time I saw the Cultural Iceberg model was in the International House, which was right across Russell

Boulevard from UC Davis. One of the speakers displayed the picture to show us the complexity of intercultural communication. The Cultural Iceberg looks like an iceberg floating in the ocean. Above the sea level is merely 10% of the information related to a culture, such as the language, the cuisines, and the holidays— relatively superficial elements. Below the sea level is the bulk of information that an immigrant needs a huge amount of time to grasp, for example, beliefs and assumptions, nonverbal language, and religion. These implicit dimensions of a particular culture can hardly be described even by the natives. You have to live in that atmosphere as a minority and observe the behavioral differences. Then you regurgitate your experiences until you feel them.

This graph was eye-opening for me because it provided me with targets to look for when I navigate a different culture. In the meantime, I once took a course called International Business Culture in college. The textbook was written by a British scholar. While it tried to compare many cultures across the globe, the information reflected in those variables was overly theoretical and disconnected from reality. To be more specific, there were outdated stereotypes all over the place and very little behind-the-curtain truth to be told, so as not to offend any single culture. For instance, the author believed that America is a low-context masculine culture and that Americans are pretty straightforward. That was from a British perspective, and I was misguided by that! In fact, consistent with the impression of immigrants from many countries, and even the impression of some US citizens, today's adult Americans (boomers and millennials mostly) aren't that straightforward; to some, they are even a little fake. I'm not comparing American culture to those who primarily speak euphemisms and metaphors or those who constantly use sarcasm to convey negative messages. No one is implying that everybody wears a sparkling smile and hides behind a strong façade, but it's simply untrue that everybody would comfortably speak their mind.

I believe that these international folks I have made friends with tend to be the most open-minded individuals with an international mindset and often some gift to learn a foreign language called English. Sometimes they are also tech-savvy. However, they don't represent the majority of the citizens in their countries of origin. I know that because I am this type of outlier myself. By the same token, if you are an expat, people you meet through InterNation might carry some characteristics of their home culture, but not completely. In my opinion, one single individual can never represent a whole culture unless they are selected and trained to play that role as a public delegate. Besides, no one can resist partial assimilation after staying in a different environment for a long time.

After that talk, I asked another speaker about the perceived "fakeness" of mainstream Americans. The person who answered me was Latino, and she offered her explanation: the P.C. culture in modern America. That was my first time learning the phrase "political correctness" after moving to California. People cannot speak their minds freely, and they have to conceal their true feelings and opinions, and inevitably they would look nice and fake to foreigners. For instance, a racist cannot tell you directly that they don't like you because of your skin color, so they have to find some pretext to turn you down. This explanation was somewhat convincing, considering the influence of P.C. culture has grown so much in the past decade.

Later, she must have forwarded my question to the main

speaker, for the latter alluded to it in a meeting on campus. She said, "'All men are equal' is an ideal, not a fact. We Americans are known for being honest and straightforward, but there are exceptions, due to a variety of reasons such as political correctness." She didn't delve deep, as this talk was intended for new international scholars and students. I happened to be there. For me, back in 2016, her on-campus talk was already kind of superficial. Understandably, she couldn't speak negatively about her home country's mainstream culture.

What a shame, I never learned about the concept of political correctness until I moved to California. Did Ohioans not take it seriously? They surely did. According to my American friends, people in the Midwest tend to be more "polite" and avoid explicit bigotry, unlike those in the South or Southwest. Is that necessarily a good thing for foreigners and minorities? Of course not. Many people would rather choose the blunt style that requires less cognitive processing. In retrospect, P.C. was consistent with the covert discrimination I perceived in the Midwest, particularly while hunting for housing.

Months later, at the International Center of UC Davis, through a brochure, I learned a model that illustrates how American culture handles relationships differently than some other cultures. In a nutshell, Americans seem friendly to strangers but are actually difficult to form deep connections with; people from some other cultures remain cold to strangers but will treat you with intimacy once you earn their trust. For this distinction, some people use these terms: "peach culture" versus "coconut culture." Naturally, "coconut" folks may perceive "peach" folks as fake, while the latter may perceive the former as rude.

Jeremy embodied the peach culture to some extent, although this theory couldn't fully explain his behavior. These cultural stereotypes may hold some truth, but I'm afraid a habitual liar or player can use cultural relativity to justify their lack of credibility in front of immigrants. Meanwhile, I still believe in the cultural diversity in the United States.

Of course, I can think of additional answers that could somewhat explain the "fakeness" in mainstream American culture as perceived by international folks.

First, are we mainly talking about the service industry, such as health care and higher education, as America is a pretty developed country? Of course, in the service industry, everybody has to act nice in order to earn five stars.

Second, if you're dealing with bureaucracy in higher education, this phenomenon is not unique to America.

Third, the fierce competition in the land of America. If you are too transparent, you are also an easy target.

Fourth, the lack of gun control in America. Don't piss anybody off, just in case.

Fifth, no one has an obligation to include you in their inner circle. You can't say someone is fake simply because they don't want to confide in you, just like you can't say someone is a lone wolf simply because they don't want to develop an intimate connection with you.

Above all, if you are new to a culture and don't understand the connotations or subtext underlying people's language, you will certainly feel that people are deliberately masking their ideas. Maybe you think people in your home country are more genuine because you are already immune to the gimmicks and euphemisms in that culture, or you have internalized it.

I'm aware that I'm not in an authorized position to criticize the mainstream American "culture," as a lot of American patriots will get irritated. If you can't understand why, let me make an analogy for you. Alex and Charlotte once told me that their ferocious black cat Infinity was a "loser" because he would often lose in a fight against their friends' cats.

I teased Infinity, "Hey Infinity, you are a loser."

Then Charlotte stopped me in a drawling voice, "Hey Slim, we can call him a loser, but you can't."

Then I adjusted my tone and said, "Infinity, you are so adorable." They were happy.

Alex and Charlotte treated Infinity as their kid. As I see it, no parent should ever call their kid a loser in front of their friends, as that would hurt the child deeply. Don't ask me how I know.

Under the same logic, Americans will only allow Mark Manson to write about the negative side of American culture because he's a mainstream American. If I openly criticize mainstream American culture, I will probably receive sharp arrows targeted at me, as Colin Kaepernick did. Why so hostile? Mainstream America will consider me an outsider. Humans are obsessed with "them" versus "us" based on certain superficial variables but not others.

To be honest, this Cultural Iceberg model still fascinates me as it did initially. It looks dreadful, though, when I realize we can never fully understand one another.

15.7 Final Curtain

July 2017 – Covid-19 pandemic, Smoke City, China

To sum up, my life in the US was like two theatre plays: one was a tragedy (2012-2014), and the other was also a tragedy (2015-2017). No exaggeration; no sugarcoating. In fact, the second tragedy was what enabled and motivated me to reveal the first tragedy — the main storyline of this project. These five years of ups and downs helped me understand America deeper but left me with a body that can no longer be called wholesome. I have learned many first-hand lessons, but I wish I hadn't or had learned in a less traumatic way:

—The first obvious lesson: Inspect the new place in person before you move there. Get to know what the city looks like under the worst weather condition. Sometimes it isn't that hard to spot the red flags as long as you go there. If the new place is worse than your current place, then you should refrain from leaving and find other opportunities. When an on-site tour is impossible, it's almost inevitable that you will fall for the skew or calibrated information through the Internet. Besides, human beings tend to see what they want to see when not provided with sufficient information.

—Pull yourself out of any love-hate triangle before the inner conflict drives you crazy. For example, when person A hurts you deeply, person B, who is close to A, would rather ask you to forgive A unconditionally than ask A to admit their wrongdoings. That indicates person B has chosen their personal interest over justice. In that case, it's only healthy for you to distance yourself from B in addition to A, at least psychologically. The principle can apply to the group level as well.

—If I could afford it, I would give up any desire to enter a high-ranking institution in exchange for legal residence in a first or second-tier city of my choice. Resources of this world aren't evenly distributed. There is a distinction between convenient places and inconvenient places. Those who tell you otherwise are not trustworthy. Admittedly, the 2020 pandemic has redefined what a good city means. While big cities are presumably more resilient, given their abundant resources, the high population density in cities like NYC also appears to be their Achilles' heel during the pandemic. However, don't forget that epidemiology, virology, and public health don't represent the entire medical field. Big cities are still strong in other aspects.

—Another important realization is that almost all the happy moments or events in life were bought with money when I played the role of a consumer. Trips, I paid for them. Music shows or football games, I paid for them. Interesting books and drinks, I paid for them. When you consider my voluntary work in the autism clinic, which brought me some kind of intrinsic reward, I had to pay for gasoline or public transportation. Donations? I only donate to those I care about or feel grateful to because they are valuable to me. But for whatever type of worthy expense, to receive the money first, I had to work on or study things I wasn't intrinsically motivated to. In fact, to be eligible to work in my desired field, I had to spend extra time studying additional material by myself. Like actor/comedian Jimmy O Yang's dad told him, "you work on something you hate, and then use the money to do what you love." That's almost antithetical to the Pollyannaish slogan: "just do what you love and love what you do."

Rewarding jobs probably won't come to you automatically but will require long-term exploration or research from you, and eventually, only a small fraction of the population can get close to self-actualization. A significant proportion may also suffer from occupational hazards; very unfortunate cases like mine may involve debilitating injuries at the burgeoning stage of one's career. Beware that most people only dare to post positive stuff online, but that doesn't mean they constantly feel positive.

—In retrospect, all these characters in my story have to stay muted sometimes for self-preservation. Outside of the nice Canadians, who do you think is relatively candid in my tragic story? The answer should be understandable to you: Mr. Williams and Mr. Hoffman. These were established professors with their tenure, so they had more free speech than others. Although they didn't always speak directly, they were not afraid to point out that something was hazardous or someone was stupid.

Mr. Williams graduated from the Ivy League, so he definitely had the stamina to criticize wrongdoings, just like my former colleagues who graduated from Stanford.

Mr. Hoffman was stringent. When he was reviewing the manuscript of my Master's thesis, a report on the research project based on Mr. Osman's theory, he commented on the final section, "Clinical Implications," with one single word: "None!" With his decades of experience, he had seen through it that the idea of studying an unpopular topic in basic science to benefit clinical practice was a long shot, if not a complete fantasy. Conjectures or implications are often proposed by career scientists with no clinical experience yet wanting to apply for healthcare-related grants. The word "Implication" is full of uncertainty and subjectivity. So how did I respond to Mr. Hoffman's brutal comment? With no hesitation, I pulled the entire section out of my thesis. I wasn't doing that to yield to the senior professor. From my standpoint, if deleting one section could help me keep my integrity, then I was absolutely down with it.

In the meantime, it's understandable that individuals who are still climbing up their ladders cannot be expected to be the most candid. They cannot afford to stand on the side of justice whenever they want. That being said, some of my activist friends are exceptional. They help generate some light in the darkness.

—Do yourself a favor: don't ask anyone such a dumb question as "is your current/former boss a good person?" You know the risk of giving an honest and negative answer to a stranger. A lot of us have faced this type of question before, and honestly, I still don't know how to answer both ethically and diplomatically. Sometimes I ask myself: is my work-related injury a result of karma? Am I being punished by Mother Nature because I didn't disclose my disappointment at Mr. McCarthy to some grad school applicant and did let them make the same wrong choice as I did?

—Life is never fair. The concept of life is a social construct, after all. When I was younger, I used to mourn over my miserable life. For example, why could American kids' parents get arrested for child abuse while my authoritarian parents could go unpunished and even justify their atrocities with cultural relativism? This disparity set the foundation for my eternal love for Western civilization.

— Not everybody is qualified as your sounding board. While it's good to be humble and open-minded, when it comes to decision-making, one should really discuss with mature people with relevant experience and wisdom, or at least with an independent and sophisticated mind, not the privileged Pollyanna. Keep in mind that age, level of education, and level of empathy aren't reliable indicators of rationality. If one has to choose between empathy and a solution, choose the latter.

Once I accepted that no one is entitled to anyone else's privilege, I felt at peace. Similarly, I stopped struggling once I embraced my recurring pain as part of life. Once I accepted that the culprits would rarely acknowledge their sins, I no longer worried about not forgiving.

Seriously, after losing a series of significant values, including a healthy dominant hand, healthy legs, and the original American dream, I locked myself up on the top floor of a dilapidated apartment building, physically and emotionally, for a long time.

To recap, I was misguided by my psychotherapist Layla to quit the job that sponsored my visa and gave me the chronic injury, when I only planned to take a month-long vacation to my country of origin. Just like a dismissive surgeon can make you die on the operating table, an overstepping therapist can make you drive off the cliff in a happy mood.

I remember crying in front of my laptop that evening when I announced my decision to take an indefinitely long break outside the US. In that sad Facebook post, I only referred to Layla as "professional guidance." That stupid decision caused me to lose my legitimate way to return to the US regardless of my health condition. The debilitating and recurring pain prevented me from returning to the US through either grad school or employment. With pressure and manipulation from people in Smoke City, I lived through severe emotional tumult and despair. Fortunately, I survived these episodes with a combination of external service (traditional herbal medicine) and self-administered interventions (expressive writing, songwriting, digital art creation, etc.). While I am emotionally dissociated from the collectivist culture here, I have to cope with the bad memories induced by everyday stimuli from human interactions and media. So how could I avoid schizophrenia under such pressure and as an ideological minority? I connect my true self to the Internet and stick with my global communities. When you overlook the distances, the world becomes a matter of topology.

However, the Covid-19 pandemic has changed everything from double difficult to quadruple difficult, as people like me tend to receive extra discrimination because of our race. That being said, I'm sincerely grateful to those open-minded individuals who see my worth and respect me all along, whether or not they know my ongoing suffering. During the worst period of the lockdown, I resonated greatly with Quasimodo, the ugly protagonist in *The Hunchback of Notre Dame* by Victor Hugo. I wanted to get out, but I couldn't, physically or mentally. I mean, to get out of the neighborhood at least, if not to get across the national border. Sadly, reality has imposed double-layered "home" confinement on me.

If only I could belong with these local people. If only I could get down there and enjoy everything under the sun like everybody else. My emotional struggle was mirrored in the lyrics of *Out There* from the Disney musical *The Hunchback of Notre Dame*. Quasimodo spoke for me in that "I want" song.

During this period, I also realized that Hunchback/Quasimodo shares something in common with two other famous musical characters. One is Elphaba, the green-skinned witch from *Wicked*. Another is Phantom, the defaced man wearing a half-mask, from *Phantom of the Opera*. All three of them face discrimination from the general public because of their atypical appearance. When individuals are isolated from the "normative" society, they have fewer options than people would think; they may try over and over again to be accepted by the mainstream until they develop "learned helplessness," which is an academic way to look at the psychological cause of depression.

When Frollo told him Hunchback, "the world is cruel, the world is wicked," he wasn't kidding. My life was destroyed by my first full-time job in America because of a stingy boss Mr. Osman. He, a green card holder, would never ask a same-aged US citizen to do the same harmful task he asked me to do. Immigrants are easy to squeeze and easy to sacrifice because of our contingent status in the first world.

Finally, I have realized that in this complex human society, unless you protect yourself deliberately and vigilantly, you will likely be victimized as an easy target. I know the word "victimized" may trigger a knee-jerk reaction in some people again.

As for these musical theater characters, I resonate with them partially because their experiences are reminiscent of real-life human relationships. To be more specific, the story of *Wicked*, Emerald City in particular, reminds me of the spurious side of academia: it isn't uncommon for the incapable to put up a glamorous façade to attract the capable and then to swallow the credit of the latter. Meanwhile, the situations faced by Phantom and Hunchback are consistent with what we see in our society: your physical disadvantage will create substantial roadblocks in your pursuit of companionship, despite your impeccable talents and benevolent nature, if you have any, to begin with. The truth is so bitter that the "positivity cultists" will never have the gut to acknowledge it openly.

After all these years of being blown here and there like a fitness ball, through both meaningful and futile struggles, I choose to extract and dispense the truth against all odds. I'm not an influencer or some kind of authority, let alone a whistleblower with a sense of mission, just a storyteller. What if my story happens to generate a splash? Maybe just a tiny one? Will the hypocrites send Internet mobs to "cancel" me? Will the autocrats send some hitmen to assassinate me? Am I ready for that? In the story of Wicked, Elphaba, the whistleblower with solid sorcery skills, was labeled as "evil" by the authority, Oz. Not surprisingly, on this battlefield called life, the brave and the faithful often lose to the powerful by a large margin. In that situation, the best way of self-preservation is to disappear from the battlefield, leaving only their hat to the world as a souvenir.

Now back to reality, I have a bit of imposter syndrome. I mean, have I been overestimating the significance of my story? Have I offered much novel information to the public? Isn't it common sense to minorities that white supremacists exist? Isn't it well-known to innocent people that unpleasant professors, clinicians, football coaches, and cops exist, as in every other glorified or dignified profession? Isn't it understandable to the competent ones that the charismatic, narcissistic, and muscular ones tend to gain popularity more easily? Have I been telling you cliché all this time? I hope not.

This whole experience I've shared with you is a multi-layered tragedy, and there's no way to sugarcoat its negative impact on me. Positive thinking cannot turn a tragedy upside down, even if I wish. However, I still care about America, I still believe in science, and I will always love my global friends. So, aside from the story being a story, if my experience can help some readers avoid future mistakes and pitfalls in their decision-making or help some readers suffer less from the narcissists and the hypocrites in their lives, I would be delighted.

The End.

Disclaimer (Reprise)

The story is X% real and Y% creative, where $X + Y = 100$ and $X \gg Y$. Based on American slavery history, if you have one drop of African-American blood, then you are black. Based on domestic policies in China, if one of your parents is an ethnic minority, you are a minority, which means you can get bonus points when applying to college (not me). In analogy, should my story be considered a novel so long as $Y > 0$? It's up to you to decide how much of it is real, but this memoir hasn't been written in a fictionalized flavor, in my opinion. If you think any individual you know in life matches with or resembles any character in my story, I will call it a coincidence.

I am neither licensed nor knowledgeable enough to provide medical or legal advice. Quite the opposite, due to ignorance, I have stumbled in many aspects of life, as manifested in the story. Meanwhile, theoretical arguments in this book may not bear academic rigor and should be treated with discretion. Moreover, information regarding institutions or businesses in certain regions may be outdated and thus should NOT be used as reliable references. The purpose of sharing the story is to help people understand the complexity of human nature and make better choices for themselves. It's not in favor of any race, gender, sexual orientation, career choice, etc.

Acknowledgment

I couldn't have finished this project without whoever made my actual life experience in the story possible and delightful. There are so many of them, including some established figures, so I decided not to name them one by one. Whether or not someone's image has appeared in this story as a character, they have made an impact on my life. Even those who have brought me long-term difficulty or misery have taught me valuable lessons.

I want to thank those who have taught and mentored me in writing and publishing. I also thank those who have shared tips on motivation and time management.

I'm grateful for a number of competent healthcare professionals from multiple countries and many knowledgeable fellows in my online support groups, especially the repetitive strain injury community and the speech recognition community.

It's worth mentioning that folks in my Objectivist community have continued to offer intellectual stimulation all these years. They have taught me what public education and academia can never provide. I miss these people.

Additionally, I want to thank those who appreciate my recent creative projects published on Youtube, Instagram, and Smule. These likes, comments, and mini collabs keep me motivated and connected with global creative brains.

Finally, we all owe a lot to those who have dedicated their lives to combating the Covid-19 pandemic and maintaining the world's order, which would otherwise be drowned in endless chaos. Health, safety, security, justice, environmental protection, and technological advance don't come at no cost. Without the general stability of human society, I wouldn't have been able to finish this project with an imperfect body.

Tribute: In memory of my feline brother, Seth O'Shea. As I worked on the multiple drafts of this book, he brought his furry and ferocious vibe to the writing process. When the readers see this book, he is no longer with us. Grateful for his companionship and inspirations. (December 19th, 2023) His photos are available on my Instagram page @stanthefeline if you care to meet him.

About The Author

Stanley O'Shea, a.k.a. @stanthefeline on social media, used to work in cognitive psychology/neuroscience, relying on his engineering background. He has co-authored 4 SCI journal articles and co-invented one patent. In his private life, he used to write indie rock/folk songs. He became unable to continue any of those activities after his work-related repetitive strain injury turned chronic, thanks to his former job at UC Davis.

To some extent, his enthusiasm for singing on the Smule app provided him with an escape from the physical and emotional pain he experiences now and then. On those days with a sore throat, he listens to podcasts, such as *The Psychology Podcast with Scott Barry Kaufman*, in a quiet park instead.

He is an empiricist, an individualist, an Objectivist (a.k.a. rational egoist), and a globalist.

Appendices
Appendix A: List of Characters

There are so many characters in the story, so I prepared these spreadsheets for your reference. This may not be an exhaustive list, as some of the characters are too trivial compared to the rest, objectively speaking.

THE SNOWY BATTLEFIELD OF OHIO

(in categorical order)

Character	Category	Location	Annotation
Mr. Hoffman	Academia	OH	Prof.; TA Supervisor
Mr. McCarthy	Academia	OH	Prof.; mentor
Mr. Osman	Academia	OH; CA	from the Middle East; boss
Mr. Williams	Academia	OH	department chair
Ms. Foster	Academia	OH	Osman's superior
Mr. Shapiro	Academia; Colleague	CA	Postdoc w/ Osman
Mr. Anderson	Academia; Musician	OH	Canadian
Slim Sun	Academia; Protagonist	OH;CA;CN	Protagonist
Elvis	Cat	OH	Live with Chris
Infinity	Cat	OH	Live with Alex & Charlotte
Samuel	Cat	CN	Live with Mandy & Doug
Dr. Clark	Clinician	OH	MD; primary care
Dr. Gallagher	Clinician	OH	MD; Sports medicine
Frankie	Clinician	OH	PT
Melissa	Clinician	OH	PT
Emily	Colleague	OH	TA
Ali	Friend	OH	From Malaysia
Antonio	Friend	OH	Cognitive psychology
Brian	Friend	OH	Former tenant; math
Caleb	Friend	OH	Evangelist
Chris	Friend	OH	w/ cat Elvis, Redditor
Lily	Friend	OH	From China
Lindsay	Friend	OH	Evangelist; w/ Carl

Owen	Friend	OH	w/ Ashley; engineering
Rachel	Friend	CN; CA	From Shanghai
Takashi : 高志	Friend	OH; CA	From Japan
Stacy : Anastasia	Friend; Antagonist	OH	Med student w/ Jeremy
Carl	Friend; Musician	OH	Evangelist; w/ Lindsay
Kelly	Friend; Musician	OH	Singer-songwriter
Kevin	Friend; Musician	OH	Singer-songwriter
Alex	Friend; Neighbor	OH	w/ Charlotte
Charlotte	Friend; Neighbor	OH	w/ Alex
"Likert"	Group Therapy	OH	Organization psychology
"Mark Twain"	Group Therapy	OH	Literature
"Stud"	Group Therapy	OH	Earring; literature
"The alchemist"	Group Therapy	OH	Biochemistry
"The Buddha"	Group Therapy	OH	Occupational therapy
"Titan"	Group Therapy	OH	Quantum physics
"Turing"	Group Therapy	OH	Latino; software engineering
Magistrate Turner	Legal	OH	Ohio court
Mr. Ivanovski	Legal	OH	Immigration lawyer
Mr. Parker	Legal	OH	OSU staff
Ms. Wilson	Legal	OH	Criminal lawyer
Ashley	Musician	OH	Lab mate from Florida
Edward	Musician	OH	Lab mate from California
Natalie	Musician	OH	Lab mate from New Jersey
Sophie	Musician	OH	Lab mate from Canada
Joe : Joseph	Musician; Colleague	OH	Undergrad RA

THE SNOWY BATTLEFIELD OF OHIO

Julian	Musician; Neighbor	OH	Vocalist; Latino
T1; Teresa	Psychotherapist	OH	Individual therapy
T2; Jacob	Psychotherapist	OH	Group therapy director
T3; Layla	Psychotherapist	CA	Individual therapy
T4; Noah	Psychotherapist	OH	Group therapy
T5; Maria	Psychotherapist	OH	Group therapy
Doug	Relative	CN	bio-dad w/ Mandy
Lulu	Relative	CN	Female cousin
Mandy	Relative	CN	bio-mom w/ Doug
Kayah	Roommate	OH	Native American
Shannon	Roommate	OH	Vet student
Mr. Li	Roommate;	OH	From China; statistician
Jeremy : Jeremiah	Roommate; Antagonist	OH	Med student w/ Stacy
Jessica	Roommate; Antagonist	OH	Digital art student
Mr. Frost	Staff	OH	Student conduct
Mei	Teacher	CN	Elementary school Chinese
Tao	Teacher	CN	High school math

(In alphabetical order)

Character	Category	Location	Annotation
Alex	Friend; Neighbor	OH	w/ Charlotte
Ali	Friend	OH	From Malaysia
Antonio	Friend	OH	Cognitive psychology
Ashley	Musician	OH	Lab mate from Florida
Brian	Friend	OH	Former tenant; math
Caleb	Friend	OH	Evangelist
Carl	Friend; Musician	OH	Evangelist; w/ Lindsay
Charlotte	Friend; Neighbor	OH	w/ Alex
Chris	Friend	OH	w/ cat Elvis, Redditor
Doug	Relative	CN	bio-dad w/ Mandy
Dr. Clark	Clinician	OH	MD; primary care
Dr. Gallagher	Clinician	OH	MD; Sports medicine
Edward	Musician	OH	Lab mate from California
Elvis	Cat	OH	Live with Chris
Emily	Colleague	OH	TA
Frankie	Clinician	OH	PT
Infinity	Cat	OH	Live with Alex & Charlotte
Jeremy : Jeremiah	Roommate; Antagonist	OH	Med student w/ Stacy
Jessica	Roommate; Antagonist	OH	Digital art student
Joe : Joseph	Musician; Colleague	OH	Undergrad RA
Julian	Musician; Neighbor	OH	Vocalist; Latino

THE SNOWY BATTLEFIELD OF OHIO

Kayah	Roommate	OH	Native American
Kelly	Friend; Musician	OH	Singer-songwriter
Kevin	Friend; Musician	OH	Singer-songwriter
Lily	Friend	OH	From China
Lindsay	Friend	OH	Evangelist; w/ Carl
Lulu	Relative	CN	Female cousin
Magistrate Turner	Legal	OH	Ohio court
Mandy	Relative	CN	bio-mom w/ Doug
Mei	Teacher	CN	Elementary school Chinese
Melissa	Clinician	OH	PT
Mr. Anderson	Academia; Musician	OH	Canadian
Mr. Frost	Staff	OH	Student conduct
Mr. Hoffman	Academia	OH	Prof.; TA Supervisor
Mr. Ivanovski	Legal	OH	Immigration lawyer
Mr. Li	Roommate;	OH	From China; statistician
Mr. McCarthy	Academia	OH	Prof.; mentor
Mr. Osman	Academia	OH; CA	from the Middle East; boss
Mr. Parker	Legal	OH	OSU staff
Mr. Shapiro	Academia; Colleague	CA	Postdoc w/ Osman
Mr. Williams	Academia	OH	department chair
Ms. Foster	Academia	OH	Osman's superior
Ms. Wilson	Legal	OH	Criminal lawyer
Natalie	Musician	OH	Lab mate from New Jersey
Owen	Friend	OH	w/ Ashley; engineering
Rachel	Friend	CN; CA	From Shanghai
Samuel	Cat	CN	Live with Mandy & Doug
Shannon	Roommate	OH	Vet student

Slim Sun	Academia; Protagonist	OH; CA; CN	Protagonist
Sophie	Musician	OH	Lab mate from Canada
Stacy : Anastasia	Friend; Antagonist	OH	Med student w/ Jeremy
T1; Teresa	Psychotherapist	OH	Individual therapy
T2; Jacob	Psychotherapist	OH	Group therapy director
T3; Layla	Psychotherapist	CA	Individual therapy
T4; Noah	Psychotherapist	OH	Group therapy
T5; Maria	Psychotherapist	OH	Group therapy
Takashi : 高志	Friend	OH; CA	From Japan
Tao	Teacher	CN	High school math
"Likert"	Group Therapy	OH	Organization psychology
"Mark Twain"	Group Therapy	OH	Literature
"Stud"	Group Therapy	OH	Earring; literature
"The alchemist"	Group Therapy	OH	Biochemistry
"The Buddha"	Group Therapy	OH	Occupational therapy
"Titan"	Group Therapy	OH	Quantum physics
"Turing"	Group Therapy	OH	Latino; software engineering

Appendix B: List of Songs

The following songs have been mentioned in this story because they fit my mentality in the specific scenes. I recommend that you check out these songs or musicals, wherever/however you can, if you are interested.

Location	Song title	Source
5.6	Elephant Love Medley	Moulin Rouge, the musical
12.0	Parachute	Original
13.3	Penitentiary	Houndmouth, US
13.4	Sweet Mary	Weezer, US
13.7	Make It Right	Prince of Egypt, the musical
15.7	Out There	The Hunchback of Notre Dame, the musical

For your convenience, I have prepared a Spotify playlist including all the songs mentioned above, except my original song *Parachute*. That song is available on SoundCloud (full version ; light version) for free.

Readers of the printed version of this book can access the links through this webpage:

https://tinyurl.com/snowy-lyrics

Appendix C: Questions for Readers/Listeners

The following questions are designed to help you regurgitate after reading the story.

*I would encourage my readers to share their answers publicly by **leaving a review on Amazon and Goodreads**. Additionally, you can discuss the book on social media, with the hashtag #snowymemoir.*

Q1: What are the characteristics of Jeremy?

Q2: What are the characteristics of Stacy?

Q3: Which psychotherapists were mentioned? How helpful were they?

Q4: Which lawyers/attorneys were mentioned? How helpful were they?

Q5: Which professors were mentioned? How do you like them?

Q6: Which musical theatre characters were mentioned?

Q7: What would you do if you were in my house drama?

Q8: What would you do if you were in my legal drama?

Q9: How would you cope with the bad reviews from the undergrads?

Q10: Do you agree that Chinese international students should ideally study Statistics in the US?

Q11: Would you try the cockroach powder to treat any chronic gastrointestinal problem you may have?

Q12: If you were Asian, would you choose to live in the Midwest?

Q13: With no regard to political correctness, do you think that Asians should go back to where they are "really" from?

Q14: What do you think of the American dream and American exceptionalism?

Q15: What is the "cultural iceberg" model?

Q16: Do you consider it fraudulent to overpromise or to give false hope?

Q17: Do you believe in justice in this human society?

Q18: How would you evaluate a person who is viewed as an elite by common standards yet treats you badly?

Q19: How would you evaluate a country that is believed to be the best country in the world yet treats immigrants like you cruelly?

Q20: Those who don't speak English and don't embrace American values may successfully immigrate to America through multiple channels, while those who want to be assimilated may be bullied, exploited, and then jettisoned. How do you view this irony in immigration?

www.ingramcontent.com/pod-product-compliance
Lightning Source LLC
LaVergne TN
LVHW040132080526
838202LV00042B/2874